BUSINESS ANALYSIS FOR BUSINESS INTELLIGENCE

BERT BRIJS

CRC Press
Taylor & Francis Group
Boca Raton   London   New York

CRC Press is an imprint of the
Taylor & Francis Group, an **informa** business
AN AUERBACH BOOK

CRC Press
Taylor & Francis Group
6000 Broken Sound Parkway NW, Suite 300
Boca Raton, FL 33487-2742

© 2013 by Taylor & Francis Group, LLC
CRC Press is an imprint of Taylor & Francis Group, an Informa business

No claim to original U.S. Government works

Printed in the United States of America on acid-free paper
Version Date: 20120620

International Standard Book Number: 978-1-4398-5834-9 (Hardback)

Library of Congress Cataloging-in-Publication Data

Brijs, Bert.
　　Business analysis for business intelligence / Bert Brijs.
　　　　p. cm.
　　Includes bibliographical references and index.
　　ISBN 978-1-4398-5834-9 (hbk. : alk. paper)
　　1. Business intelligence. 2. Decision making. 3. Strategic planning. I. Title.

HD38.7.B75 2012
658.4'72--dc23
2012005257

Visit the Taylor & Francis Web site at
http://www.taylorandfrancis.com

and the CRC Press Web site at
http://www.crcpress.com

Contents

Preface

Running a business from a Business Intelligence (BI) point of view is like setting up research strategies to accept or reject hypotheses, prejudice, or generally accepted theories, refining and improving models, illustrating and reinforcing these with actions and stories to build the foundation upon which your organization's strategies are built.

LINEAR SHORTCUTS

But for lack of time, budget, or other reasons, we tend to create "linear shortcuts" and restrict ourselves to empiric, rule-based business intelligence. And even on that level, things can go seriously wrong. Maybe the drawing in Figure F.1 says it better than words. The shaded ellipse is the linear shortcut, ignoring or, worse, denying the existence of other possible causes and only grasping part of the problem and the solution. Management is satisfied with an explanatory power expressed by the 0.65 of the correlation coefficient and does not have the level of sophistication to push the envelope farther. One direction is to get more root causes in the model, increasing R, and the other—equally important if not more so—is to monitor the root causes on a continuous basis because nothing is more ephemeral than analysis results based on transactions that are dimensionalized, aggregated, and ranked according to the organization's paradigms.

These linear shortcuts are cause and effect chains that are easy to communicate to the organization. Thus, management deprives itself of thorough and methodical Business Intelligence methods and systems that take the "horizontal" approach to its success or failure drivers. As the decision maker is seeking a satisfactory outcome rather than the best possible, he is paying an opportunity cost that is not seen in the books but might lead to the organization's premature demise. The history of the rise and fall of many great companies shows a constant in their behavior: the strategic patterns, ploys, and posture that led to their success also lead to their downfall as they keep clinging to their linear shortcuts. These linear shortcuts undermine the potential of business intelligence and, as a consequence, the organization's strategic potential.

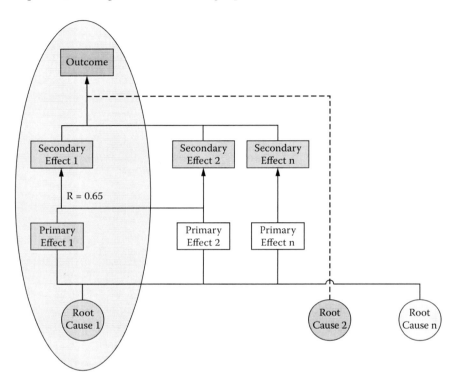

Linear shortcuts lead to oversimplification in decision making.

THERE IS NO SILVER BULLET IN BI

I am not claiming to have found the silver bullet that will produce the ultimate Business Intelligence model. The only promise I can make to the reader is that he or she will discover the complexity of aligning the organization's information management with its strategy process. My hope is that the organization's information management will develop a broader view of Business Intelligence, broader than the Information Technology (IT) aspects, broader than the business aspects, and broader than the interaction between the two and that this will lead to better performance of the strategy execution, which is essential for the organization's survival.

As Business Intelligence becomes more and more pervasive, the competitive edge will go to those organizations that implement and develop Business Intelligence in close harmony with their specific culture and their strategy process. When I read Tom Davenport's article (2006) I did a double-take. Davenport described what I was doing 20 years ago in a large German mail-order company. Long before the Internet, we touted that "One day all marketing would become direct marketing," meaning we would be able to individualize our customer relationship management on all aspects: product, price, promotion, cost, and profit. Because of our more scientific and analytic approach, we had information of which our brick-and-mortar competitors, the general stores, could only dream. Now, our creed is becoming true for even the smaller organizations, and analytical power and skills are becoming the new competitive frontier. Let me take you on a tour to inspire you to turn your organization into an analytical competitor.

Acknowledgments

A well-known African proverb says, "I am but a man because of other men," which is so right for this book. So many clients, colleagues, friends, and even totally unrelated people have contributed to this book that I will certainly forget to thank many of them. So, if your name is not on the list, send me an e-mail at bert@ba4bi.com and I will list your name in the next edition.

The first men on this planet who led me to the technical aspects of Business Intelligence were Christian Heusquin, who combined studies on renewable energy with theories on decision support systems in the early 1980s, and Gert-Jan Van Oers, head of the analysis department at Neckermann mail-order, but the man who really widened my technical view of the subject was Ralph Kimball, a great teacher and a fine human being. He was always there to answer my questions, rebuke my theses and, although he was involved in many startup innovative companies, he never let these interests take over from his value-free, scientific approach to Business Intelligence.

In my everyday practice I had great support from many colleagues at Datamotive, a BI specialist in the Benelux, especially from Jochen Stroobants, business analyst at Datamotive. Jens de Wael, Human Resources Management (HRM) manager at BIS Industrial Services gave inspiring advice on HRM and BI, and Luc Bouquet from TEKA Info Pilots proved a critical reader, pressing me for clear and concise formulation of my ideas. He also contributed to the section on knowledge transfer and the template for the best practices interview. Koen Van Waeyenberghe, a certified data vault modeler challenged my opinions on the modeling techniques and Paul Merckx, regulatory director of Agfa, also convinced me to formulate my ideas for a broader audience as he enthusiastically argued this book would be of interest to a lot more people than I expected.

1

Introduction

WHY THIS BOOK?

Books on management and information technology have a half-life of maximum six months. Fads and fashions follow each other in rapid waves and leave few impressions, just like real waves. So why bother? Why go through the trouble of spending more time to write a book than it will remain on the shelf in the bookstore?

Maybe it is because I hope to have unveiled a few universal truths about translating strategy into Business Intelligence (BI) architectures and certainly because I haven't met with any course, book, or consultant who really pays in-depth attention to this crucial aspect of successful BI projects. Sure there are the obligatory checklists and the people going through the motions, but as soon as possible, discussions focus on data models, processing capacity, and tools. Even the more tenacious who try to push the business analysis issues to the limit often miss the point behind the questions as these are abstractions missing the organization's context and its impact on strategy formulation and implementation.

Few business analysts demonstrate deep knowledge of the strategy process and its interaction with information management. There you have the value proposition of this book: to open up the potential of understanding this interaction.

ICT Has Grown Up

Information and communication technology (ICT) have reached a mature stage. The signs are clear: the majority of organizations no longer consider information technologists as the plumbers solving the problems created by the business. More and more organizations use ICT as a strategic asset, be it to support decision making or to generate surplus revenue, redefine market conditions, redefine processes and systems, or even redefine the rules of the game.

Here and there, an ICT professional makes it to the board of a non-ICT company. The demand for a methodical approach to translating strategy development and implementation into an appropriate Business Intelligence environment is growing. This book aims to contribute to this demand.

A Practical Approach

I am not a management scientist, first and foremost, because I don't believe there is such a thing as management science as there is no distance between the research object and the researcher as in physics or other positive sciences. "Management scientists" often present their study results as cookbook recipes, tricks, algorithms, and control instruments. The few really scientific studies on strategy, organizational behavior, and the organizational aspects of information management often reinvent the wheel but their theories never make it to everyday practice because a humanist approach needs to add context to the theories during implementation.

Another reason for failure to translate theory into practice are first and foremost flaws in the theory that remain unchallenged as the "management scientist" is too busy promoting his theory and evangelizing the business community to deal with such trivialities as proving his theories work. I remember getting courses from a direct-marketing guru who himself had the most unsuccessful mail-order company in the business.

A last reason for failure lies in the fact that many theoretical constructs are developed for *das Idealtyp* in Max Weber's definition as the combination of all features in optimal condition and therefore not suited for application in day-to-day management.

Hands-On Issues, Questions, and Methods

I do not bother the reader with impracticable theories. I prefer to share real experience about practices that work. They have proven their value in various sectors including banking and finance, industrial environments, logistics, and retail, among others. This book offers a framework for the practice of business analysts responsible for translating strategic management into information management strategies. It also provides senior managers with a better understanding of the strategic potential of information technology. And remember: it is you who has to interpret these practices and enrich them within the context of your organization.

Where appropriate, I address business analysis issues, not by providing the reader with extensive checklists but by suggesting questions that open a conversation. Business analysis for Business Intelligence is the art of well-structured conversations supported by deep and practical knowledge of the subject. Checklists ensure airplanes take off or your car maintenance is complete but they don't lead to meaningful analytical exchange of information that business analysis for Business Intelligence needs.

In the Appendix of this book we do have a checklist-like questionnaire. But this serves only the purpose of preparing the interviewee. Thus, he gets the impression he controls the process as he can come prepared to the interview. World-class interviewers will leave the interviewee with this perception while extracting information she is not even aware she was going to share. Don't forget, for some, business analysis interviews carry the message: "Lo and behold, change is coming!" This book can't help you to penetrate the defensive barriers, tricks, and tactics your interviewees will use. I refer you to many good books on interview techniques to help you with that problem. Authors like Michael Porter (1980), Henry Mintzberg (1989), and Peter Senge (1990) have provided me with workable concepts and frameworks.

My approach to the strategy process offers an eclectic background of theories for those who want to acquire more knowledge of the subject. By no means has this background pretended to be complete or original. Some of the authors and articles were not the first to promote an idea or a theory. But they certainly were the most outspoken and marketed their ideas better than others. But I do also try to expand this theoretical background with authors from the non-English-speaking community whose work remains unknown for lack of translations.

Someone once said: "Consultants get paid for the answers; academics get paid for the questions." Being a consultant I beg to differ and see the question–answer dilemma on the same level as the chicken–egg question. This book is my attempt as a nonacademic practitioner, being very busy delivering answers, to start up a dialogue with academics who have raised interesting questions on strategy and information management. This book doesn't hold all the answers but I hope it asks all the right questions.

Figures Don't Explain Everything

This is not your classical management handbook full of optimism. The more insights I find on why organizations are successful or fail, the more I am convinced that the old adage, "What you can measure, you can manage," does not hold the complete truth any more in our Western organizations. There are transcendental immeasurable aspects about an organization's performance. Henry Mintzberg tries to pigeonhole it in the ideology aspect, which partly holds truth. I have tried to map Western organization's maturity on Abe Maslow's old pyramid (Maslow, 1943) but that doesn't explain everything either. But does this lack of explanatory power relieve us from the obligation to at least measure and manage as much as we can? Of course not. I hope this book can contribute to a more vivid and a more complete debate on the subject and I will be delighted to receive your comments on www.ba4bi.com.

WHAT I MEAN BY "BUSINESS INTELLIGENCE"

From Decision Support to Information Democracy

Let's review a few definitions from my predecessors, Bill Inmon, Ralph Kimball, Séan Kelly, and others who laid out the foundations in the 1990s. It is amazing how most authors were still using terms from decades before: DSS (decision support systems) and M/EIS (management/executive information systems), which reveal the paradigm of centralized decision making, control, and strategy development of the various planning schools in the post-WWII era exactly at the time they were laying the foundations for performing Business Intelligence systems, propagating the intelligent enterprise! It resembles the classical technology development examples:

- Early cinema mimicking theater
- Early television mimicking cinema
- The first cars looking like a landau

A decision support system provides information to users allowing them to analyze a situation and make decisions, period. With "information" the pioneers meant "assembled and preformatted data for querying," which implied a lot of "ex ante modeling." In other words, the early DSS systems had an implicit view of the world by including certain data sources and leaving out others for various reasons: they didn't see the value or they were unable to exploit less-structured data due to technological restrictions.

The latest and fancier version of this approach is performance management monitoring software where the organization models a strategy map with its (presumed) causal relationships and defines the critical success factors and the ensuing key performance indicators to support their world view.

So, Inmon and the other pioneers relied heavily on presenting summary reports for management with drill-down functionalities to allow the executive to look for further details down the path. This concept is still valuable today but it has been broadened and enriched, not just because of better technology, but because we have learned the hard way that this form of strategic information isn't going to get us much farther in refining our strategy. (In some cases it only hastened the process of running companies to the brink of bankruptcy.) Yet, their assumptions about what management wants still make sense (Inmon, 1992, p. 163):

- Management's attention is constantly shifting.
- The shift is in a random pattern.
- Management always wants the information now!
- At the end of the data, management wants the data integrated as well.

The term "Business Intelligence" was used as early as September 1996, when a Gartner Group report said:

> By 2000, Information Democracy will emerge in forward-thinking enterprises, with Business Intelligence information and applications available broadly to employees, consultants, customers, suppliers, and the public. The key to thriving in a competitive marketplace is staying ahead of the competition. Making sound business decisions based on accurate and current information takes more than intuition. Data analysis, reporting, and query tools can help business users wade through a sea of data to synthesize valuable information from it — today these tools collectively fall into a category called "Business Intelligence."

The term "Information Democracy" is the most important one in this description because it abandons the centralized view of DSS, MIS, and EIS architectures and their underlying mindset.

A Definition

A common definition today sounds like:

> Business intelligence (BI) is a broad category of applications and technologies for gathering, storing, analyzing, and providing access to data to help enterprise users make better business decisions. BI applications include the activities of decision support systems, query and reporting, online analytical processing (OLAP), statistical analysis, forecasting, and data mining.

Business intelligence applications can be:

- Mission-critical and integral to an enterprise's operations or occasional to meet a special requirement
- Enterprisewide or local to one division, department, or project
- Centrally initiated or driven by user demand

This definition tries to make abstraction from technology and subcategories that will probably converge or change over time anyhow.

Business Intelligence is the systematic collection and preparation of data to provide management, employees, and other stakeholders with meaningful information that, combined with context-rich knowledge of the organization, improves the effectiveness of the organization's strategy process.

Business Intelligence has four important aspects that correspond in changing accentuation with classical management levels. A cybernetic, dialectic, synthetic, and an explorative approach are the ingredients of a mix on the operational, tactical or functional, and the strategic level. The business analyst who masters this mix will exploit the potential of BI to the maximum.

Scope of This Book

There are libraries filled with management literature about corporate strategy and on the other hand, there is a somewhat smaller room with bookshelves on Business Intelligence and data warehousing, the foundation of any BI system. This book brings the two together to produce a roadmap for C-level executives to position their existing or new BI initiatives in their strategy process, or vice versa: to improve their strategy process by fostering better BI systems. It is independent of data warehouse architectures: whether you're an adept of the Inmon, Kimball, or Linstedt school, this book can help you to bridge the gap between executive management and information management.

There are many fine books on data warehousing and BI but most of them treat the business analysis phase as asking a few questions and distilling the facts and dimensions from the answers, which is fine if you are only concerned with delivering a BI product at the end of a BI project. There is a need for embedding business intelligence in the strategy process in such a profound way that it becomes a competitive differentiator. This is the gap *BA for BI* is trying to fill.

WHAT DOES A BA4BI DO?

What is a business analyst for Business Intelligence (BA4BI) and how does one become a BA4BI? After 17 years in this profession, I am still amazed about the immature concepts, job descriptions, and training curricula for this important contributor to successful BI projects and processes. Experience from past projects shows that over 50% of the deficiencies in a BI system are caused by failure to produce the right requirements, to provide sufficient context, and to deliver a project charter that guides the BI team to success.

So, there is the objective of this section: to define the BA4BI job, his or her role in the project and to develop a learning and development path for candidates who want to excel in this discipline. We also refer to the Appendixes explaining the skills needed and what to ask during your job interview as we believe nobody graduates as a BA4BI.

If you type define "business analyst" on a well-known search engine, you won't get the answer to your question, other than very weak expressions such as "someone who analyzes the operations of a department in order to develop a solution to its problems." Problems? Department? Does a business analyst sit behind his desk waiting for a problem to come up and respond only when the problem is departmental?

It is obvious that when the general term "business analyst" is ill-defined, organizations are struggling to create a clear concept of "business analyst for business intelligence." This chapter is an effort to provide some clarity and a development path for candidate BA4BIs.

Defining the Concept "Business Analyst for Business Intelligence"

A *business analyst* identifies the relevant business questions and looks for answers. These answers may be confined to an IT solution but they may also lie in the process design, the organization's structure, its behavior, its culture, its planning and control process, and . . . its strategy process. A business analyst for business intelligence looks at all these aspects as he is aware of the interaction among them and is capable of prioritizing the necessary analytical steps toward finding a solution.

The tasks can be situated on the three classical levels: operational, tactical, and strategic. The scope can be as narrow as data analysis and as broad as architecture and governance consulting. So in this definition are two scope dimensions: the horizontal scope and the vertical scope. The horizontal scope looks at the playing field of the analysis job from information analysis to analyzing the strategy process. The vertical scope looks at the content of the job from data analysis up to data architecture and data governance.

I am not looking for a definition that will stand the test of time or the scrutiny of academics. I just want to share my observations with you. And what better way is there than to draw a picture first and then explain what's in it. Analysts love models, don't they? Let us take a walk through the model, following the horizontal scope: from "how" via "where" to "what–when–why."

Taking into account that this model is also an abstraction from a rich reality, it brings at least some structure to the semantic chaos that exists in job descriptions, recruitment ads, and consequently in the minds of IT and business people. On the left of the schema are the building blocks that are knowledge domains and activities that constitute the principal parts and aspects of the strategy process, relevant to a business intelligence analyst. Three arrows describe both the depth and the width of what a business analyst's job can include.

The arrows suggest a linear approach but that is only for convenience reasons. A true representation would resemble a fractal, illustrating how a business analyst for Business Intelligence always looks at the entire context, even when she is zooming in on one tiny detail such as an attribute of an entity, while the pattern remains the same. And vice versa: when she is confronted with high-level strategy presentations she knows how this PowerPoint talk relates to the transaction systems

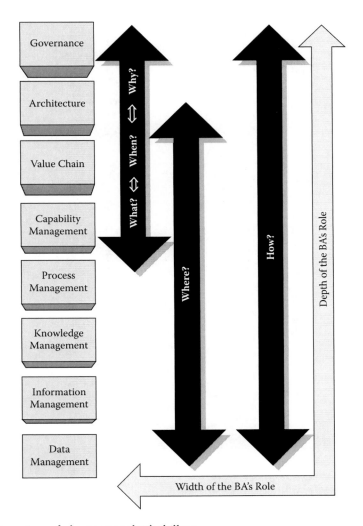

The dimensions of a business analyst's skill set.

containing the source data and the present reports and analysis models used by the organization.

"How" Career Path

The schema suggests the usual vertical career path of a business analyst, which deals mainly with the "How" question, namely, "How do we translate the business issues, questions, threats, and opportunities into a BI system that deals adequately with them?"

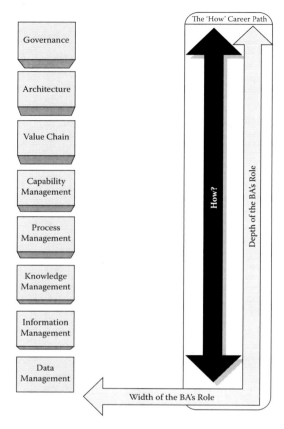

1. He starts with low-level data analysis, working his way up to: 2. Information management aspects like master data management and data quality as tools for strategy implementation. 3. He might skip knowledge management as not too many organizations are ready for KM but he will have to develop some KM skills to suggest improvements in this area. 4. He surely will get involved in some way into process management analysis: How are processes designed? What are the data created during these process steps? How do they evolve over time? Now it is time to make a big career move to a more senior role. 5. What are the strategic capabilities of the organization? In other words, what are the material and immaterial assets and what are the organization's competences that further, delay or hinder the realization of our strategy? 6. If the analyst masters the previous building blocks he will get a better and deeper understanding of the impact and importance of the value chain as the fundamental configuration of how the organization conducts its business. 7. Now it is time to move to the architectural level: the configuration of the business and the IT support for the business priorities. Configuring the BI architecture has to fit into the whole IT picture as the source systems and services produced by these systems impact the BI system's effectiveness profoundly. 8. The (senior) business analyst for business intelligence also needs to know the Business–IT governance model and how it is enforced. Governance is the lubricant when both parties diverge on the contents, context, or direction of a BI project or system.

"Where" Career Path

In this path, the analyst is capable of prioritizing the analysis issues and defining the analysis direction. Let me explain this briefly. The customer may ask you to develop a financial data warehouse and the necessary reporting environment. On this level you should be able to verify whether this is a legitimate and feasible customer demand. If, for example, the cost registration systems are faulty, how can you ever produce reliable analytical data for the cost of goods sold? Or, if the customer data are a downright mess, how can you produce reliable contribution margins per customer?

"C-Level" Career Path

The C-level career path takes business analysis to the next level: translating strategy into information strategy or—in the case of conglomerates or federated environments—information strategies. This level is about clearly communicating management's world view to the information architecture: the business architecture, the data architecture, and the application landscape. (We leave the functional aspects and the infrastructure aspects aside as these are derived from previous decisions.)

Management's world view can be made explicit by developing a map of causal relationships management uses to decide on strategic options. A business that pursues organic growth will have a completely different architecture from a business that is constantly looking for acquisitions. A business that controls an integrated end-to-end value chain will present a different architecture from a business that outsources its noncore activities.

Observation: I haven't seen too many business analysts become CEO of an organization but I would like to see more C-level executives acquire the top-level skills of a business analyst!

STRUCTURE OF THIS BOOK

The book follows a top-down approach: from the strategic level, via the functional levels, and down to operational levels. Because Business Intelligence needs a holistic approach, we deal with organizational, HRM, financial, and ICT aspects to create a picture as complete as possible. Inasmuch as

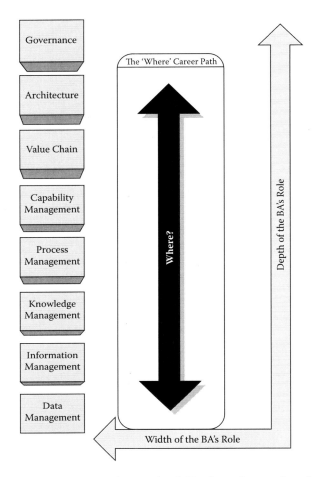

It is time to move your career to the next level. You know how to describe unambiguously the data requirements, the information requirements. You have mapped these on the various processes producing the data and you are aware of the context of these data, which is not always documented in the systems. You have experienced the influence of the organization's capabilities on the desired BI functionality. And the value chain concept together with the architecture and governance choices provide you with enough context to add meaning to the requirements and even suggest new requirements that add extra value to the client's expectations. So, now you know how to convert the strategic building blocks into blueprints and conceptual data models, BI applications delivering the desired and the necessary functionality. Observation shows clearly the distinction between a seasoned BI analyst and a junior analyst. The junior will start with what he knows: if he has a DBA background, chances are he will address the data requirements, the source to target mapping, and the likes. If he is a financial expert, he will help define finance reports, etc… The senior business analyst will first prioritize the order in which the analysis cycle will take place. Is it mainly a data conversion issue? Or do we have to get the processes right? The junior will do things right whereas the senior will do the right things.

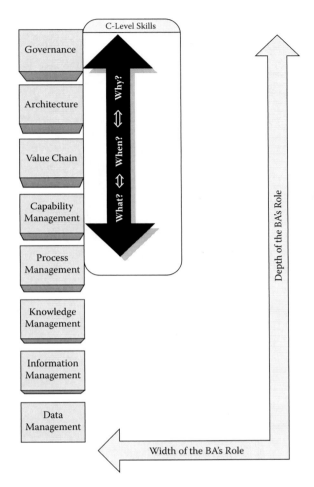

This is a place where I haven't seen too many business analysts. It is the place where the fundamental decisions are taken. As a business analyst you are on the receiving side but if you master the fundamentals of governance, architecture, the value chain, and capability management you will provide your analysis with depth and context an order of magnitude greater than the "How" and the "Where" guys. This is certainly the place where a Business Intelligence Competence Center (BICC) should operate and it should also be on the agenda of C-level management as a constant awareness. With every decision managers make, the BI impact question should be on the agenda. Let's outsource the components manufacturing. OK, but do we have sufficient level of data integration in place with the supplier to keep the information flowing to the BI system? Let's merge Wedgies BU with the Widget BU. OK, but up to now their operational reporting was only consolidated on the level of product groups and they kept the smallest grain of reporting in the BU systems. What will it take to consolidate on SKU and product line level? Let's encourage our sales reps to work from home. OK, but the sales reports will need more context as the reps will get less verbal comment on the figures.

Business Intelligence is more than an ICT project, it is the start of profound changes in the way organizations work and perform in the market.

Principal Aspects

Strategy Formulation and Formation

The Greeks gave a top-down direction to *strategos* (general), derived from *stratus* (army) and *agein* (to lead). Today's insights have broadened the strategy concept to an organizational "way of achieving things," *things* being formal objectives, personal agendas, windfalls, exploited opportunities, and other serendipities. *Strategy formulation* and *formation* are two sides of the same coin: the first deals with planning and implementing strategy, the latter with observing patterns from the past to interpret future developments, which are then either reinforced or mitigated. High-performance strategies always combine top-down and bottom-up approaches in an optimum mix for the organization.

Managing the relationship between the organization's configuration and this mix supported by an appropriate Business Intelligence architecture is the mission of what I like to call an intelligent enterprise architect. A sound business analysis methodology is the first step toward that status.

Strategy Implementation

It is clear that most ICT systems support planned strategies with specialized Balanced Scorecard software as the ultimate management platform for what I call "strategy planning, accounting, and controlling." From the above you already know that I consider this only a partial solution to a very complex phenomenon. I assemble elements for a comprehensive Business Intelligence ontology that supersedes the ICT aspects and provides management with a reference framework for the years to come. Ambitious? Yes, but we have seen the results from the alternative: haphazard IT patches for problems IT cannot solve. This attempt is an effort to support information managers in their quest for being taken seriously by top management.

Developing a Marketing Strategy

Marketing is the locomotive of the organization. No organization can survive without a market, an audience, the public, even serfs, legitimating it.

In all business analysis processes for Business Intelligence I have worked on, the customer comes after finance and operations for all sorts of reasons I won't go into here. With this observation in the back of my mind I try to introduce the customer perspective into finance, operations, HRM, and all other subject areas management deems higher priority than the one who is really paying his salary, the customer.

Modern marketing strategies are embedded in the entire organization. Yet, don't be surprised to find remains of marketing departments that are positioned as subcontractors for operations and even finance! Pity them and give them the best service you can. Maybe the insights from your customer information system will one day help them to improve their position.

Financial Perspective

Financial managers are the most predictable of all specimens in the organization. So here's the first reason why many BI projects start with a financial iteration: quick wins! Finance appreciates timely, fast, and accurate reporting of what happened during the last month from a few well-described perspectives, available in the public domain: an income statement, a contribution approach, or an audit trail. The financial perspective can be used as an important element for the cost justification of the BI project. It will reveal issues in other departments, perspectives, or functions to be addressed by the BI project.

At least one of these issues is to get a better insight to the various cost drivers in the organization. The intersection of finance and operations yields interesting information in almost any BI project.

Operations Strategy

Throughput times, capacity use, resource management, and inventory management are directly addressable issues in BI for operations. Cost analysis and asset management are in the cross-section with finance and demand an interdisciplinary approach for the business analyst.

HRM and BI

Managing absenteeism and managing competences are major BI domains in the human resources management (HRM) practice. Although HRM is not the top priority for most organizations, it can fundamentally change the way the organization operates in the market.

Business Intelligence Framework

The structure of an enterprise Business Intelligence system needs an unequivocal description of:

- The Business Intelligence product: What are the deliverables for each person or profile involved?
- The Business Intelligence services: What service does each BI deliverable provide for each person or profile?
- The Business Intelligence profession: What should each person or profile involved in the enterprise BI project be able to do, based on which BI knowledge?
- A classification of the Business Intelligence knowledge itself.

Thus, we are ready to describe both the Business Intelligence processes and the process flow of a business analysis project.

Introducing a BI Project

After many years and much hype in BI, we are left with three types of BI organizations: the disillusioned, the successful, and the fresh starters.

The disillusioned, even frustrated innovators from the early 1990s, have spent huge budgets on technology without really getting any BI value for their dollar. The successful must have done things right: optimizing customer expectations, budget, throughput time, and the actual BI deliverables. They are role models, keen on keeping their BI wisdom to themselves and may not allow external priers. The fresh starters are smaller companies who can afford BI as the infrastructure price has dropped dramatically.

Database vendors offer a BI suite as a free add-on, and storage and processing capacity continues to reduce the price–performance ratio. But the hardest part to compress is BI consultancy. So for the suspicious starters and the disillusioned it is absolutely necessary to create a confidence-building project initiation phase before the organization commits to a budget for an investment without any salvage value if things go south (see Figure 1.1).

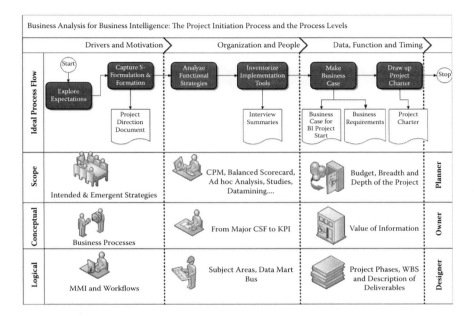

FIGURE 1.1
The project initiation process.

A Typical Business Analysis Project Flow

Ralph Kimball's life-cycle model (Figure 1.2) provides a robust basis. The business analysis aspects focus on five of the twelve phases in the model plus, of course, the project management aspects.

1. *Project planning:* The book does not provide answers to the question "How do I plan a BI project, step by step?" But it offers valuable input for planners.
2. *Business requirements definition:* The book provides tools, concepts, and straightforward questions to enhance the quality of the requirements. This is the central point of gravity of the book.
3. *Dimensional modeling:* There are many fine books on dimensional modeling but it may help here and there to link business analysis issues to modeling issues.
4. *BI application specification:* Again, authors such as Kimball, Nigel Pendse, and many others have extensively published on this aspect. A high-level positioning of BI tool types provides a direction for the tool selection phase.

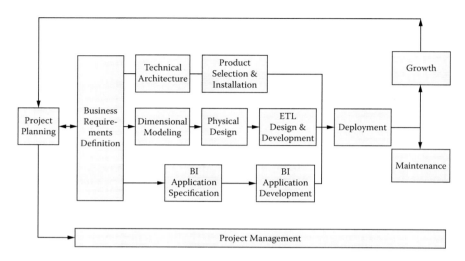

FIGURE 1.2

Kimball's life-cycle model. (Schema courtesy of R. Kimball et al., *The Data Warehouse Lifecycle Toolkit.* John Wiley & Sons, New York, 1998.)

5. *Growth:* As the growth phase is (from methodological point of view) new analysis iteration, I only address the events that signal the analyst to take an initiative even before the business users are aware there is a need for a new iteration. Aspects including knowledge transfer and keeping the BI process going are just as important.

The book presents best practices in business analysis for Business Intelligence with much emphasis on the project management aspects as this is the main issue in many BI projects: how to overcome the inertia and gain momentum so the BI project becomes a BI process.

Business Intelligence Processes

Now we widen the scope a bit to get the complete picture: from strategy formation and formulation to implementation supported by a performing BI system, delivering relevant information on time in all aspects of the organization's strategy:

- Intended or planned strategy
- Emergent or spontaneous strategy
- Realized strategy

TABLE 1.1

The Stage by Aspect Matrix

Stage / Aspect	Intended	Emergent	Realized
Formation	KPI Reporting, Environmental scanning, Explorative data mining	Customer and competitive analysis Ad hoc queries	KPI reporting
Formulation	Process-based BI KPI Reporting	Exception reporting	Process-based BI
Implementation	Process-based BI, KPI Reporting	User log files and query monitoring	KPI Reporting e-learning and knowledge management

The "stage by aspect" matrix in Table 1.1 indicates BI's contribution in each of the nine combinations. A short explanation of each term may bring some clarity to this matrix.

KPI (key performance indicator) reporting: This is an important part of Balanced Scorecards, executive dashboards, corporate performance management, or executive information systems. When management has defined the KPIs they are monitored and presented in all stages of the strategy process as management wants to control the strategy process.

Environmental scanning: This is the collecting, analyzing, and editing of structured and unstructured information from private and public sources such as from Dun and Bradstreet, Organisation for Economic Cooperation and Development (OECD), or other reports via press clippings or even street rumors. Any potentially important piece of information is assembled, verified, and distributed to management. Most BI tools do not support this kind of intelligence gathering. Document management systems with a plus or knowledge management systems support this far better.

Explorative data mining: This may be a tautology but I am using it on purpose as there is a lot of confusion in the market about data mining. Some authors position data mining as the art of spontaneously detecting causal relationships between recorded events. This is too optimistic. Data mining is the discipline of analyzing unstructured data based on the testing of null hypotheses that are accepted or rejected. It can also present trends in a numerical or graphical mode and suggest further research directions.

User log files and query monitoring: Although this does not contribute to the strategy process itself, it indicates the level of acceptance of BI in the organization and the questions asked.

Process-based BI: This is the marriage between business process management and corporate performance management. It attempts to combine cybernetic, dialectic, and explorative forms of BI embedded in process monitoring.

Ad hoc queries: This BI aspect helps users to deepen their knowledge about observed phenomena in other reports. It helps to find answers to the "why" questions. Another term often used is OLAP (online analytical processing) and its various architectures: the obsolete DOLAP (desktop OLAP), ROLAP (relational OLAP), MOLAP (multidimensional OLAP), and HOLAP (hybrid OLAP). We refer to the glossary for more information.

Customer and competitive analysis: BI can give management better insight to customer behavior by analyzing all transactions from the first contact with the customer to the last order. Lifetime value management is a mail-order concept that has reached mainstream business organizations since the 1990s. Competitive analysis is a lot more difficult for various reasons: the necessary information is not always available and most of the available information is biased. Competitive analysis needs external information such as income statements and balance sheets, market share, or surveys. These sources are either hard to interpret because they were prepared for fiscal reasons including financial reporting or they don't fit into an analytical model because they use different KPIs or the same KPIs with different definitions. The internal sources are sometimes of worse quality because of what I call "Caesar's effect."* Any salesperson who has to make a loss report will be tempted to picture the competition as a little more potent and capable than reality permits.

---

* Caesar wrote in his De Bello Gallico: Horum omnium fortissimi sunt Belgae, or "of all these [the Gauls ed.] the Belgians are the strongest." He did this not to report the truth, but to embellish his victory over the Belgian tribes.

E-learning: It makes the lessons learned from the BI system available to a broader audience via structured learning modules. Some companies use it to the full extent, managing the enrollment of their "students," taking tests, creating certification programs, and monitoring the learning effort of their students. This is an underestimated aspect (or discipline) in the BI field. If BI generates information, how do we make sure that all aspects of this information are described and understood on every level of the organization that is (potentially) affected by this information? E-learning can create the extra push to make sure that strategic information is converted into strategic behavior.

Knowledge management (KM): In the pre-KM era, I worked on a project for a Heineken brewery where all the brewing statistics were posted in what was called the "stats room." The brewing masters took their break in this room and discussed the posted information, thereby exchanging knowledge and enhancing the value of these stats. Few projects I have worked on were open to this idea, which leaves an important and valuable BI potential untapped.

Tips, Tricks, and a Toolbox

Where appropriate, the chapters conclude with some tips for digging up the truth about BI in your client organization. At the end of the book is a set of templates and guidelines to produce a quality business analysis product. In the Appendix, a short introduction to the technical aspects of data warehousing and the history of this discipline are added for those who are not familiar with the discipline.

BI System

The book uses the honeycomb metaphor of a BI system, as shown in Figure 1.3, where all components interact with each other. As a business analyst you will have to develop a consistent view of the proper use of all the components and especially that single most important component that is not in this picture: the user.

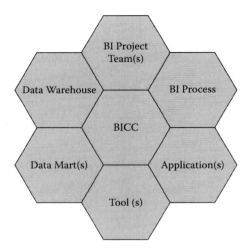

FIGURE 1.3
The BI system.

CHAPTERS OF THIS BOOK

Macroscopic View of Business Intelligence

Increasing Cycle Speed of Growth and Its Laws

As this book makes the link between the strategy process and the business analysis issues and questions to address to create a better alignment, it is crucial to illustrate the major strategic issues that drive the necessity and business value of a good analytical approach.

- First Law: The triangle of knowledge, growth, and the strategy processes.
  - This law states that when growth is the destination of the strategic journey, then knowledge is the fuel that drives your organization toward its destination.
- Second Law: Your narrow choice between two options.
  - Observation taught me that organizations always have the choice between optimizing the present strategic approach or turning it around, breaking radically with present strategies.
- Third Law: Any organization optimizes two extremes.
  - The dichotomy between economies of scale and the cost of heterogeneity has long reigned (and still reigns) over many organizations. With IT, this dichotomy disappears.

- Fourth Law: Measure only what you can measure but...
  - This section draws the analyst's attention to aspects beyond the typical measurements a BI system produces.
- Fifth Law: There is always a dominant source.
  - This important section helps the analyst determine where the organization's powerbase resides: the strategic apex, functional management, or the operational core.
- Sixth Law: IT is here to stay.
- The good news is IT has finally gained acceptance in the boardroom, where strategic directions are chosen. The bad news is the alignment between IT and the business is not always optimal. Therefore, a few issues for the analyst are raised.

Balancing the 5 Ps of Strategic Management

The chapter puts forward the best generic description of what strategic management really is, namely plan, pattern, ploy, posture, and positioning all to be placed in perspective by management. Combined with the management style it can help the business analyst determine where the center of gravity is for the development of a Business Intelligence strategy, and adapting BI to the organization's configuration.

Henry Mintzberg's (1991) observations of organization configurations led to a framework inspiring the business analyst to look for yet another important anchor point for her analysis: what are the dominant forces that drive (implicitly or more explicitly) the BI project.

Adapting BI to the Organization's Configuration

Henry Mintzberg's (1991) organization configurations provide analysts with an initial sense of the direction of the project. This small but important chapter provides useful tips for the analyst to discover—long before the customer is aware—where the project will be heading.

Understanding the 4 Cs

The foundations of true Business Intelligence lie in understanding the 4 Cs that, together with environmental factors, determine the strategic directions an organization can choose. Customer, cost, competitor, and competences are the basic drivers and levers management can interpret and influence at the same time. Understanding these basic dynamics is a necessity for a business analyst who wants to get the context of BI solutions for strategic management.

Business Case for Business Intelligence

One of the first deliverables to be developed and refined throughout the project is the business case as there can be no BI project without one. This chapter offers the analyst practical handles and guidelines to develop a business case for BI.

Business Analysis and Management Areas

BI and Cost Accounting

This chapter presents the eight steps to set up activity-based costing and discusses the potential data sources for the cost elements so the analyst knows where to start the analysis.

BI and Financial Management

Although financial reporting is pretty straightforward, this chapter points out a few methods that can help to improve the quality of the analysis and it also indicates relationships with other subject areas. Many BI projects start with a financial iteration and some look no farther, missing opportunities for improvement. After reading this chapter you will not get stuck in the middle.

BI and Operations Management

Forecasting, supply chain optimization, and outsourcing analysis are the three major subject areas in operations management. This chapter addresses the business analysis issues.

BI and Marketing Management

Business Intelligence for marketing purposes has two starting points: the process data coming from a customer relationship management (CRM) system and behavioral data coming from web clicks, observation, surveys, and the like. When these data are combined with each other and with other sources a great potential for strategic marketing improvement can be tapped. The chapter discusses BI's contributions to the principal marketing activities and the marketing disciplines, raising the right questions and issues.

BI and Human Resources Management

Two major subject areas are addressed in this chapter: managing skills in conjunction with job and customer requirements and reducing absenteeism and churn.

Business Analysis and the Project Life Cycle

Starting a BI Project

Many organizations have failed BI projects because the BI concept itself was introduced in a happenstance way and expectations weren't managed as they should be. This chapter focuses on the motivation and expectation of management but it also presents concepts to analyze the decision-making process in the client organization.

Managing the Project Life Cycle

The BI project life cycle needs interventions from the business analyst in varying intensity, depending on the phase and exogenous factors, which we discuss in this chapter. Five elements from the project life cycle get special attention as they are relevant for the analyst: project planning, business requirements definition, dimensional modeling, BI application specification, and growth.

Mastering Data Management

As soon as there is a business case for a project, the data management issue has to be addressed as this is a fundamental aspect for best practices in BI. The chapter offers a framework for data management and discusses the practical issues to be addressed by the business analyst.

Mastering Data Quality

The same goes for data quality: it pays to address the issue from the start as 99% of all data quality problems have to be tackled in the source systems.

The questionnaire suggests past, present, and future data quality issues to address as these may have a serious impact on the Business Intelligence project and the BI products it intends to deliver.

The Business Analyst's Toolbox

Project Direction Document Template

The project direction template is a high-level introduction document for the project that is used to get an analysis budget from management to prepare the project charter. Some practitioners call it a quick scan or a feasibility analysis but the latter is too much honor for this management product. The result of this document should be one of these decisions: stop the project, examine it further, or prepare a project charter. The project direction document template is typical for the incremental approach used in Business Intelligence.

Interview Summary Template

This template helps the analyst provide meaningful feedback to the interviewee assessing the quality of the interview and achieving true commitment from the interview about his vision and input for the BI project.

Business Case Document Template

This template serves as a memory aid for analysts who assist the business in drawing up a business case that will be refined throughout the project.

Business Analysis Deliverables Template

No fewer than 13 deliverables are defined to guarantee a complete overview of the situation:

1. High-level situation analysis
2. Purpose of the BI project
3. Stakeholder matrix
4. Business requirements
5. Project management constraints

6. Scope of the product
7. Data requirements
8. Presentation methods
9. Security requirements
10. Other requirements
11. Project plan and task list
12. Documentation
13. Glossary

The template provides sufficient input for a project charter, which can in its turn serve as input for a contract.

Project Charter Document Template

The project charter crystallizes the business requirements into a guide for the continuation of the project. Some customers find this a sufficient basis to start the project. Others may require a contract, which is not discussed in this book as legal aspects differ from one country to another and this subject is beyond the responsibilities of the analyst. A well-formulated project charter will form the basis of a good contract.

Best Practice Sharing Template

When the project draws to a close, the team will dissolve and the documentation left behind will not cover the lessons learned and best practices. To make sure these are spread throughout the organization we propose a specific interview template with the best practice owner(s) to make sure nothing gets lost.

Generic Interview Guide

The generic interview guide serves as a memory aid and as an introduction for your conversation with the interviewee. If you send this in advance to your interlocutor, the interviewee will be better prepared and have a more efficient process delivering the best possible information. The interview guide also contains a metadata checklist to create awareness for better metadata from the outset of the project.

Generic Business Object Definitions

Any BI system will have at least one or more of these objects in the database:

Customer
Organization
Employee
Product
Territory

We have developed a few generic definitions to get the discussion started as we have proof that nothing is more difficult than aligning everybody in the organization around concepts such as these. We also prove in this chapter that there is no urge to develop one-size-fits-all definitions as perspectives may vary within one organization.

Appendices Overview

Appendix A: What to Ask on Your Job Interview

Make sure you know where the organization is between these two extremes on the scale. Some are transferring their chaos to your desk while others are so overly structured, they will oppress any initiative for improvement.

Appendix B: Business Intelligence from 1960 to Today

A short history of BI illustrates the rapid evolution the discipline has made and helps the analyst to understand the present situation better.

Appendix C: The 101 on Data Warehousing

This Appendix is for non-IT readers who need a quick introduction to data warehousing as the foundation of a BI system but who don't want to be overwhelmed with a lot of technical mumbo jumbo.

Appendix D: Survey for a BI Project

We have left the survey out of the toolbox because it is not common practice in BI projects. Nevertheless, as it could inspire the reader, we have added a survey example to the Appendixes.

2

The Increasing Cycle Speed
of Growth and Its Laws

INTRODUCTION

Growth Has a Price

There are universal laws at work that urge organizations to respond adequately to the environment. Formulating and implementing strategy is an ongoing process based on timely, accurate, and consistent information and a management vision that directs this process yet remains open to emergent opportunities and dissident actions and opinions.

Growth is the ultimate goal of any business and the subordinate goals to growth form a menu from which the organization serves smaller or larger portions: innovation; efficiency increase; productivity increase; market (share) growth; customer loyalty increase; market, price, and or cost leadership; product value added; quality management; economic value added; and risk reduction; all these goals support growth. And all of them require adequate information to formulate goals and provide measures of success.

Useful Lifespan of the PLC

History proves that product life cycles (PLC) may not be shorter than they used to be but they certainly have a smaller window of opportunity. In other words, due to faster and global communication channels and methods competitors respond quickly to new technological developments and in the case of technological platform improvements they wage life and death battles to get the lead in the market. Compare the number of car manufacturers in the early years of the automobile to the number of mobile phone producers in the early years of Global System for Mobile Communication (GSM) technology and the argument becomes clear: fewer but larger organizations cause faster changes in the market.

As the cycle speed of growth increases over time, the response time to environmental changes is reduced drastically. The first reason for this slump lies in the organization's growth itself where the initial hands-on strategy makers move away from the theater of operations or are replaced by "mercenaries" or more euphemistically, "professional managers" who bring their MBA models and methods but lack the ideological vigor and rigor of the founders. The second reason may occur in environmental change that is noticed too late as people have a tendency to believe that tomorrow will be the same as today.

Three Deltas

So growth comes at a price and managing growth takes respect for five basic laws I have observed, combined with a keen sense of timing and knowing when you know enough to act.

Years ago, I took a master class from one of the gurus of planning, Igor Ansoff. Ansoff has been *the* planning advocate in management science (although I consider that to be an oxymoron, as explained in the introduction of this book), introducing his concepts in giant organizations, including Boeing and NATO, but I had the impression he was no longer fanatically sticking to his guns. During the master class we developed a contingency approach to planning that no longer blamed turbulence for not achieving the planned goals but used it in the planning equation.

Schematically we came up with the diagram in Figure 2.1, which represents the shape, recognizability, and predictive value of data and information collected. In a turbulent environment the information is fragmented, inconsistent, and sparse. The more we move away from stable predictable environments, the less we need planning and the more we need adequate response mechanisms in the field organization.

It is clear that the left side of the diagram represents the situation of more stable markets such as museums or processed food production, and the right side illustrates the situation of innovative companies such as biotech or stable markets where disruptive technological advance is changing the rules of the game drastically.

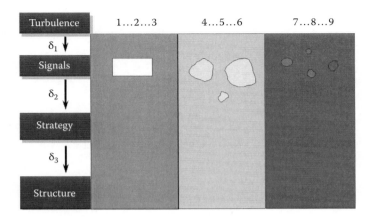

FIGURE 2.1
The planning–response time dilemma.

Time, the Essential Strategic Factor

It is also clear that the time lapse between the occurrence of the signals in the environment and their registration becomes longer as the company grows because information goes through more management layers and filters, often adapting the signals to their agenda. So unless your organization has the time to wait for the whole picture to come up on the radar screen, you are faced with serious potential danger. That is the first delta in your strategy process.

The second delta describes the time lapse to interpret the signals and formulate an adequate strategy update. During this process, additional information is needed to validate the strategic alternatives. In some cases organizations order market or expert studies to look for extra risk reduction and build support for their plans. Entrepreneurial intuition is replaced by inquiries as there is some reckoning to be done for the board and the shareholders.

The third and greatest delta is the time needed to adapt the organization to the new strategy. Capital investments have to be planned, financed, and integrated into the organization, skills have to be developed and learning curves start at a high level of cost per unit. New procedures originate and cause conflicts with existing procedures, processes, and structures.

Sometimes people are made redundant because they can't adapt to the new reality or there is no room for their skill set in the new configuration.

Needless to say this can have a negative impact on the people who stay on board, although I have seen situations where the latter sighed, "Good riddance," as people were made redundant.

Business Analysis Issues

Throughout the interviews and assessments, you should analyze historic and recent examples of the time lapse among these deltas.

Opening questions that cover this issue:

- When did the company have to adjust its plans to unforeseen events?
- When and how was the last time your company was taken by surprise and had to readjust quickly?
- What factors helped to speed up your response time and what didn't?

But you can also take a look into the future:

- Suppose the technology you use to realize your sales becomes obsolete in one to two years. How would you prepare for this foreseen evolution, starting today?
- Suppose the sales and marketing method you are using today gradually becomes ineffective. What information would you like today to prepare for this evolution?

According to the context you are working in, the questions may change. But they will always have to probe for the degree of adaptiveness and the available information resources to support far-reaching strategic decisions.

FIRST LAW: THE TRIANGLE OF KNOWLEDGE, GROWTH, AND STRATEGY PROCESSES

Various authors have demonstrated the relationship between knowledge and growth. Adam Smith (1723–1790) postulated growth as a necessity so man can devote himself to education and science. If you have seen African children spending their days walking miles to get water for their families and thus missing an education that would liberate them from this generation-old treadmill of poverty, you see Mr. Smith's point.

Benjamin Friedman from Harvard University states that prosperity is parallel to tolerance, which in its turn is parallel to democracy.

Anyone studying recent history and present developments in China will see these parallels. Joseph Schumpeter (1883–1950) justified growth with a simple and unavoidable truth: if savings on government bonds yield more than shares, then that is where the money goes. Schumpeter recognized the value of technical innovation causing disruptive changes that create and destroy wealth.

Paul Romer from Chicago University (at present teaching at Stanford University) studied the relationship between knowledge and growth and formulated the endogenous growth theory in his article "Endogenous Technological Change." According to Romer (1990), knowledge grows in small controllable processes and is a major driver in economic progress:

> The model presented here is essentially the one-sector neoclassical model with technological change, augmented to give an endogenous explanation of the source of the technological change. The most robust welfare conclusion from the model is that because research projects exchange current costs for a stream of benefits in the future, the rate of technological change is sensitive to the rate of interest. Although all the research is embodied in capital goods, a subsidy to physical capital accumulation may be a very poor substitute for direct subsidies that increase the incentive to undertake research. In the absence of feasible policies that can remove the divergence between the social and private returns to research, a second-best policy would be to subsidize the accumulation of total human capital. The most interesting positive implication of the model is that an economy with a larger total stock of human capital will experience faster growth. This finding suggests that free international trade can act to speed up growth. It also suggests a way to understand what it is about developed economies in the twentieth century that permitted rates of growth of income per capita that are unprecedented in human history. The model also suggests that low levels of human capital may help explain why growth is not observed in underdeveloped economies that are closed and why a less developed economy with a very large population can still benefit from economic integration with the rest of the world.

William Baumol from New York University states in *The Free Market Machine* (2004) that the battle between oligopolistic companies is the engine of innovation and thus, growth. No one at Airbus,

Intel, or Pfizer will counterargue. Let us end this argument for the coexistence of knowledge, growth, and strategy processes on a lighter note from Patrick O'Rourke in *Eat the Rich* (1998):

> I had one fundamental question about economics: Why do some places prosper and thrive while others just suck? It's not a matter of brains. No part of the earth (with the possible exception of Brentwood) is dumber than Beverly Hills, and the residents are wading in gravy. In Russia, meanwhile, where chess is a spectator sport, they're boiling stones for soup. Nor can education be the reason. Fourth graders in the American school system know what a condom is but aren't sure about 9 x 7. Natural resources aren't the answer. Africa has diamonds, gold, uranium, you name it. Scandinavia has little and is frozen besides. Maybe culture is the key, but wealthy regions such as the local mall are famous for lacking it.

Politicians in the Western democracies insist heavily on the knowledge economy stressing innovation—and by extension information and education—as the primary raw material for economic growth. Several conference papers stress the value of knowledge for world economic growth including, "Indeed, as it has been explained, knowledge is the public good for a future of peace and better life for a majority of people whichever is their civilization" (Verlaeten, 2002).

The final goal of strategic management is profitable growth, free of as many risks as possible, and since the ecological debate started in the late 1960s, more and more business leaders have added the adjective "sustainable" to their growth goals.

So, can anyone explain to me why managers are very good at managing money, resources, technology, people, and all other assets one can imagine except information and knowledge? Sure, every company has a customer relationship management (CRM) system, but what about the data quality? I worked for a multinational software company selling CRM software that had not cleaned its business data for more than six years. But keeping a basic level of data quality is just the beginning. How many companies rise above the basic level of marketing sophistication you notice in messages such as, "It is three months since we heard from you, so here is an offer you can't refuse: 30% discount on your next order." At best, organizations have some idea about their costs from their enterprise resource planning (ERP) systems and can develop growth–cost impact scenarios based on these data.

These are two examples of the lowest level of analytic strategic information: cost and customer information. Higher-level information such as the other two Cs, "competitors" and "competences," is already a lot harder to find in most Business Intelligence (BI) systems, let alone synthetic information covering the 5 Ps (position, posture, perspective, plan, and ploys).

The Knowledge Exchange Process

To ensure maximum effectiveness of the strategy process, the exchange of knowledge among all stakeholders is of vital importance. Yet, in my consulting experience I have met with very few organizations where knowledge exchange was part of the corporate culture. Those that were successful had a democratic leadership and dealt with few external parties. They had no shareholders because they provided their own funds, they had no trouble with pressure groups because nobody from outside really understood what was going on in the company (although that is often a good reason for pressure groups to fire up their fundraising–activism–public relations machine), and they were able to synchronize the personal agendas of their employees with the company's agenda. But these were rare examples, exceptions to the rule, the rule being that the major part of larger organizations is just not ready for knowledge exchange.

Many factors hamper this knowledge exchange process and most organizational structures survive by the "none of your business" adage. The principal barrier to reach knowledge exchange Nirvana in larger organizations is the impossibility of synchronizing the agendas of shareholders, the board of directors, executive management, functional management, the workforce, labor unions, government, pressure groups, and the like. But how do you measure the degree of knowledge exchange in an organization?

How do you measure something that materializes only during the exchange and sometimes much later, hidden in the results of the process? And what about the dark number, the untapped potential? I was happy to find at least one researcher who is tackling this question systematically.

Knowledge cooperation, according to Karin Moser (2002), can be defined as "the willingness with which and measure in which co-workers contribute their knowledge to the business processes and support each other with their knowledge even when there is no direct and immediate personal benefit for it." By extension this holds a lot of truth for the strategy process. In the same article, Moser presents three preconditions for knowledge cooperation: reciprocity, a long-term perspective for the employees and the organization, and breaking the hierarchical barriers. I agree with some but not all of these preconditions.

Reciprocity

I learned about reciprocity the hard way during the implementation of CRM systems. The only way to get good information from a reluctant sales executive is to provide her with more and better information than she could ever come up with herself and giving full credit to the CRM system for that information.

Long-Term Perspectives

Be it for individual development programs or the future of the business and its position in the branch, I have my doubts about this precondition. If this were true, why are there so many sad examples of "*la guerre des flics*" or "the police wars" as we knew them in Belgium, France, the United States, and other countries? These are exemplary organizations for Professor Moser's criteria: they have a dominant position in their branch and they offer cradle-to-grave development perspectives for their employees. And the picture gets even grimmer when you realize that knowledge is exploited as a raw material in all primary processes of the police force. Or, what to think of very short-term successes in knowledge sharing of interdisciplinary research startup companies, with no position at all and no long-term perspectives either, except the rigor and vigor of the founding entrepreneurs?

Fewer Hierarchies

Moser also stresses the need for high autonomy for the co-workers and participation in decision making as well as flat hierarchies and low intra-company barriers. The last condition is very important to make it happen and clarifies the argument. I know of many organizations that interpret "exchange throughout all hierarchical layers" as passing through information from one layer to another where the source acts as a filter for the receiver. And that exchange process is a lot closer to politics and manipulation than knowledge cooperation.

Measuring Reciprocity

Moser's vision of knowledge cooperation rejects machine bureaucracy*
as a barrier to information exchange and—implicitly—as a roadblock for
high-performance information management with a Business Intelligence
infrastructure as a cornerstone for decision making. In her knowledge
cooperation inventory she makes a thorough study of individual, organizational, collective, and knowledge cooperation mentality and practices to
define the degree of readiness for knowledge management.

Among the individual factors of competence, motivation and self-
starter aspects are charted and the organizational factors include level of
satisfaction with the infrastructure, financial aspects, and the perceived
reciprocity. The collective aspects deal with expectations about knowledge
management's (KM's) effectiveness, trust in the professional future, and
the level of autonomy in the organization.

Among the 24 drivers for knowledge management Amrit Tiwana (2000)
sums up, five organizational and four personnel drivers support the idea
that the machine bureaucracy is incompatible with sophisticated business
intelligence and knowledge exchange for strategy development.

Organizational Drivers

Tiwana (2000) distinguishes functional convergence, emergence of
project-centric organizational structures, challenges brought about by
deregulation, companies' inability to keep pace with competitive change
due to globalization, and convergence of products and services as organizational drivers. The emergence of project-centric organizations supports
my critique of Moser's long-term perspective as a preliminary for knowledge exchange. A sense of urgency for a short-term project may well be as
powerful as any driver!

Personnel Drivers

Tiwana (2000) sums up widespread functional convergence, the need
to support effective cross-functional collaboration, team mobility and

---

* The machine bureaucracy is one of the organizational archetypes as defined by Henry Mintzberg
in his works such as *The Structuring of Organizations* (1979), *Mintzberg on Management* (1989),
and the like, where the operating core dominates organizational behavior. Simplified: the primary
process dominates the way decisions are prepared and taken.

fluidity, as well as the need to deal with complex corporate expectations. Many other authors (Leliveld and Vink, 2000; Davis and Newstrom, 1989) support the idea that knowledge exchange based on reciprocity can only take place in organizational forms that present the whole picture to their employees and that keep the distance among coworkers and the company's vision, objectives, customers, and so on, as small as possible.

I am not a psychologist trained in projection techniques and in-depth interview methods to measure the emotional and motivational aspects of reciprocity. And even if I could come up with relevant and significant data, the question about practical implementation methods would remain. My reciprocity measurements are based on the organizational assumption that interdependency between people and organizations is the key factor that creates reciprocity.

Business Analysis Issues

The very simple questionnaire in Table 2.1 helps you to pinpoint the level of reciprocity. On a five-point Likert scale a representative sample of employees can express their perception of interdependency in the organization. The more the average moves toward five points, the more interdependency and need for information exchange exists.

TABLE 2.1

Pros and Cons of Economies of Scale

Question: How do you reach your objectives?		
1: By individual effort	3: By coordinating efforts of colleagues	5: By coordinating efforts from other departments
Question: What is the nature of the exchanged information?		
1: Information directed at my job description	3: Information also directed at adjacent functions or departments	5: Interdisciplinary information
Question: How are decisions being made?		
1: By individuals	3: In small teams	5: Organizationwide consulting and feedback loops
Where appropriate you can add the following question:		
Question: How are resources, funds, and assets allocated?		
1: By arbitrary decisions from the top	3: After consulting various experts in the organization	5: By mutual adjustment processes

SECOND LAW: YOUR NARROW CHOICE BETWEEN TWO OPTIONS

Depending on various factors, such as the life-cycle phase of the organization, the market conditions for resources, the level of resistance to change in the organization, and so on, strategic choices boil down to two:

- Optimize the existing situation because it yields maximum growth at a minimum risk.
- Change the present situation because it will lead to negative growth, higher risks, or even disaster.

During my almost 30 years of business practice I observed that the bigger the market share, the more inward-looking organizations become. It is as if these organizations consider a large market share as a synonym for market control, which it isn't. In their opinion, internal improvement initiatives yield better results than paying closer attention to the customer. The natural development and growth of a business goes through four consecutive phases: focus—conquer—retreat—redeploy. Let us examine these four phases in detail and look at the predominant strategic choice organizations make in each phase.

Note: We stress natural development as there are many companies being created through mergers, turnaround operations, or what I call "project businesses," a phenomenon we saw a lot of during the Internet bubble. CEOs moved from one pre-IPO to the other, taking companies to the NASDAQ and then moving on to the next prey. Their salaries and bonuses were paid by the often gullible private investor.

Focus

How does a business come into being? The founder, or the founding team in high-tech environments, has a specific skill that holds promise for success. By focusing on this skill, the business proves its viability and grows. A heavy focus on serving the market better than the competitors through superior services and products is key to the early success. As it grows, new skills are acquired by hiring professionals, contracting consultants, and internal development.

Tolerance for inefficiencies in the customer serving process diminishes. The need for standardization, total quality management emerges, and the organization shifts from a missionary organization to a more formalized configuration. We refer to the 7-S model as described by Robert Waterman Jr., Thomas Peters, and Julien Philips in their article, "Structure Is Not Organisation" (1980) to describe the changes that are taking place as the business grows:

- The "S" from systems takes over from style as the need for management control grows.
- The "S" from structure takes over from superordinate goals as power struggles are channeled into business units, job descriptions, and salary scales.
- What remain relatively unchanged are strategy, staff, and skills. That is why, although the configuration of a business may change over time, its culture evolves a lot more slowly. Because the values and beliefs that led to the organization's growth date from the early days, they remain engrained in these three Ss.

Conquest

As the company gains sufficient control over internal matters, thereby often eliminating dissidents, it gradually directs its attention to increasing the number of market segments served and gaining maximum share in these segments. Strategy development is basically optimizing the existing processes in an incremental way so strategy control is being introduced via corporate performance systems based on Balanced Scorecards. In our Fourth Law we elaborate more on these measurement systems.

Because growth is essential for a business, it may come in different flavors. Optimism, or innate bonus plans for top management, majority shareholders, or venture capitalists who want to bail out at a maximum P/E ratio (price/earnings ratio) might be the cause of low-quality growth. But even high-quality growth can have unwanted side effects that cause the company to retreat.

Retreat

The growth of the organization has caused some side effects that might divert the business from its original focus. The reasons are obvious:

- Shareholders expect increasing returns every year so quarterly reports prevail over the rest (and believe me, this happens also in organizations who have introduced the Balanced Scorecard!).
- The law of diminishing returns forces the company to develop new initiatives and new product/market combinations that are riskier.
- The company profits attract new competitors attacking the company's cash cow.

In his seminal book *The Rise and Fall of The Great Powers*, Paul Kennedy (1987) introduced the concept of the "imperial overstretch" and more than 20 years ago predicted the relative decline of the United States as the leading world power. A somewhat simplistic reduction of his arguments can easily be transplanted to market leaders: because of strategic obligations from the past, a business can get into trouble as new challengers come into the market. Imagine a company like Ford or General Motors who developed their distribution system more than 80 years ago now under attack from an Internet-based car sales company delivering ambulant car maintenance services at your home. How could GM and Ford respond to this threat without hurting their existing distribution system? We saw similar situations in the financial sector where "bricks-and-mortar" banks responded poorly to the first Internet banks before they became "click-and-mortar," only to attract fickle, promotion-sensitive customers at a higher cost than pure Internet players.

Other than distribution configurations, these obligations vary from joint ventures to capital investments in technology becoming obsolete, and so on. And last but not least: social obligations. Especially in Western Europe social obligations lay a heavy burden on a business. Take the Belgian example where a white collar worker with five years' service receives a year's salary or more when made redundant. Everyone remembers the Volkswagen Brussels' restructuring that led to redundancy payments of up to €100,000 per worker. Including tax and social contributions the cost could rise to a whopping €190,000. That makes you think twice about reinvesting in Belgium. Yet the Volkswagen Group did it because of the skills level of the workforce. But it is no exaggeration to state that some companies are bankrupt without their accounts showing it because if they restructure to adapt to new realities, they can't afford to make people redundant and so continue to suffer losses.

Redeploy

Already in the previous phase, management is looking for new per-spectives and horizons to redeploy the company's assets. To identify opportunities, the Business Intelligence infrastructure is of strategic importance. Where are new revenue opportunities? What can we learn from successful departments? Redeploying the business means redefin-ing the mission, redirecting and reorienting the organization's skills. The better the BI system is developed, the more intelligent and the smoother this process will be. During these four phases the organiza-tion chooses between optimization or change of its plans, positioning, posture, perspective, and ploys. A discussion on these 5 Ps is presented in the next chapter.

Strategy Continuum

The diagram in Figure 2.2 illustrates the path(s) an organization can fol-low when pursuing a growth strategy. Change and optimization are the boundaries of a continuum between strategic turnaround, revitalizing, and efficiency improvements of the present strategic choices.

Figure 2.2 suggests "exclusive OR" choices but that is a misinterpreta-tion of these descriptive terms, classifying strategic directions. We can all classify horses and donkeys but we are also aware that a stallion and a jenny can breed mules. In the same way, you should interpret this scheme as a continuum of mixed forms between drastic change and stability.

The extremes occur rarely; most of the time, management is busy revitalizing the strategic directions for all sorts of reasons: new employ-ees come to the organization, new market segments are entered, or new products are developed, among others. All these tactical moves can affect

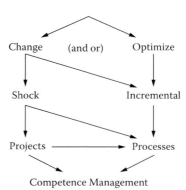

FIGURE 2.2
The strategy continuum as a path.

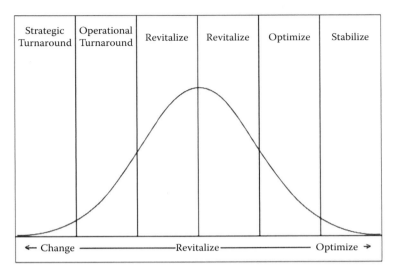

| Strategic Turnaround | Operational Turnaround | Revitalize | Revitalize | Optimize | Stabilize |

← Change ——————————Revitalize—————— Optimize →

FIGURE 2.3
The strategy continuum and general directions.

the organization's strategy so management has to take action that moves between dotting the i's and crossing the t's and adapting some external aspects of the strategic direction such as "customers served," "priorities reshuffled," and the like.

As shown in Figure 2.3, change and optimization are the extremes on a continuum between strategic turnaround and stability, or between restoring effectiveness and efficiency increase. A good business analyst should be able to capture the dominant strategic direction in an organization.

Business Analysis Issues

To check the company's attitude and BI infrastructure to adapt to change, these questions might open up an interesting debate:

- How do you perform "what if" analysis today?
- Can you scale up minor cost savers or minor revenue sources?
- Does your BI infrastructure allow freewheeling and unstructured data exploration? If so, are we talking online analytical processing (OLAP), data mining, text mining?
- What is the procedure for the creation of new reports, analyses, and thorough studies of the data in your organization?
- Is there a procedure to add new data sources to the BI system? If so, what are the criteria to accept or reject the change?

- Suppose a new front-end tool would expand the possibilities of your existing data with a large factor. What scenario would you prefer:
  - Do a Big Bang introduction of the new tool, replacing the old front-end tool.
- Test it and look for users that are "mature" enough to handle the new tool, leaving the old tool to the others.

When the ice is broken, probe a little bit deeper. Don't use a checklist or ask for points on a Likert scale unless you can do a companywide anonymous inquiry. And when you do, you will still need interviews to look for context and poignant stories that give color to the cultural sketch of the attitude toward change.

- What do you consider important in your organization?
  - Clear goals and procedures.
  - Task orientation.
  - Every individual is responsible for his own achievements.
  - Critiques and remarks are accepted in the organization.
  - After discussing the ideas and reaching a conclusion we expect all parties to support the results of the discussion.
  - Dissidence, if used to prove a point beneficial to the organization, is allowed.
  - Teamwork is preferred over individual excellence.
  - Every worker has access to top management.
  - There is a high level of trust among colleagues.
  - Colleagues support each other in the case of problems related to the job.
  - Change is perceived as part of the business.
  - A good atmosphere is more important than meeting today's targets.
  - Meeting the monthly targets is more important than job satisfaction.
  - We put the customer first (make sure you get examples because every company pays lip service to this slogan!).
  - Entrepreneurial spirit is preferred over acceptance of orders.
  - Job security combined with lower wages is preferred over a higher salary with no job security.

THIRD LAW: ANY ORGANIZATION OPTIMIZES TWO EXTREMES

A few years ago, I was swept away by the scientific argumentation on an issue most politicians' pre-scientific gut feeling recognizes: the size of an organization is an optimum between the economies of scale and the cost of heterogeneity. Admittedly, Alesina and Spolaore (2003) developed the argument for nations as they work in the field of political economy but the parallels are clear as businesses show the same mechanisms internally and, of course, businesses are important actors in the economy and in politics.

Apply this theory to the value chain and to generic competitive strategies as described by Michael Porter and you come up with a very interesting and practical reference framework. But before we do, let us list the advantages and disadvantages of both extremes as shown in Table 2.2. When Michael Porter wrote his "Competitive Strategy" (1980) there was no Internet and 90% of all U.S. retail sales went through classical distribution channels and the rest via mail order. So it was logical that he represented his three generic competitive strategies as three separate entities.

Figure 2.4 still offers us a reference framework except that today companies are capable of passing the crisp barriers among the three strategies at almost no cost because of information and communication technology (ICT). ICT has turned this diagram upside down. Mass customization makes it possible to offer one car model in over 5,000 combinations. The extended enterprise business model makes it possible to broaden and differentiate the product or service offerings at a far lower entry cost than before.

Nevertheless, the typology remains relevant, so from an analyst's point of view it is necessary to translate these strategies into skills and resources and organizational requirements as Porter does, adding specific ICT skills as a third dimension of these strategies. Therefore, one is no longer "stuck in the middle" as Porter put it but has the possibility of combining the best of three worlds. Henry Mintzberg (1989, 1991) points out that ideology can be the *trait d'union* between opposing strategies such as differentiation and cost leadership; we believe ICT facilitates this ideological binding agent.

TABLE 2.2

Pros and Cons of Heterogeneity

Economies of Scale	
Advantages	**Disadvantages**
Basis for cost leadership	As soon as the market matures, customers leave you for more sophisticated (read: diversified) products
Creates entry barriers for head-on competition	Opens possibilities for lateral (flanking) competition and new entrants with new technology as the commitment of assets to economies of scale can be enormous
Works great in market skimming strategies	
Works great in emerging markets	May provoke a technology and marketing "lock-in" at a premature stage, which needs expensive corrections when the market matures
Heterogeneity	
Basis for diversified competition and risk spread	Spreading resources too thin
Creates entry barriers for competition in mature markets where diversification comes as a natural evolution	Opens possibilities for sideways competition and new entrants with new technology as the commitment of assets to economies of scope can be enormous
Customer lifetime value increases as the customer evolves with the diversified product range	Fixed costs to be absorbed by a smaller revenue basis
If the majority of the heterogeneous products or business units covers their market segment better than the competition this strategy yields high margins	

Value Chain Revisited

The other powerful concept introduced by Porter in the 1980s was the value chain, a decomposition of value-adding activities in a company to convert raw materials into products and services, servicing customers. Porter made the distinction between the primary processes producing the products and services and the support activities such as Human Resources Management (HRM), finance, and facility management. More and more of both activity types are being supported by ICT, rendering a feeling of

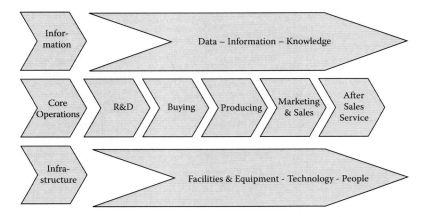

FIGURE 2.4
A modernized version of the value chain, integrating the information aspects of the value chain.

control. The old rationalization and control paradigm as old as Henri Saint-Simon's, Henri Fayol's, and Frederick Taylor's theories on management re-enters management practice. With the Balanced Scorecard introduced as the ultimate strategy accounting system, management is rekindling the positivist image of management sciences and creating a false feeling of controlling the uncontrollable. But I am digressing.

Consider this value chain as an assembly of building blocks that no longer need to be managed centrally. Outsourcing entire processes to specialized companies, co-sourcing processes with competitors, and pushing processes to the self-serving customer have all been made possible through ICT.

Conclusion: there is no dichotomy between economies of scale and heterogeneity in the modern business environment, providing the ICT infrastructure is implemented effectively. The world's most famous example is Amazon.com using ICT to create economies of scale in the back office to support a strategy of cost leadership while supporting a strategy of differentiation in the front office using CRM, Business Intelligence for better targeting, and exploiting even the smallest niches in the market economically. For people with a short memory, let us not forget that only because of the easy money provided by investors during the Internet hype was Jeff Bezos able to learn from his mistakes and build this huge marketing machine over quite a long period. Today in 2012, no investor would allow him that amount of time to spend and money to burn.

TABLE 2.3

Consequences of Cost Leadership

Commonly Required Skills and Resources	Common Organizational Requirements	ICT Requirements and Systems
Sustained capital investment and access to capital	Tight cost control Frequent detailed control reports	Asset management support systems, cost monitoring, and reporting
Process engineering skills	Structured organization and responsibilities	Skills management, e-learning, HRM systems, process management support, ERP
Intense supervision of labor	Incentives based on meeting strict quantitative targets	Manufacturing automation, access control systems, and time registration

Business Analysis Issues

What Defines Overall Cost Leadership?

Please see Table 2.3.

When discussing strategy with managers you can address the subject from one or more of the three perspectives in Table 2.4.

TABLE 2.4

Consequences of Differentiation

Commonly Required Skills and Resources	Common Organizational Requirements	ICT Requirements and Systems
Strong marketing abilities Product engineering Creative flair Strong capability in basic research	Strong coordination among functions in R&D, product development, and marketing	Customer relationship management, configuration management Groupware, project management
Corporate reputation for quality or technological leadership	Subjective measurement and incentives instead of quantitative measures	Quality management, process management, and ERP systems
Long tradition in the industry or unique combination of skills drawn from other businesses	Amenities to attract highly skilled labor, scientists, or creative people	Knowledge management
Strong cooperation from channels	A profit-sharing culture	Partner relationship management systems

What Defines Differentiation?

What Defines Focus?

In Porter's (1980) terms it is the combination of the above policies directed at the particular strategic target. The same goes for the ICT systems. The scale and depth of these systems depend on the profitability of the organization and the level of systematic processes and structures in the organization. The latter criterion depends on the growth possibilities: does the niche have growth potential or will it remain a marginal market segment. If the niche is very promising, we will see larger organizations focusing on this niche as a transition phase toward either a differentiated market leader in a mainstream market or a cost leader in a mass market. In that case, the organizational and ICT requirements will have the traits of the differentiated organization or the cost leader.

FOURTH LAW: MEASURE ONLY WHAT YOU CAN MEASURE BUT . . .

. . . don't forget to manage the immeasurable. As stated before in this book, management has a long-standing pedigree of rationalization geared at obtaining maximum efficiency. This efficiency Eldorado is expressed as the greatest measurable benefit for the smallest measurable cost. Everyone knows the adage, "What you can't measure, you can't manage," but I am afraid we will have to do better than that to become really successful managers. The history of entrepreneurial success is full of stories of people who didn't have a clue about the theories MBA adepts adore but they became very successful by constantly learning and adapting. One of my favorites is the story of Ben & Jerry's, who started their first ice cream parlor in New Jersey, one of the colder states in the United States, and obtained a bank loan by doing a "find and replace" of "Pizza" by "Ice cream" in a Word document of a business plan for a pizza joint.

Closer to me is the example of Janssen Pharmaceutica, a company driven by the enthusiasm, the genius, and the drive of Dr. Paul Janssen that permeated the entire company. The company didn't only excel in discovering more useful molecules per number of experiments than any other pharmaceutical company; they were also the first to invest in China as early as 1980 when nobody saw the enormous potential of the sleeping giant.

Examples like these stress the importance of commitment, hands on management, looking for the facts behind the figures and seizing opportunities before they could ever show up in the figures.

During my mission at Robeco, one of the largest asset management firms in Western Europe, I met with Gerard Wolfs, an analyst who stated, "Always look for the story behind the figures." What Wolfs meant was that figures are just abstractions of reality and to manage only by these figures is like describing Provence by reading aloud the names on a roadmap. So my message is: go see Provence and use the roadmap as a mnemonic support. And moreover, do not always trust your roadmap.

Many psychological experiments confirm what any manager knows intuitively: people adapt their behavior to that part of it observed by their peers or superiors. A few lessons are to be learned from this:

- Avoid redundant measurements.
  - Ex.: The time a salesperson spends on each customer
- Avoid inconsistent measurements.
  - Ex.: Effective machine hours and average cost of series
- Avoid quasi-measurements.
  - Ex.: Results of peer reviews
- Avoid one-dimensional measurement systems.
  - Ex.: Only focusing on cost

Make sure your measurements convey the right message about the company's mission and give an answer to the "What's in it for me?" question from the employees.

Experiment

In the chapter "A Note on that Dirty Word Efficiency," Mintzberg (1989, pp. 330–334) refers to an experiment in an MBA class to demonstrate that efficiency is related to measurable data. I expanded this experiment to a distinct target group of ICT professionals. They were asked to reflect on four simple questions:

- What is an efficient restaurant to you?
- What is an efficient house to you?
- When do you consider you are working efficiently?
- On a scale of 1–7, how efficient are you in general?

Results

In total, 85 ICT professionals were interviewed. More than 80% of the respondents defined efficiency in terms of measurable throughput and output:

> It is a restaurant that serves what I want in a short time after ordering.
> It is a house where I can "house" all the functions I need: eating, sleeping, studying.

It was clear that ICT people are trained in objective figures to gauge a medium complex reality like a house or a restaurant. Imagine this reductionism applied to something as complex as a medium-sized organization with 800 employees, 15 departments, and at least 20 stakeholder types.

Almost nobody referred to less tangible but equally important aspects such as feeling comfortable, at ease, or coziness. Most ICT professionals considered themselves rather efficient (average score of 4.2) and defined efficiency in terms of achieving the objectives, in our terms, when their plans were met, regardless of what happened on the way to achieving these plans.

Conclusion

Business Intelligence is more than presenting neatly scrubbed figures on a desktop. It is about providing context and making sense of the numbers but also enriching these same figures with strong motivational appeal. These immeasurable aspects may have a stronger impact on the company's decision-making behavior than the naked truths reflected in the numbers.

Business Analysis Issues

Try to find out about the Business Intelligence mindset in the company. Is it a healthy mix of a cybernetic, a dialectic, a synthetic, and an explorative approach, or merely geared toward increasing the efficiency of the strategy process instead of increasing its scope by introducing alternatives the organization would never have considered without Business Intelligence?

> Is the BI architecture the result of a demand for more control or does it allow creative holistic thinking to grow the numerator instead of constantly reducing the denominator?

Are the results from the Business Intelligence system used to engage further thinking, brainstorming, and exploration instead of presenting canonical truths about the organization?

What is management's tolerance for decision making under uncertainty?

Do the results from the BI system lead to formulating hypotheses that are validated or repudiated by management after talking to various people in the organization?

Does the system contribute to the development of new models or improvement of existing ones?

A Few Tips

Ask your interviewees about their definition of management. If you get the planning–organizing–coordinating–and–controlling cliché you may contribute to a successful BI project but you are far away from a successful strategy process. Don't forget to check on his or her views on efficiency; it will clarify a lot.

Let us conclude this section with a wonderful quote from Albert Einstein: "Not everything that counts can be counted; not everything that can be counted counts."

FIFTH LAW: THERE IS ALWAYS A DOMINANT SOURCE

Strategy can emerge in all corners and parts of the organization but depending on its configuration, you will have to look for the dominant source:

- The strategic apex where top management suggests, sells, or dictates the strategy, depending on the corporate culture and leadership
- The functional management where the leading department initiates the strategy process and the rest follow suit, or (and I hope your organization is not in that situation) use sabotage to oust an internal competitor in the race for the throne
- The operational layer where—at best—formal groups, such as trade unions, or informal groups are leading the way, introducing strategic questions and taking new initiatives

Strategic Apex

The presentation mode can differ depending on the company's culture but the results are equal: a centrally developed strategy with a level of detail that impairs free interpretation for middle management. Companies like Microsoft have a strong centralized leadership. This shows even in operational details. Microsoft's global customer database is physically stored in the U.S. offices. So, as soon as the U.S. East Coast offices fire up their computers in the morning, performance in the European offices decreases in the afternoon hours.

Exploring Alternatives and Options

Leadership is very much about looking for untrodden areas and exploring possibilities beyond the present scope and mindset of the organization. The question remains as to what extent a BI infrastructure can contribute to exploration. This process relies heavily on soft information and outright guesswork, far beyond the scope of BI. We are in the realm of knowledge management where an important process of turning implicit or tacit knowledge is turned into explicit knowledge. That is when BI assumes its responsibilities again.

Functional Management

Often two departments lead the way; either in conjunction or as fierce opposites do they dominate the strategy process. In my experience the main power plays were between three functions in changing combinations:

- Marketing versus finance
- Finance versus operations
- Operations versus marketing

I refer to the chapters on BI and financial management, BI and operations management, and BI and marketing management for more details.

In many organizations my colleagues from Lingua Franca Consulting and I have worked with, the CEO mainly plays a role of conflict handling, mitigating the effects of ambitious managers clashing with their colleagues as they optimize their department's output at the expense of others. The first case I remember was of a mail-order company where marketing was responsible for sales promotion. There are lots of ways of boosting your sales as you temporarily change the marketing mix elements: more aggressive advertising, gifts, sweepstakes and contests, packaging with an added value, and, last but not least, temporary price reductions, or TPRs, as they are known in marketing jargon. In this particular company, marketing decided on which sales promotion tactics were used but the purchasing department was responsible for pricing the product.

Result? It was better for the marketing budget to maximize the TPRs instead of using more creative promotions because these were at the expense of the purchasing department. I remember an executive saying: "We are all very profitable departments sharing the company's losses." This may be an extreme example (one that was remedied after a reorganization exercise), but there are many subtle variants.

Marketing versus Finance

Finance is focused on issues such as cost accounting, balancing the books, audit trails, cash management, capital budgeting, and the like. When marketing proposes pricing strategies that do not cover the present direct costs to buy market share, it has a hard time convincing the finance department that this is the way to go. Sophisticated data analysis is needed to determine who is right.

Finance versus Operations

Finance and operations may quarrel over investment in machines and other capital goods that increase capacity but also risk, commitment, and decreased flexibility to adapt. How all this relates to lower unit cost is not always clear. And then there is asset management, the intersection between economical and technical aspects of an asset. To develop effective asset management strategies, an integration of maintenance, operational, financial, and even sales data is necessary to provide decision support.

Operations versus Marketing

Marketing wants the highest service level possible but operations has to reduce stock levels to an operational optimum, often supported by the finance department as they adhere to the "cash is king" adage. To determine the real optimum between marketing and operational effectiveness, complex data gathering and calculations are needed.

Operational Layer

Bottom-Up Strategy Formation

In organizations where operations are in the hands of highly skilled workers or craftsmen, academics, consultants, and other professionals with a high degree of knowledge, skills, and experience often inaccessible to outsiders (as managers are), the strategy formation process is in their hands. Because these people have very short feedback loops between learning and doing, management is often unaware of the strategic change under way and their BI systems fail to detect and report this change.

The only help BI can offer management is the monitoring of outliers in every aspect of the business, asking the right questions. Are these outliers random or are they caused by deliberate action from an individual stakeholder? Can we repeat the event? Are the underlying processes known to anyone in the organization? This is about as far as the BI system goes. The rest depends on the interpersonal skills of managers in their interaction with professionals. Management's response is the simple choice between accepting the new strategic initiative and creating a favorable environment or rejecting it and running the risk of the professionals leaving the company to pursue their dream.

The Dutch BSO, founded by Eckart Wintzen, was an example of an organic growth management style, keeping high potentials within the company and balancing between entrepreneurial freedom for these managers and a common sense of direction for the company. His idea was to grow by remaining small. Wintzen didn't want to become the CEO of a large impersonal company and when his enterprise reached the 50 FTE mark, he split it into two cells of 25, so the manager of the second cell would know every employee by name and take responsibility for the group. Every time a cell became too large, it split roughly in half, so in less than 10 years the self-employed Wintzen created an IT company with 10,000 employees. But when he left the company, new management soon let go of the cell growth idea, proving that individual leadership can be an important factor in strategy formation and formulation.

This translation from "Eckart's Notes" (Wintzen, 2007) illustrates his vision about growth through cell division:

> Let's put all boring theory aside: a company can only function perfectly when everybody knows what is expected of him and when the job gets done in the team.
>
> To me, the word "team" means everybody knows his co-workers, knows what the others can and cannot do and is willing to take a piece of his colleague's work without moaning or grunting. All this in the spirit of consensus and harmony. That is the reason for the conveniently arranged cells. The family business idea. But togetherness is also an emotional matter; you have to be willing to be together. And that works only when there is a fit, when you think it's a good idea to go for a beer together.
>
> Therefore the co-workers in a cell determine who can join the cell, someone who fits in the team. Other than that, cell management knows best which sort of knowledge and experience is more important than academic degrees or vice versa (fat chance!).
>
> Thus it is pragmatic to let the companies recruit locally. The candidates will be scrutinized by their future colleagues (peer interviews) and these colleagues will assess if the new hire will fit in the team.
>
> The problem with recruiting via the H.R.M. Department is that candidates may comply with the technical/academic "specs" but as a person don't fit in the team.
>
> By the way, a "computer nerd" with practical experience will establish whether a candidate's experience is real or he has read "How to bluff your way in IT, without really knowing" ten times as fast as a recruiter.
>
> We have seen it elsewhere, it is like a marriage and you don't have your partner selected by an H.R.M. recruiter, do you?

The Cybernetic Feedback Loops

In this environment, the image of driving a car is often used. The Business Intelligence system delivers clear steering instructions for areas such as operations, finance, and marketing, for example. Key assumptions to make this work are that all business rules are explicit and unequivocal and all business processes are documented and understood by the people who have to execute them.

To deliver this feedback loop, all relevant variables have to be measured and logged. Whether they are explicitly presented depends on the level and amount of exceptions defined in the business processes and the rules governing the process. The latest buzzwords are business rules engines (BRE) that interact with BI in a SOA (service oriented architecture).

We have three kinds of variables:

- Control variables: They define the criteria for the process to be successful, for example, "Make a trip to Luxembourg," according to four control parameters:
  - Destination: Rue de Wirtz, 2, Luxembourg
  - Estimated time: Two to three hours' drive from Brussels
  - Safety parameters: Respect the traffic code, especially the speed limits
  - Budget: Standard cost per kilometer is €1,09
- Essential variables. In this example we foresee five essential variables that help the driver to make decisions:
  - Kilometers to go
  - Fuel level
  - Elapsed time
  - Speed
  - Position
- Action variables: These define the scope of decisions, c.q. actions needed to reach the control variables based on the observation of the essential variables:
  - Steer (left, right)
  - Brake (brake power dosage)
- Accelerate (acceleration power dosage)

It is clear that this vision of Business Intelligence is a very narrow and mechanistic one and people who have seen the effects of program trading on the stock exchange in Fall 1987 will know what I mean. Nevertheless, the applications of this BI application level are worth examining.

Examples of Operational BI in Marketing

1. Customer reactivation: Any customer who hasn't ordered an item for six months receives an e-mail with an offer especially targeted at her.
2. Customer potential: Based on customer data and comparisons with similar customers, the customer potential is calculated.
3. Tailor-made couponing: Based on the customer's purchase behavior, he receives coupons before or after going to the supermarket.

4. One-to-one marketing: The accumulated customer data drastically improve the service and the personalization of the service and the products, thus raising the entry barrier for competitors by increasing the switching costs for the consumer.

Examples of Operational BI in Finance

1. Credit limit calculation: Based on customer and accounting data, the credit limit is increased or decreased.
2. Automatic cash management: Combining historical accounting data, forecasts, budgets, and optimization algorithms dealing with risk, availability, and interest returns, the system prepares the necessary financial transfers.

Examples of Operational BI in Operations (Supply Chain Management and Manufacturing)

1. Automatic inventory replenishment: Based on algorithms taking into account present usage, forecasts, and lead times, inventory orders are automatically placed.
2. Demand forecasting: From simple smoothed averages of historic data to the sophisticated BI variant that may be a combination of massive amounts of data from all sorts of sources, including:
   - Indices of consumer confidence
   - Temperature
   - Hours of sunlight
   - Unemployment figures
   - Proxy sales figures
   - Sales pipeline
   - General market data

These forecasts provide input for staff planning, procurement, and so on.

In the operations world this type of BI is also called "structured decision systems." These systems use the transaction data in procedures that are fully formalized and structured around unequivocal rules. Inventory management systems, payroll systems, invoicing, warehouse management systems, and maintenance systems are typical examples. These systems have extensive operational reporting facilities and alerts when things get out of hand. Events such as late deliveries or machine failure (or imminent failure) are reported in clear terms to key users.

SIXTH LAW: IT IS HERE TO STAY

My interest in the value of IT started in the 1980s when I was a manager at a mail-order company. These guys were very much aware of the strategic potential of IT: customer analysis, targeting, research, promotion testing, invoicing, and dunning; at Neckermann Mailorder in Frankfurt, Germany they and their colleagues from Otto, La Redoute, 3 Suisses, Sears, Great Universal Stores, and others were way ahead of the nondirect marketers. It was no coincidence that the IT manager from the Dutch Neckermann subsidiary became general manager. More than 20 years later, "regular" business has caught up with the direct marketers and started to use IT as a strategic facilitator and, in some cases, as a strategic differentiator.

IT Can Create Competitive Advantages

No manager will counterargue this adage yet there are caveats: timing is essential and budgets are to be managed tightly. Many IT fads had little to do with competitive advantage and they used up budgets that could have been more productive. Excuse me for not summing them all up with their buzzwords; I want to remain on speaking terms with the vendors but see if you can recognize these situations:

- The ERP introduction held great promise but soon it became clear that the 1.0 version was a hodgepodge of loosely connected island applications with incompatible processes, no metadata, weak reporting features, and a steep learning curve for the user community.
- The Balanced Scorecard application was a nice package for an old application: instead of interconnecting the KPIs and revealing causal relationships between them, the tool did nothing more than use Robert S. Kaplan's graphical representations for what were still four unconnected reports.
- The CRM introduction would make all sales processes transparent and would lead to better sales management, better customer retention, and more marketing effectiveness. It led to chaos in the salesforce and chaos in the customer data.
- According to a recent survey from Accenture (2008), 40% of business executives rely on their gut feeling for decision making instead of BI. The survey of more than 250 executives is the basis of a report,

"Competing Through Business Analytics," that studied companies' use of and investment in analytics to remain competitive.

But let us focus on the positive examples:

- No organization needs to accept information silos yet there will always be tension between delivering a quick and pragmatic solution to the business and policing a strict charter of architectural and technical standards.
- More and more applications are assembled from reusable components. Instead of reinventing the wheel, developers realize that speed can be the determining success factor.
- Organizations' view of IT is shifting from a project-based to an asset-based approach. IT has become just as structural and pervasive as the other assets an organization uses to realize its strategy.
- IT has left its ivory tower and embraces strategic processes such as account management and business alignment management instead of selling the users an IT solution or, worse, enforcing the solution.

The Alignment Movement

I don't know whether there can be talk of an official movement but I use Arlo Guthrie's definition, as stated in "Alice's Restaurant," "And can you, can you imagine fifty people a day, I said fifty people a day walking in singin' a bar of Alice's Restaurant and walking out. And friends they may think it's a movement." I bet any professional can find at least 50 people in his ecosystem who consider alignment as an important and continuous topic on the agenda. Henderson and Venkatraman (1993) wrote a groundbreaking article and later Weill and Ross (2004) made a case for formalized IT governance. They consider IT governance as board and management responsibility and describe the major components: leadership, structures, and processes.

What I learned from it for my BI practice was to approach a BI project step by step without yielding to the pressure to produce results as fast as possible and it inspired me to draw my own conclusions and produce a derived matrix for BI projects.

Figure 2.5 shows the top-down version of strategy/BI alignment: C-level management, including the CIO, formulate a strategy and define the

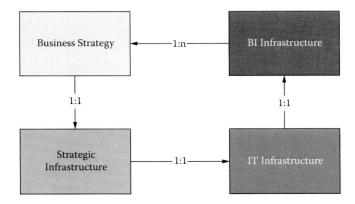

FIGURE 2.5
Strategy BI alignment roadmap. (Inspired by Henderson and Venkatraman, 1993.)

necessary strategic resources (money, competencies, resources, partnerships and alliances, etc.). This affects the IT infrastructure, which in its turn has an influence on the BI infrastructure. The outcomes of the BI infrastructure, in their turn, will affect strategy formulation and, preferably also, the strategy formation process.

Unfortunately, however hard I try to impose this rational step-by-step translation process on the organizations I work for, my experience is a little bit murkier. A BI tool presented in a seminar to the CEO may turn this process into a muddle of tool selection tug-of-war that leads the organization nowhere. A well-known European telecom company spent more than a year testing at least 11 front-end BI tools. By the time Version 4.0 of tool vendor Z was found best in class, tool vendor Y had overtaken Z with Version 5.3. Needless to say, the money spent on meetings, infighting, proofs of concept, software rent, opportunity cost, and training was enough to implement at least two completely different BI tools. This would have satisfied at least two factions and it would have got things moving in the organization.

Business Analysis Issues

The importance of a good project charter to start up the BI project with an approach to strategic and operational return on investment (ROI) cannot be underestimated. But once the project is finished, new BI iterations should become routine. The diagram in Figure 2.6 gives a high-level overview of the business analysis process of iteration with a

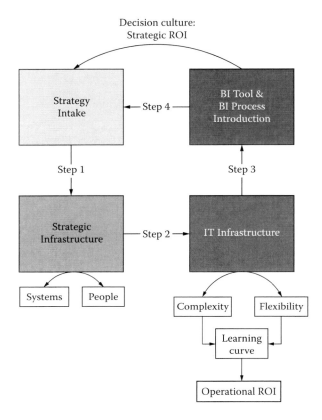

FIGURE 2.6
Iterative approach to BI strategy alignment.

focus on the ROI aspects. We refer to the chapters on the major business analysis processes for more details.

This diagram shows the approach to iterations in the BI process, focusing on the strategic and operational ROI. As this becomes a routine the analyst focuses on the systems and people aspect at the strategic infrastructure level and on complexity and flexibility of the IT infrastructure to determine operational ROI. Strategic ROI comes from the impact of the new BI processes or the new available information on strategy formulation and the decision culture as a whole. The principal question on that level is: "To what extent does the BI infrastructure support both crisp information needs and fuzzy, holistic conceptual exploration?"

3

Balancing the 5 Ps of Strategic Management

INTRODUCTION

Strategic management relates to military strategy as a fruit salad does to an apple. It has elements of military strategy but it is far richer and subtler. Management strategies are a lot richer and far more sophisticated than military strategies. In the military version, you either win or lose whereas in the business version all combinations are possible: win–win, win–lose, or lose–lose. In the military version it is one side versus the other and although coalitions may change over time, no military strategy can cope with the concept of competitive collaborators, such as seven Japanese electronics companies, the French Thomson, Philips, and Time Warner, who co-developed electronic formats for DVD recording and the technology that uses these formats.

Is it a form of conceptual laziness that managers like to see themselves as the commander-in-chief of an army? Or is it the infantile remains of the war games managers played when they were five? In this chapter I assemble the elements that constitute business strategies and draw important conclusions about the contribution of Business Intelligence (BI) to this complex interaction of the 5 Ps, as defined by Henry Mintzberg (1989) which I reduced to the Business Intelligence aspects:

- *Planning*: This is the most common known element for any strategist. Military plans like the Von Schlieffen Plan to invade France via a route that was considered impenetrable because of natural obstacles and the neutrality of Belgium are common knowledge in any military academy. In business, planning combines three disciplines: plans that describe future action which you will certainly undertake, scenarios dealing with certain future events, and forecasts describing uncertain future events and actions.

- *Patterns:* These relate to the sensitivity with which signals from the battlefield are captured and interpreted and the flexibility of response is rather simple in the military version: it's the job of the platoon commander to deal with these patterns. In the business version it should also be the job of the CEO.
- *Position:* This is a concept describing the economic, financial, and marketing position of the company. This is where elements including economies of scale, balance sheet and income statement ratios, learning curve, brain positioning, share of mind, market share, and so on determine how sustainable your competitive advantage is.
- *Posture*: This has to do with how the company sees the world and determines the direction and course of the organization's actions. It relates to corporate culture, ideology, and in its simplest form it is "the way we do things around here."
- *Ploys:* This may be seen as mini-strategies (or *stratagèmes* as the French call them) or short-term diversions from the "grand strategy" to delude adversaries or to adapt to changing situations.

Now that we have defined the 5 Ps, let us see how they interact and how skilled managers combine these 5 Ps into one grand P that invigorates the entire organization: perspective. Successful managers can put all the issues, ideas, and analyses about these Ps in perspective so the organization understands the big picture. This can and will also give direction to the BI project, providing the business analyst can reverse-engineer this big picture into the BI elements that contribute to the 5 Ps.

THE 5 Ps AND THEIR INTERACTION

The schedule in Figure 3.1 sums up the major strategy formulation and formation elements and how they interact. Strategy formulation always takes input from the environment:

- What are the trends?
- What do our (potential) customers want from us?

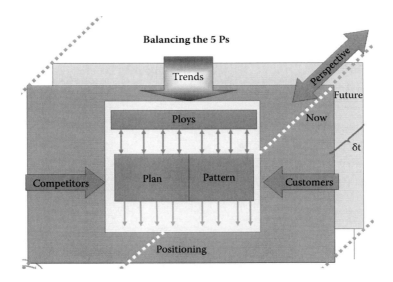

FIGURE 3.1
The interaction among the 5 Ps.

- How do they perceive our added value?
- What are our competitors up to?

Positioning leads to statements of how the company wants to respond to these inputs, which you can simplistically describe as attack, defend, or run away from the scene. This leads to three interacting Ps: plan, pattern, and ploys.

The main issue for management is to put all this into perspective and do so in a clear, understandable, and actionable way to give a sense of direction to the organization and create a decision-making basis for most issues at hand. The speed (the δt) with which an organization can adapt itself to the changing perspective determines the effectiveness of the strategy formulation, formation, and execution. Speeding up this learning loop among all the Ps is the essential task of an effective BI system.

I gladly refer to Peter Senge's (1990) publications on the learning organization for an in-depth discussion. Suffice it to say that many successful strategies have been formulated after the facts to wrap up a step-by-step learning process that led to success.

MANAGING STRATEGY

In the previous section we described the building blocks of management strategy. How do they interact? What can the manager influence? Where does she have to adapt to situations, undergo events, or prevent things from happening? How does he insure the organization against unavoidable risk? What part remains systematic uninsurable risk? These are the big questions and I humbly acknowledge I only give part answers to these questions as the complete answers would lead to perfection or worse: management as a science.

In my 30 years of business experience I have seen three approaches to strategic management, depending on the culture of the organization and the leadership style of the CEO: linear, judgmental, or bargaining. Depending on the strategy management style, the BI system will shift its focus on various aspects.

Three Strategy Management Styles

Although many MBA professors advocate the linear style, I have found no evidence that this leads to better results than the others. The only discriminating factor I have observed is the measure with which the organization is ready to learn; that is, the shorter the feedback loops and the integration of this feedback into the strategy formation, formulation, and implementation processes, the more successful is the strategy.

Linear Style

The classic or linear approach, shown in Figure 3.2, is where analysis leads to conclusions that are presented to the folks who should execute the plan and the ploys, stick to the position, and report regularly to headquarters (HQ). This is what we all have been taught: strategy as a step-by-step cookbook execution of analysis, formulation, execution, and measurement. Yet this schedule represents only part of the picture: the planned or intended strategy can be defined and executed but as John Lennon said, "Life is what happens while you're making other plans," so the measurements do not entirely relate to the outcome of the plan.

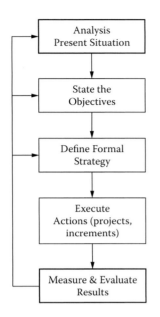

FIGURE 3.2
The linear strategy process.

Judgmental Style

In the face of uncertainty and unpredictable events, the only possible approach is judgment, that hard to define combination of knowledge, insight, *Aha Erlebnis,* coherent thinking, and . . . intuition. Intuition? Isn't this a concept for women's magazines or esoteric discussion groups? No, if analysis is about decomposition into explicit knowledge, judgment is about the Gestalt, the holistic approach based on deep, pre-scientific, implicit knowledge. If analysis is vertical thinking, then intuition is lateral thinking, spontaneous combinations of patterns that reveal their relevance to us in an unknown and unaware way. Judgment is also the art of coping with paradoxes, inconsistent data, and fuzzy signals in the environment.

Bargaining Style

Bargaining as a strategy can have its merits as the result can be that everyone in the organization gets involved and the strategy process itself is used to build coherence and better sharing of the vision, the objectives, and goals of the strategy. At the risk of unfairly generalizing, my experience with Dutch companies adhering to the "polder model" is generally positive. This polder model stems from the Middle Ages, when people had to work together to overcome nature's threat of flooding the area. It is a decision-making process based on building consensus. The main disadvantage is the time- and effort-consuming aspect but its greatest merit is a better shared sense of direction for the organization. Prerequisites for a successful bargaining style are complete transparency and placing the general interest before self-interest or else we are in the middle of politics rather than open communication channels for open minds.

Conclusion

What is the basis of these management styles? It could be the CEO's curriculum. One can imagine an engineer preferring the analytical approach whereas a lawyer might prefer a judgmental approach and a social scientist might prefer a bargaining style.

Although I have found some confirmation of these clues, I believe we are giving too much credit to the CEO who is not as almighty as shareholders believe. Strategic management is the combination of formation, formulation, and implementation. In the first two phases, the CEO may have maximum impact but in the implementation aspects even the best executive dashboard will only give her the illusion of strategic control as worker, customers, and competitors will play their roles fully. The main reason for choosing (or being forced to choose) one of these strategic management styles is the combination of two interacting phenomena:

- The certainty in the organization about causal relationships: Does a customer leave the company because of the competition, flaws in our service, the general economic climate, the announcement of a substitute technology in the coming years, and so on?
- The level of goal sharing in the organization: Are we looking at a loosely stitched together fabric of acquisitions or are we at the other end of the scale, looking at an organically grown enterprise with directors stemming from the pioneering days?

Observe the signs of these two aspects and you will be able to distinguish the PR version (which is, of course, analytical) from the real version. The grid in Figure 3.3 shows four decision-making situations. The arrows indicate the path management wants to follow to arrive in management's

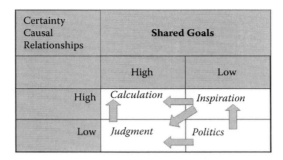

FIGURE 3.3
Decision-making situations.

heaven: analytical calculated decisions showing rationality and control of the situation.

When there is a high certainty about what causes what and everybody in the organization shares the same goals, the analytical approach shows its value. When causality is low, yet the organization knows where it wants to go, judgment should be the leading style. We often observe this in turnaround situations or in entrepreneurial environments. When both causality is low and there is no clear path accepted by the organization, politics come into play and strategic management becomes a bargaining game. This is where market research firms stand a good chance of tapping into an interesting market. When they deliver the information, the bargaining game may become more inspired and the strategic management style may evolve toward judgment or calculation, depending on the results of the "inspired strategy."

Strategy Management Styles and Plan–Pattern–Ploys

Let us have a look at the outcome of any strategic plan before we address the issue. All strategy formulation efforts start with a blank sheet of paper, which is being filled with situation analysis, formulation of objectives, action plans, and measurements. In short, the linear approach appeals to stakeholders because it is Cartesian logic: it avoids ambiguities and it gives a sense of direction to the organization. Then comes the reality check: to what extent is the planned strategy to be realized on the shop floor, with partners, distributors, and customers? Did everybody understand the mission–vision–objectives statement? And did the competition react as we expected?

Although Michael Porter (1980) has a nice logical framework for this question, it doesn't always come out that way. We may be aware of what is being communicated about our competitors and even in the case of inside information of former employees (industrial espionage) we are still not clear on the underlying motives and intentions and we are certainly in the dark about our competitor's assumptions about himself and the industry. Some competitor analysis makes a competitor unpredictable by presenting information based on inadequate data such as financial statements. I remember a customer who, year after year, showed alarming balance sheets and income statements but who was capable of mobilizing millions of dollars to realize new projects and launch new products. Many multinational companies have financial capacities that do not show in the balance sheet and in what is now commonly known as "the networked economy" these networks can be well hidden and only reveal their power in case of calamities or new business opportunities.

Last but not least, emotions also play their part. The Belgian margarine market is dominated by two players who have historic ties. Any move from either of them causes immediate and vigorous response from the other party, which does not always stand the economic test.

The last thing you want from a Business Intelligence system is the creation of false information leading to wrong decisions. This brings a pertinent question to the table: how do you validate and evaluate the strategic value of the system? We address this in the chapter, "The Business Case for Business Intelligence."

Figure 3.4 illustrates the complexity of this simple schema where the intended strategy thrives in an environment of strategic control, based on negative feedback functioning like a thermostat. It is of a Newtonian system, seeking a balance and the stability of a steady-state model. The Balanced Scorecard as an accounting system for strategic analysis fits wonderfully in this ecosystem, thereby ignoring reality. Its major problem deals with a disconnect between reality and planning because of the time gap between the two.

The emerging strategies are focused on opportunistic discoveries of the silver bullet. They grow in an environment of positive feedback where successful strategies survive the scrutiny of colleagues and the market. Its major problem is consistency. The realized strategy is only the Platonic image of what you wanted to measure. Concepts outside the measurement scope will not influence future strategy planning processes until they

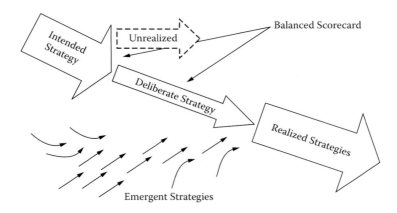

FIGURE 3.4
A comparison between the two inputs.

appear as "unavoidable" and the organization becomes the victim of this strategic myopia.

Choosing the Center of Gravity

Each management style in strategy formulation affects the center of gravity but the bargaining style may cause problems as they go in all directions. Sometimes the planners prevail, sometimes the ploys clan dominates the strategy process, and in fewer cases the pattern pundits take over the process. Any BI consultant who has worked in this environment will recognize the symptoms: scope creep, change requests, and lots of unfinished tasks. The simple matrix shown in Table 3.1 gives a hint of the direction your BI project is going. In the next chapter we describe the approaches to choose the appropriate starting point for the first iteration and give a few tips to keep the project on the road.

TABLE 3.1

Management Style/Priority	Plan	Pattern	Ploys
Linear	1.	3.	2.
Judgmental	2.	1.	3.
Bargaining	1–3	1–3	1–3

4

Adapting BI to the Organization's Configuration

INTRODUCTION

Henry Mintzberg (1989) spent a great deal of his academic research on the study of organizations and how they adapt (or don't adapt!) to the environment. He described five consistent "Idealtyps" based on their coordinating mechanisms and the forces working within and around the organization. In reality, you will meet mixed varieties and combinations of up to three types. By designating the key part of the organization type, Mintzberg also gave us a hint of what a Business Intelligence (BI) infrastructure would look like depending on these configurations. I reuse a few of Mintzberg's schemes with a strong caveat: read and reread his books and articles and check his findings with your clients' situation to get an in-depth comprehension of what Mintzberg really means. The alternative is mindless verbalism taking your BI project up the creek.

MINTZBERG'S CONFIGURATIONS

Depending on where the key part of the organization resides and what kind of coordinating mechanism is dominant, Mintzberg (1989) describes five configurations and two (what I would call) aberrations: the entrepreneurial organization, the machine organization, the professional organization, the diversified organization, and the innovative organization (see Figure 4.1).

What I see as temporary organization forms or aberrations are the missionary organization and the political organization. From a BI point of view these two are not concerned with Business Intelligence; they are

Six Basic Parts of the Organization

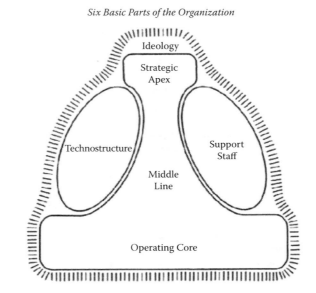

FIGURE 4.1
These are the key part elements of an organization: Ideology pulling the organization together, the strategic apex with a strong pull to lead, to give direction, the middle line with a pull to balkanize and to create little kingdoms, the operating core with a pull to professionalize, to grow in their job, the technostructure with a pull to rationalize and the support staff with a pull to collaborate. Not in the picture but often very present is the force of politics, pulling the organization apart.

concerned with proving a point and anything goes to do just that. If anyone feels interested in doing research on my hypothesis that missionary and political organizations have a higher fraud incidence rate than the other organization forms, I will be glad to be of service. Nevertheless, any organization type can be more or less bound together by ideology or pulled apart by politics but as an "Idealtyp" these are simply not the kind we need in profit organizations (see Table 4.1).

MINTZBERG'S LESSONS FOR BUSINESS INTELLIGENCE

The "Idealtyps" of organizations have dominant business case themes that come from the way they view the world and how they should adapt to—or control, as some think—the environment. The entrepreneurial organization's leadership has a strong focus on the organization's expansion,

TABLE 4.1

Configuration	Prime Coordinating Mechanism	Key Part of Organization	Type of Decentralization
Entrepreneurial	Direct supervision	Strategic apex	Vertical & horizontal
Machine	Standardization of work processes	Technostructure	Limited horizontal
Professional	Standardization of skills	Operating core	Horizontal decentralization
Diversified	Standardization of outputs	Middle line	Limited vertical decentralization
Innovative	Mutual adjustment	Support staff	Selected decentralization
Missionary	Standardization of norms	Ideology	Decentralization
Political	None	None	Varies

Source: "Mintzberg on Management" 1989.

realizing the dream of the entrepreneur. BI should deliver the entrepreneur the reality checks for her strategic direction as entrepreneurial leaders do not often accept criticism from their subordinates. A BI system, presenting the facts, can remedy entrepreneurial persistence beyond reason. Mike Saylor, entrepreneur and founder of Microstrategy, a leading BI tool vendor, once said in the early days of his company: "Strategy is very much a matter of perseverance." I agree, but it takes good information and courage to decide when perseverance has turned into stubbornness, leading to defeat.

The machine organization tries to control the environment by exerting influence on its community, taking over suppliers, customers, or simply by the sheer volume of people, money, and goods it controls. In such an environment, Business Intelligence is primarily a stable reporting environment spitting out key performance indicators (KPIs) of all sorts, often not interrelated or examined for their consistency, as one middle manager uses his KPIs to check out another department. In a machine organization, politics are always playing a role and control is the key word. The same goes for all the divisions of the diversified organization, but if you look one level up, there is a great drive for consistency to compare performance of the divisions. The Balanced Scorecard approach is very popular in these organizations.

The professional organization combines close client contact from their professionals and pigeonholing to route the consulting services through the organization. Business Intelligence often comes in a "lite" version, especially in politicized organizations. But even in coherent environments with a strong ideological pull, the professionals rely on very few Business Intelligence contributions, such as time sheet analysis, skills matrices, support incident analysis, and customer share-of-wallet analysis, to name the principal ones.

The innovative organization is a real pain to work for as a BI person. Management constantly shifts focus in their BI strategy. My advice is, "Go with the flow," and make sure you are as versatile as the organization, doing a lot of quick and dirty work as timeliness prevails over accuracy and learning is the key process in Business Intelligence. If you want me to give it a name, would you settle for "Explorative Business Intelligence"?

Excuse me for not bothering to give directions for *pur sang* missionary or political organizations. My advice is, "Stay away as far as you can from them." Failure of your BI project is almost certain; who will pay your bills is very uncertain.

Business Analysis Issues

Try to establish as soon as possible in what type, or mix of types, of organization you are operating. Examine the prime coordinating mechanisms on all levels and in all departments or divisions of the organization as these can change for various reasons:

- The primary process
- Leadership styles (get the [Curriculum Vitae] CVs of the decision makers!)
- Historic reasons, most of the time cultural remnants of past operations, positions, and posture

Determining the key part of the organization is a lot harder. The answer is not always to be found in the numbers although a comparison between competitors may give you a hint, providing you have access to these data. Most of the time, the answer lies in the subtleties of what I call the roots of decision making. What did the CEO do before he made a decision?

- Did the decision maker rely on studies and advice from his staff?
- Was the decision maker heavily involved in the priorities of the technostructure?

- Did he have regular and long meetings with middle management?
- Did he get his hands dirty in the operating core?

Even harder is the task of determining the type of decentralization. You may not be able to do it in a short time. As Mintzberg defines decentralization as the diffusion of decision-making powers, either vertical via delegation to managers or horizontal to nonmanagers, it sounds simple, but the answer is not always in the formal structures of the organization. Informal leaders, advisors, and influencers often play an important role and they are hard to detect at first glance. You need to be an organizational tracker to locate diffused sources of decision-making power by finding the answers to these questions:

- Who are the first to be informed about new developments?
- Who are the persons you are referred to "for more details"?

5

Understanding the 4 Cs

INTRODUCTION

If you simplify Business Intelligence (BI)—and you know consultants just love that—then it all amounts to knowledge and insight in the dynamics of four subject areas or perspectives:

- Cost
- Customers
- Competitors
- Competencies

Cost is an important perspective for a data warehouse: it can be traced over long periods of time, illustrating how fixed costs can become variable over time and vice versa, proving trend lines that can help you with your long-term planning. Cost is the most pervasive and at the same time the easiest perspective to measure.

The customer perspective may be the most important but it is a lot harder to get the complete picture for decision making as you can only measure derivatives of the second- or even the third-order when you capture what I call "partial externalizations of behavior," which in their turn are an externalization of intentions, emotions, and so on, which in their turn, and so on. You get the idea, right? One important externalization is, of course, revenue.

Why not make it harder on ourselves and try to capture competitive behavior in our BI system? Your customer relationship management (CRM) source may trace win–loss analysis of sales opportunities but the major sources for competitors are aggregated data such as market share overviews, pricing comparisons, product feature comparisons, income statements, balance sheets, and other vague indicators of their potential to harm your organization. Yet the alternative to neglecting these data may prove more disastrous than struggling to register their blips on your radar. Check if you have sufficient detailed data available for automatic loads over a longer period of time, that is, win–loss analysis in your CRM system, inflow from new employees in your Human Resources Management (HRM) system, and public data such as accounting data and sector data. If this is not the case, competitive analysis will keep the characteristics of a periodic study instead of readily available Business Intelligence reports and analysis.

Competencies are an even broader concept, present in all your processes, people, and systems. Your HRM system may manage a competence matrix, personal development plans linked to appraisal systems where the corporate objectives may be stated in general terms and in measurable performance indicators.

Whether you use these 4 Cs as perspectives on other subject areas or as subject areas on their own depends on the complexity of your organization. A subject area is either a business process, a group of similar business processes, or a function within the organization, such as:

- Cost accounting, with a focus on activity-based costing (ABC)
- Financial management
- Operations
- Marketing
- HRM
- R&D
- Legal

In the next chapters we use the function approach for clarity purposes. Every organization has some traits of each of these functional aspects that can be treated as a generic subject area. The business process approach would imply a level of detail and a number of variations exceeding the scope of this book. A good business analyst performing a business process analysis will be able to map the functional aspects of the processes and make the switch. Keep in all analysis tracks these 4 Cs as placeholders that are independent of organizational change as these are the fundamental drivers of any organization's behavior in the market. Make sure you get as much information about them as possible, even if the present demand is not focusing on certain objects or characteristics of these 4 Cs.

APPLYING THE 4 C PERSPECTIVE ON FUNCTIONS

What are the principal issues when applying the 4 Cs to the principal management domains? The matrix in Table 5.1 lists them. Of course, the priorities depend on the situation of the organization. The added value of this schema is simple: it forces analysts to produce clear definitions, terms, and measurements at the very beginning of the analysis because this matrix shows them from the onset that there is more than meets the eye. Suppose the analysis begins with a cost of quality subject area. Then you'd better define vague concepts such as "quality" and "cost". You may even want to make the distinction among measurable and immeasurable cost and quality as the latter might be of equal or greater importance for decision making.

THE 4 Cs: THE FOUNDATION OF A BALANCED SCORECARD

I consider the concept of a Balanced Scorecard known to the reader. Technically speaking it is a Business Intelligence approach where data are aggregated on various levels around the four perspectives (market performance; learning, innovating, and growth performance; financial performance; and operational performance) using at least two feedback mechanisms: between the perspectives (i.e., cause–effect assumptions between Key Performance Indicators (KPIs) that are modeled in the scorecard) and between the users of the balanced scorecard: to make comments on the reports and exchange knowledge and ideas.

Before you can start building a Balanced Scorecard, analyze the 4 Cs to systematize your analysis. The schedule in Figure 5.1 illustrates the relationships between the foundation and the construction of the Balanced Scorecard.

Before you can put flesh to this skeleton and make sure the interconnected perspectives yield usable information, you need to chart the 4 Cs, as shown in Figure 5.2, where each perspective is linked to at least two "root causes" from an analytical point of view. Not every organization needs a full-blown Balanced Scorecard. This intermediate layer provides a methodological step toward the Balanced Scorecard and protects the

TABLE 5.1

Overview of the Applicable Processes, Activities, Analyses, and the 4 Cs

	Cost	Customers	Competitors	Competencies
Cost Accounting	Collecting cost data; assigning costs in a meaningful way	Activity-based costing per customer; Lifetime value management	Target costing; competitive analysis	Cost of quality
Financial Management	Risk analysis	Customer lifetime value management	Relative financial strength analysis	Not applicable
Operations	Asset management; activity-based costing per product/service	Customer self-service analysis; Customization analysis	Industry efficiency benchmarks	Cost of quality; SPC; ISO
Marketing	Lifetime value management; target cost per order; market information value	Basket analysis; Customer analysis; market penetration analysis	Market penetration analysis; competitive analysis	Customer satisfaction analysis
HRM	Human capital; employee lifetime value management		Employee turnover analysis	Skills analysis
Research & Development	Product life-cycle cost	Co-engineering analysis	Patent research	Skills analysis

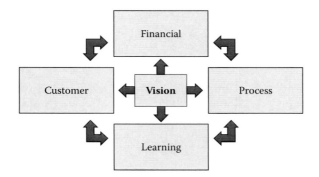

FIGURE 5.1
Schematic representation of Kaplan and Norton's Balanced Scorecard.

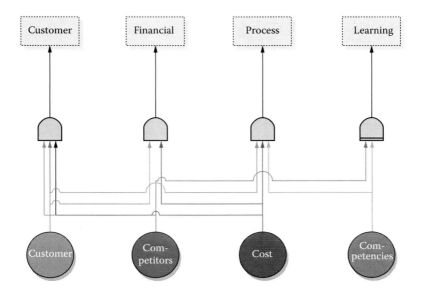

FIGURE 5.2
How 4 C analysis provides input for the Balanced Scorecard.

client's investments in business analysis should he, at a later stage, need to develop the scorecard or formulate new requirements.

Business Analysis Issues

However narrow the scope of your analysis may be, never skip this exploration phase to get the fundamental driving forces behind the organization's success (or failure). Make sure the causal relationships are clearly divided into two categories: the explorative category, which contains hypotheses, hunches, and other gut feelings and by its nature remain to be challenged, and the justifiable category (usually the smaller one), which contains reproducible and verifiable causal relationships, resilient throughout the planning cycle. All probabilities are subjective so a group consensus is needed. Be wary of the following phenomena that may cause bias:

Too great an initial divergence is resolved via authority.
There may be dependencies between the opinions of the various contributors.
There is probably a lack of calibration between the various predictions and their outcomes, so again, authority may take over.

6

The Business Case for Business Intelligence

INTRODUCTION

In his article "Competing on Analytics," Thomas Davenport (2006) paints a picture of analysis-savvy organizations:

> Organisations are competing on analytics not just because they can—business today is awash in data and data crunchers—but also because they should. At a time when firms in many industries offer similar products and use comparable technologies, business processes are among the last remaining points of differentiation. And analytics competitors wring every last drop of value from these processes. So, like other companies, they know what products their customers want, but they also know what prices those customers will pay, how many items each will buy in a lifetime, and what triggers will make people buy more. Like other companies, they know compensation costs and turnover rates, but they can also calculate how much personnel contribute to or detract from the bottom line and how salary levels relate to individuals' performance. Like other companies, they know when inventories are running low, but they can also predict problems with demand and supply chains, to achieve low rates of inventory and high rates of perfect orders.
>
> And analytics competitors do all those things in a coordinated way, as part of an overarching strategy championed by top leadership and pushed down to decision makers at every level. Employees hired for their expertise with numbers or trained to recognise their importance are armed with the best evidence and the best quantitative tools. As a result, they make the best decisions: big and small, every day, over and over and over.

Our job as a business analyst is to support them on their path toward Davenport's (2006) analytical Valhalla. But first, we have to convince the

CEO with more than just a description of the ideal Business Intelligence (BI) user; we also have to present concrete verifiable estimates or calculations of the added value Davenport so eloquently describes.

We have discussed the strategic management aspects of Business Intelligence in general. This should provide you with enough background for a cost justification of a BI project for the CEO. In this chapter, we discuss the information economics (IE) approach and some alternative methods we have developed in our practice. We illustrate the mechanism with a real business case.

THE BASICS OF INFORMATION ECONOMICS

Information, economics is part of microeconomic theory and at the end of the 1960s, when computers became a commonplace technology for information management in large organizations, it also addressed issues concerned with the economics of information technology.

Originally, information economics was used to justify the investment in management accounting systems but by extension IE is now used for any investment, enhancing the information asymmetry to the advantage of the investor. Information is considered as an economic good (as the laws on insider trading clearly illustrate), reducing the risks involved in decision making. Information has a value and comes at a cost to supply it. To determine the value of information we need to assess the following aspects:

1. The business environment.
2. An overview of the options, the decisions, and their possible outcomes.
3. The likelihood of each outcome as a function of the possible states of nature.
4. How the BI system* reports on the state of nature and simulates the outcomes depends on the capability of the system to capture signals, information about the possible states of nature, and the

---

* This may be a superfluous clarification in a book that deals with many human aspects of BI but just to make sure: a BI system is—like all information systems—a combination of technology and people. This means the performance of the BI system is not the sole responsibility of the tech people; the users and managers play an equally important role.

conditional probability of the occurrence of each signal as a result of each possible state of the environment.
5. If all aspects are charted, a payoff matrix concludes the assessment.

These assessments are not cookbook recipes. Therefore, we would like to illustrate them via a real-life case of cost justification for a financial institution.

ILLUSTRATING IE WITH A BUSINESS CASE

A major financial institution experimented with Business Intelligence on a technical level: tool selection and a proof of concept. Once these were finished they didn't exactly know what the next steps could be and they asked for advice. The central question was, "How could Business Intelligence further the development of the organization and could we also quantify this so the IT guys could ask for a budget?" The mission statement of this organization gave us great inspiration:

> (. . .) And that is exactly what our Company is: a concept. It is an idea, moreover an idea that is kept together by people. There is no concrete foundation, no piles underneath, it doesn't come from machines (. . .) What our Company realises from day to day is determined by the interaction between the people from the Company and their relations (. . .)
>
> Because if we don't make sure we all have the same understanding of that concept, it will not work.

This mission statement gave direction to the cost justification research: a better understanding of relationships between the company and its clients would increase its profitability. How? That was to be examined.

We looked at the strategic objectives, the generic strategy, and the methods and processes used to pursue these objectives, and calculated the added value of Business Intelligence to these processes. We focused on the attraction, development, and retention of customers for this financial asset management company and the related processes:

1. Qualifying prospects
2. Understanding customer behavior

3. Managing relationships with customers
4. Customer-oriented product development and service delivery
5. Managing the quality of service
6. Managing and exceeding the expectations of the customers
7. Monitoring and exploiting customer satisfaction
8. Maintaining a learning experience for the customer and the organization
9. Translating the previous to a strengthened competitive position

This was quite a challenge for both the organization and the technology. After interviewing several people from marketing, customer service, portfolio management, product development, and general management we reached five important strategic conclusions that could justify the investment in a Business Intelligence system for the organization.

From a Process to a Marketing Culture

At the time of our mission, the evolution was under way; the classical wall between back office and front office (for so long the *modus vivendi* in the financial world) was coming down, yet typical back office activities such as the mail room, master file management, financial mutations, internal control, archiving, management, and information procurement were considered as cost centers to be charged out to the business units that were various types of asset management divisions: bonds, savings, stock, futures and options, property, and so on. The company uses six different distribution channels and management reporting consisted of the portfolio situation per distribution channel and the cash flow statements of each channel/portfolio combination.

First Conclusion: Save on Reporting Operations

These monthly statements were a massive time consumer for three full time employees (FTEs) who could easily save 40–70% of their time doing a more intelligent job than collecting, cleaning, validating, aggregating, and presenting the data before they were analyzed. We left the quantification of these figures to the client for the simple reason that there is not much added value in having a consultant calculate a percentage from a salary cost.

TABLE 6.1

Relevant High-Level Customer Information That Could Be Produced Automatically

Group	Existing Customers	Acquisition Goal	Acquisition Costs (€)	Development Costs (€)	Retention %	Income per Customer/ Yr (€)
Fund A (high incomes)	1,000	150	850	50	96.05	1,500
Fund B (medium incomes)	350,000	45,000	100	25	97	500

Second Conclusion: Churn Reduction through Better Customer Analysis

The present reporting of cash flow per distribution channel gives the company no insight to customer acquisition development and retention economics. The present churn percentage is 3.5% but nobody in the organization knows about the who, what, where, and how of this percentage. By "de-averaging" the customer base, the company can focus on critical customer groups. Table 6.1 shows that, with a BI system, if we drill down on Fund A with 1,000 customers we get the analytical information shown in Table 6.2.

It is clear from Table 6.2 that segments 3 and 6 will get special attention from the customer service people, who might even examine and analyze these figures to the individual customer level, considering the yearly income per customer. A manual and painstaking study of these two asset management funds led to the following hypothesis: we can increase the lifetime value (LTV) of Fund A from €6.250 to €6.374 and

TABLE 6.2

Fund A

Fund A: Segments (%)	Total Market	1	2	3	4	5	6
Segment	100	12	16.1	7	23.8	19.4	21.7
Profits	100	6.2	12.4	19.1	22.8	13.5	26
Churn	3.95	0.1	0.9	5.9	2.3	2.1	3.8
Profit per population	1.00	0.51	0.77	2.73	0.96	0.70	1.20

for fund B we can lift it from €2.217 to €2.258. The LTV calculation used the following assumptions:

- Revenue in the first year = 50% of the second year.
- Cost per customer remains constant over time.
- A discount rate of 15% is used to calculate the net present value of future revenue streams, which reflects a high risk level (inflation +11% at the time of calculation).
- The horizon is 10 years.
- The churn rate was given as 3.95% and could be reduced to 3.08%.

On a customer base of 1,000 for the high income fund A and 350,000 for the medium income fund B, the total revenue was €14,327,793 in 10 years as shown in Table 6.3. The table is based on a high retention rate (96.05%) but also a high discount factor expressing risk, resulting in €6,250 LTV per new customer. By reducing churn from 3.95 to 3.08% the company could increase the LTV to €6,374 per customer for the high income fund.

Third Conclusion: Better Prospect Qualification

This is where the IE approach will play its role to the full extent. If a prospect approached a fund manager (or vice versa) how would the fund manager know what the customer potential of this prospect is? Would he look at the car she's driving? I know people who drive super cars and live in a rented apartment with no luxury. Would he look at the size of the prospect's house? Maybe the owner has a killing mortgage. Would he look at the yearly income? What about inheritors of a fortune with no income? Or a high income earner with three divorces to pay off? It is clear that correct prospect qualification can improve the company's income.

Table 6.4 represents a payoff matrix of a given strategy combined with the state of nature: a high income prospect gets a high income or a medium income treatment or a medium income prospect gets a high income or a medium income treatment. There are four combinations possible, each with its own payoff.

If management chooses the MAXIMIN criterion, it would choose a medium income treatment (MIT) for all prospects because there are about 350 times more of them among their existing customers and still 300 more are foreseen in the prospection targets which are, of course, based on demographic data and analyses.

TABLE 6.3

LTV Calculation for 1,000 High Income Customers

Note: Revenue in Yr 1	€650	1,500 income – 850 acquisition cost
Development and retention cost	€50	
Revenue in the following years	€1,500	

Year	Total Customers	Retention Rate (%)	Total Revenue (€)	Variable Cost (€)	Contribution (€)	Net Present Value (NPV) at 15%
1998	1,000	94.00	650,000.00	50,000.00	600,000.00	600,000.00
1999	940	94.46	1,410,000.00	47,000.00	1,363,000.00	1,185,217.39
2000	888	94.91	1,331,818.04	44,393.93	1,287,424.10	973,477.58
2001	843	95.37	1,264,033.29	42,134.44	1,221,898.85	803,418.33
2002	804	95.82	1,205,452.18	40,181.74	1,165,270.44	666,247.15
2003	770	96.28	1,155,072.96	38,502.43	1,116,570.52	555,132.89
2004	741	96.73	1,112,056.88	37,068.56	1,074,988.32	464,747.12
2005	717	97.19	1,075,704.63	35,856.82	1,039,847.81	390,917.31
2006	697	97.64	1,045,437.10	34,847.90	1,010,589.20	330,363.40
2007	681	98.10	1,020,779.84	34,025.99	986,753.85	280,497.03
Stepwise loyalty increase	0.455	96.05			€ 10,866,343.09	€ 6,250,018.20

TABLE 6.4

Payoff Matrix for the First Year Income of a New Customer

Strategy	High Income Prospect (HIP; €)	Medium Income Prospect (MIP; €)
Fund A: High Income Treatment (HIT)	1,500	–(250)
Fund B: Medium Income Treatment (MIT)	200	500

But as you can imagine, there will be medium income prospects (MIPs) posing as high income prospects (HIPs) and as financial advisors try to give the best service possible to their relations, the chances are high that the prospect is just trying to maximize her value for money and the company ends up waiting for the big money transfer that is not coming. So, the business case here is clear: what are the probabilities for HIP and MIP to make sure that the expected outcome of both strategies is equal? In other words, what is $P_{(HIP)}$ and what is $(1 - P)_{(HIP)}$ or $P_{(MIP)}$?

If we use the data from the payoff matrix to solve the equation, the results are rather alarming:

$$P(1,500) + ((1 - P)(-250)) = P(200) + ((1 - P)(500))$$

$$1,750P - 250 = -300P + 500$$

$$2,050\ P = 750$$

$$P(HIP) = 0.3658 \text{ but in reality it is } 0.0028!$$

$$P(MIP) = 0.6342 \text{ but in reality it is } 0.9972!$$

Now we can calculate the expected monetary value (EMV) of the information delivered by a BI system to improve prospect qualification and apply the correct treatment (HIT/MIT) to the qualified prospect:

$$EMV(HIT) = (0.0028)1.500 + (0.9972)(-250) = -245,1$$

$$EMV(MIT) = (0.0028)200 + (0.9972)500 = 499.16$$

$$EVPI = (0.0028)1500 + (0.9972)500 = 502.80$$

This means that the added value of a BI system for prospect qualification is €502.8 minus €499.16, or €3.64 per prospect within a one-year term. With a prospect target of 45,150 there is an extra revenue bonus of 45,150 times €3.64 or €164,346, which is somewhat better than a MAXIMIN approach to this problem.

But there is more. You can expand this equation by calculating the lifetime value of a customer in both cases: treated on the basis of correct or incorrect prospect qualification. Using the same methodology, you can calculate the LTV of a HIP with a MIP treatment and that of a MIP with a HIP treatment. We found it decreased from €6,374 to €5,974 for the HIP and from €2,256 to €1,633 for a MIP.

Imagine (and we did more than that) examining the revenues from thousands of customers over a period of 10 years, who the company deals with yearly, with 5% of what I call "inflation prospects," people who like to pretend they belong to the high income segment in the hope of getting VIP treatment; what is the cost of these terrorist consumers? Remember, we would only meet with 0.28% high income prospects instead of five. So here's the math:

$$((5\% - 0.28\%) * 45,150 * (2,256 - 1,663)) = 1,131 * €623 = €1,327,.662.84$$

Over a million euros in savings in one year, just by better prospect qualification? This was more than enough to make the decision for an investment in BI.

GENERIC ADVANTAGES OF BUSINESS INTELLIGENCE

Although I am not a great fan of checklists for BI analysis, here is some form of a checklist with what I would define as advantages that should come with any BI project. And the inverse also goes: any BI project with one or more of these advantages missing is either not well managed or your organization already has a BI system in place and you are unaware of this.

Improved Communication Effectiveness

The exercise of building a BI system will further the cooperation between information and communication technology (ICT) and the user community, inasmuch as both parties will have to think about their data strategies. One of the minimum results is improved report quality, which also contributes to better communication in the organization. Data strategies in the user community have much to do with master data management, a simple application of the rule, "Do it right the first time." Whether we are discussing product data, customer data, employee data, or any other set that is used in various processes and departments, master data management becomes an ongoing issue in BI. And even the tiniest improvement will result in better customer service and cost reduction.

Improved Data Quality

One version of the truth is the biggest promise of a Business Intelligence system, based on a data warehouse. Many of its dimensions contain non-transactional data describing entities such as customers, components, and products. A few examples of standardized data definitions are:

- Common engineering models
- Product data models
- Customer data models
- Corporate data models

These can be consolidated in a corporate information repository to enhance internal communications and provide a direction in the strategic thinking of an organization. In the section "Generic Business Object Definitions" we work out an example of customer definitions.

Common Engineering Models

In a production environment where engineer-to-order or build-to-order production runs are the case, there are common engineering models. This approach, which is based on hierarchical decomposition and standardized interfaces, provides a flexible component-based representation for systems, subsystems, and components. It allows new models to be composed programmatically or visually to form more complex models. Common engineering models support integration of a hierarchy of models that represent the system at differing levels of abstraction. Selection of a particular model is based on a number of criteria, including the level of detail needed, the objective of the component or subsystem, the available knowledge, and given resources. In most production organizations, these models are available as the cost of neglecting this is simply prohibitive.

Product Data Models

In an assemble-to-order environment, product and component catalogs are the source for normalized definitions and descriptions of entities. Also there, the business case for master data management is obvious. This is not always so in a commercial organization where management is concerned with moving the goods out of the inventory as quickly as possible and considers master data management as "some fancy IT frill," as one customer once told me. But also commercial organizations may have good product data sources. If the organization is in e-commerce, they are probably starting on a good basis. If there is no tradition of centrally managed product data, the BI process will force the organization to adapt.

Customer Data Models

These very volatile entities require special attention. From my mail-order experience I have seen changes of up to 25% per year, depending on the market segment. In the consumer market segments, people move, get married, divorce, or change their name (even their gender is not a static datatype anymore). In the business segments, people change function, departments, business units, or change companies, and often their mail is read and handled by other people long after they are gone, so you are not even aware you are addressing the wrong person.

And there is more than just the accuracy issue. Who owns the customer data? Watch out for political ploys. What are the different perspectives or views of the customer data for the different users? Consult an expert on privacy issues to make sure you are not heading for a lawsuit. What is the cost and benefit of each attribute registered? These attributes are nontransactional data that have to be assembled via inquiries, dialogue with the customer, or external databases and may require a lot of effort and cost to capture and maintain currently. With a good Business Intelligence system, you may get more insight to the true value of these data. Discriminant analysis, partial correlation analysis, and other methods can give you valuable information about the value of these attributes.

Better Understanding of Available Data

Once the BI system is in use, statistics will indicate data usage intensity and will give directions as to which data are worth storing. It will also indicate new directions for data capturing strategies. And, in turn, this will lead to savings on one hand and better information.

Smarter Extraction and Exchange of Data

"Build it once; use it many times" is the message. Instead of tolerating time, money, and resource-consuming ad hoc research and ad hoc queries, the BI system will cover these business questions, from routine to highly specialized and unstructured discovery paths, so they can be asked over and over at no extra data collection cost. With the BI system in place, the learning curve will work to the advantage of the users. The graph in Figure 6.1 illustrates an anonymous but real-life example of how a BI system saves money on managing data independently of the amount. As the BI system develops and captures more data attributes, the cumulative savings increase, breaking even after six months. The key factor is the number of attributes processed and stored. The example shows a calculation on the basis of 500 captured attributes, which represents a level of data sophistication well under the present standards of most organizations. The curve shows a breakeven point after six months when the BI system uses a well-architected environment for storage, retrieval, and analysis. Of course this calculation is organization dependent.

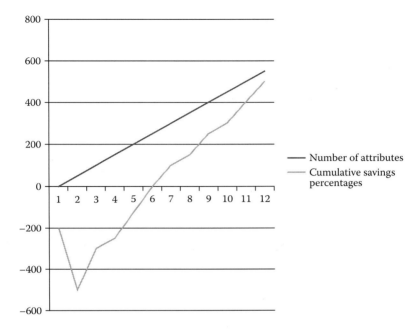

FIGURE 6.1
The savings over a period of only 12 months.

Better Understanding of the Business Processes

I admit, this may not apply to all organizations but in many industrial organizations, there is a clear disconnect between the sales processes and the production processes where production is only occasionally confronted with the customer dimension. Another disconnect is often found between cost accounting in the sales department and the production and after-sales departments. BI empowers the organization to move from a purely process-oriented culture to a more customer-oriented culture and method of operating.

One of the important issues for the analyst is to assess as soon as possible whether the various departments use different hierarchies for the strategy-defining inputs such as customer dimension, product dimension, channel dimension, and in some rare cases geographic dimension. If this is the case, the BI system can contribute to better communication between the various departments by providing insight to all

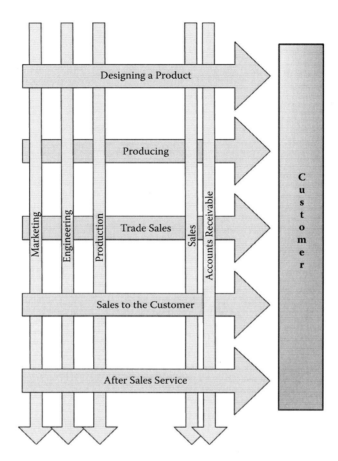

FIGURE 6.2
A unified view of the customer data and data specific for their function of the departments.

organizational perspectives. Figure 6.2 shows the value of increased customer awareness throughout all business processes. Today end-to-end process management is widely accepted but the old functional silos are still there as no process owner is capable of mastering all the disciplines used in the process.

7

BI and Cost Accounting

SETTING UP AN ABC SYSTEM USING BI

Activity-based costing (ABC) has been around for 20 years or more but without the help of Business Intelligence (BI), this is an almost impossible goal to achieve. Even with the help from BI, it is still a daunting task. Most organizations start ABC as a project, a learning experience. When the added value of ABC is established, it becomes embedded in day-to-day management processes. There are five phases in an ABC project:

1. Assemble all sources of cost registration
2. Validate the consistency of the registrations
3. Assign the sources in a meaningful way
4. Express assumptions
5. Communicate the results and validate them in the field

An in-depth discussion of these source systems will reveal the issues for a Business Intelligence project focusing on cost accounting.

Assemble All Sources of Cost Registration

In most organizations cost information is to be found in many transaction systems:

- The accounting system
- The enterprise resource planning (ERP) system
- Product data management (PDM) systems
- Budgeting systems
- Time registration and access systems

- Payroll systems
- Warehouse management systems (WMS)
- Inventory management systems (IMS)
- Document management systems (DMS)

Validate the Consistency

A simple method is to determine the relevant measurement units (minutes, kilograms, units, liters, events, etc.) and compare the results of these registrations with observations. I know of very few of the above registration systems that are designed for ABC cost registration. Make sure you discuss the following aspects with all parties concerned:

- The planning horizon
- The update frequency
- The level of aggregation

These aspects have a great impact on the consistency between the various source systems. For example, a bill of materials (BOM) is used for the internal production facility and expresses a production cost based on present equipment. If management has decided to replace certain machines or update certain process steps then this information has to be known in advance to allow users to adapt their calculations: quotes, capacity management, and the like. As for the level of aggregation, I advise everybody to look for the lowest level of detail. In case of aggregated data you not only run the risk of missing the point, you may also assign costs in an inconsistent way.

Assign the Sources in a Meaningful Way

Costs can be assigned to a product, a customer, and a process. Most insight is gained from the three combinations of product–customer, customer–process, and product–process as they reveal the weak spots in the production or service delivery process due to product or customer specifications.

If we only focus on the process as an assignment method, period costing can reveal interesting information. We use fixed time intervals such as a week, a month, a quarter, or a book year and focus on the spending for the process, not on the products nor the customers. This is where we deal with issues including throughput time and cost of quality as a function of throughput time. When sufficient data are available management may be able to optimize throughput considering at least the following constraints:

- The higher the throughput, the fewer fixed costs to allocate to the product, and the lower the unit price
- The higher the throughput, the higher the investment in resources and quality management
- The higher the throughput, the more inventory buildup

Eight Steps for Cost Assignment

Step 1. Make an inventory of all activities in the company and determine the relevant period for each activity and the activity rate, for example, number of orders or number of machine hours. Examples of activities are: production order acceptance process, production planning, direct material purchase, inventory reception, order picking, production run setup, die changing, production run, production equipment maintenance, quality control, shipment, invoicing, cash receipts, and so on.

Step 2. Get the data:
- How many minutes or hours will be spent on each activity?
- What is the total direct cost of operating each of the activities?
- What amounts of fixed costs are incurred during the relevant period of the activity?
- What is the total operating cost per activity (fixed and direct costs)?
- What is the normal activity rate (i.e., the total cost of activity divided by the number of cost driver occurrences = the cost per occurrence or cost driver rate)?
- What is the cost variance as a function of 100%, 90%, and so on capacity use?

For more details on the source data, see the next section.

Step 3. Make process diagrams for each standard product or service, including all costs per process step: direct labor, direct material, purchases, and so on.

Communicate these diagrams with all parties concerned, especially those people who control throughput time and costs.

There is nothing worse than planners detached from the actual workforce.

Step 4. Make customized process diagrams per large customer. This is of utmost importance when margins are low and salespeople make quotes by the seat of their pants.

Step 5. Assign activity costs to cost targets (jobs, products, customers). Use the formula "Actual number of activity occurrences times the Cost Driver Rate (from Step 2) = Assigned (Traceable) Costs."

Step 6. Track the evolution of the costs in a regularly scheduled report. There will be price increases of components, inflation will play a role, unions will have their say on the labor costs, government regulations will affect your costs, and so on.

Step 7. Establish a 1:1 relationship between activities (and their known costs) and your pricing and invoicing system. This will please the auditors who love to make comparisons between activities and invoicing, making sure that all activities are beneficial to the organization and not to individuals in the company.

Step 8. Monitor the validity of your assignments with a budget–actual report. In Step 5 you already set up the monitoring of the unit costs of each item on the BOM. Now you are including the capacity use in the equation.

Consider the Alternatives during the Cost Assignment Process

Consider alternative methods for identifying activities:

- Top-down: Senior management identifies what is done.
- Participative approach: The operating core identifies what is done.
- Recycling method: Use what is already documented in ISO or other process documentation.
- Time–motion studies: Observe what is done and measure the execution and throughput time, the variance, and the reasons for variance.

Consider alternative classification of activities:

- Value added versus non-value-added activities (Just-in-Time processing)
- Various levels from the bottom to the top:
  - Unit level
  - Batch level
  - Product level
  - Customer level
  - Facility level

Note that the higher we move up the ladder, the more we are absorbing non-manufacturing costs such as repairs and maintenance, supplies, utilities, rent, insurance, taxes, and depreciation incurred outside the factory or plant.

Express Assumptions

What will be the behavior of these costs over time, fixed, semi-variable, and variable?

With what rate, geometric, linear, random, or exponential? And what will cause a change in behavior, volume, quality, specifications, legislation, and so on?

How do we estimate the machine versus labor intensity and what are the substitution possibilities?

How do we treat sunk costs, depreciation, depletion, and amortization, among others?

What is the level of precision needed to serve a valid business purpose? For example, in a price-sensitive competition such as milk production, any hundredth of a percent miscalculation on 10 million liters of milk is still 1,000 liters.

Communicate the Results and Validate Them in the Field

Large bureaucracies have always emphasized the control aspects of costing but modern management reformulates this vision into feedforward and learning from cost control as there is no added value in moaning after the facts have been produced. Make sure sales and marketing people can use the results for better targeting purposes and better price quotes, and R&D people can use ABC for smarter product development by using existing production processes and their cost as a proxy for new products.

Pros and Cons of Activity-Based Costing

Pros

ABC identifies non-value-added activities and it identifies cost savings opportunities, namely the untraceable costs that have no added value in the customer serving process.

ABC provides very detailed cost/profitability information down to the individual level of a process step, a work instruction, a product component, a customer, a supplier, or a production worker, among others.

ABC differentiates complex versus simple processes, thus allocating a more just amount of overhead than in the "peanut butter spread" method of absorption costing.

More cost and production data can lead to more information and as a consequence, better decisions.

Cons

ABC is very costly to implement and maintain and should only be used in organizations where the lowest level of activities (at unit level) is unambiguous, stable over time, and all cost driver factors of these activities are well known and remain so over time.

ABC also uses historic data to establish a cost structure. This is no different from traditional absorption costing but if the feedback loops can be kept short, trends will emerge and suggest forward-looking cost structures as management can adapt the process better to the desired cost levels.

Some authors claim that ABC encourages activity but with the right checks and balances (i.e., inventory management, order management, and production management) this should be no show-stopper.

Joint costs and joint revenues remain a problem for analysis purposes and correct attribution of profits to the right product as they assume equal and proportionate gains from shared activities.

ABC may discourage novel approaches to processes as process innovation is a move away from the secure path of known costs but that depends on the attitude of management. In an innovative, professional, or entrepreneurial organization this may not be too big a problem but in a diversified organization or a machine organization, change disrupts daily routine and these structures are not designed for that.

A CLOSER LOOK AT ABC SOURCE SYSTEMS

Accounting System

An accounting system is designed for reporting on the state of assets and liabilities and the profit and loss of the company. In its records, you can find useful data about subcontractors, wages and salaries, overhead costs, and the like. Make sure you check whether there is a difference between the reporting requirements demanded by U.S.–GAAP (Generally Accepted Accounting Principles), IAS (International Accounting Standards), and IFRS (International Financial Reporting Standards) and what the organization considers realistic and attainable. Take depreciation periods from production assets under scrutiny and make sure you calculate on the basis of economic reality.

Enterprise Resource Planning System

A common starting point to track ABC is the bill of materials or the bill of services (BOS). These are the "recipes" for a product or a service. Each component has its own BOM so you can detect the hierarchy and the order of the process steps and materials and resources used should the client have no process description. An example of a BOM is in Figure 7.1. Work orders, including the BOM and the routing of the production flow, are a more accurate source of information.

Product Data Management Systems

Labeled product lifecycle management (PLM) systems, and most ERP systems also include this application but in the case of older source systems, the PDM can be a separate entity, such as PDM Works from Dassault Systèmes or Plexus. PDM systems manage all products, components, and their process steps, raw materials, and designs.

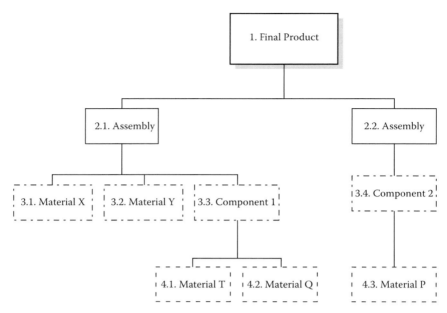

FIGURE 7.1
The typical structure of a bill of materials.

According to PLM practitioners, PLM is both a repository for all information that affects a product and a formal communication channel among product stakeholders: marketing, engineering, manufacturing, and field service. The PLM system is the first place where all product information from marketing and design comes together, and where it leaves in a form suitable for production and support.

Current PLM solutions typically represent the convergence of capabilities from earlier configuration management (CM), electronic document management system (EDMS), product data management, and computer aided design (CAD) file management systems. At a minimum, a PLM system will address:

- Revision management for requirement, design, and process documentation, part identification and description
- Identification and management of vendor sources and their approved parts
- Product structure (bill of material) construction and control
- Electronic file repository (data library or vault)
- Materials content identification for regulatory compliance Waste Electrical and Electronic Equipment directive/Restriction of Hazardous

Substances directive/End of Life Vehicle (WEEE/RoHS/ELV) and economic control

- Definition of custom part and document metadata ("attributes")
- Workflow for formally approving data changes, multiuser secured access, including "electronic signature"
- Data export to downstream ERP/SCM/CRM (enterprise resource planning/supply chain management/customer relationship management) systems

Budgeting Systems

Budgeting systems come in all flavors but the master budget and the flexible budget are the minimum sources you must examine. Most companies use either the accounting system or a spreadsheet application. Specific budgeting software will also include features such as forecasting, verification and control, and functionality.

Time Registration and Access Systems

From the basic functionality of these systems, activity measurement per job, per department, and per individual, this includes transport management systems that track the activities of a transportation mode and its crew in all levels of complexity from a truck to a cargo vessel. These systems record the exact start and finish times of all staff; in some cases they also use the electronic timesheet data to automate payroll to save significant administrative time and effort and streamline existing processes. Via real-time job costing it attributes staff time to jobs to allow comprehensive job costing on a real-time basis.

Payroll Systems

Any payroll software will take over the routine calculation of ordinary payroll requirements such as tax and contributions for unemployment and health insurance. It will also calculate the contributions the employer has to pay. Payroll software will also:

- Calculate all sorts of legal deductions.
- Produce pay slips for the employees.
- Produce payment reports to allow you to pay employees, showing the amount to be paid to each employee.

- Keep records of payments and deductions.
- Produce year-end reports and documentation for employer and employees.
- Produce the necessary figures or documentation when an employee leaves.

Payroll systems provide information either on paper or electronically to update nominal ledgers, and a whole range of other reports is possible. Some will allow a high level of detail in the information passed to the ledgers, allowing accounting to distinguish among departments, managers, and even individual jobs.

Warehouse Management Systems

Its basic purpose is to follow all movements of stock: reception, racking, order picking, shipping, and so on, and it tracks all physical storage over defined periods. If the WMS measures all throughput times it can monitor the direct costs for handling the inventory. Don't underestimate these costs. For example, the order costs for parts can easily add up to amounts between €50 and €150 per order.

Inventory Management Systems

These systems deal with issues including the economic order quantity, backorders, and cost analysis throughout the entire supply chain. The main objective of an IMS is to reduce costs by removing inventory from the supply chain, reducing obsolescence, decreasing operational assets, lowering network operations cost, and decreasing transportation costs combined with effective customer response. Data produced by these systems enhance the relevance of any ABC analysis as inventory is—other than physical stock—also a stock of person-hours produced.

Document Management Systems

Administration and written communication absorb more costs than most of us imagine. Document management systems trace who has worked for how long on which document. Using this information combined with the project or client information, a DMS contributes to the analysis dataset: execution time and throughput time being the basic measurements leading to derived measurements (cost per document per client, communication intensity, or share of administration costs per client, etc.).

SETTING UP ABC ANALYSIS IN THE DATA WAREHOUSE

As a business analyst you sometimes have to dive into the technical aspects of Business Intelligence. I assume the reader is familiar with the concept of a data warehouse. If not, I refer to Appendix C: "The 101 on Data Warehousing." During the data staging process, codes that have no meaning to the business user are converted into meaningful labels for the measures and dimensions. One of these codes is the handling, or instruction code, and the corresponding invoice code. If these are well conceived as described in Step 6 from the cost assignment process, this should give you meaningful information providing you create a lookup table that contains at least four columns, namely the general ledger code and description and the activity code and its description. I have an example of a cleaning company that wants to apply ABC analysis and this is the minimum information they need to analyze their cost and revenue:

General ledger group category code:

- General ledger label (e.g., sales of cleaning services, sales of cleaning products, travel, etc.)
- Activity code
- Activity description (e.g., carpet cleaning, dusting, window cleaning ground floor, window cleaning first floor, etc.)
- Throughput time
- Execution time
- Waiting time
- Travel time
- Unit of measurement
- Unit cost
- Unit standard sales price
- Other relevant codes such as:
  - Location code
  - Location description (e.g., city center, suburbs)
- Premises description (e.g., free/occupied at time of cleaning)

The standard SQL code would be something like:

```
CREATE TABLE Invoice_Code_Lookup
(General_Ledger_Code char(10) UNIQUE NOT NULL,
```

General_Ledger_Label char(50) UNIQUE NOT NULL,
Activity_Code char(10) UNIQUE NOT NULL,
Activity_Description char(50) UNIQUE NOT NULL,
Throughput_Time integer,
Execution_Time integer,
Waiting_Time integer,
Travel_Time integer,
Measure_Unit char(25),
Unit_Cost decimal(4,2) CHECK (Unit_Cost > 0),
Standard_Sales_Price decimal(4,2))

CONCLUSION

A data warehouse support for ABC can be of immense value to the company. Instead of costing and quoting on the basis of yearly standard cost revisions, the ABC system can adapt on a monthly basis in highly volatile business environments and improve competitive pricing in such a way that better capacity use leads to a higher return on assets and sharper margins with higher turnover, holding back the competition.

As a business analyst, your job is to assess the value of this complex system before anyone signs off on the project. Creating a business case for ABC that sticks is a challenging task. Before large portions of money are spent on the building of the BI system, it may be a good idea to start a "manual pilot" using spreadsheets and calculators for a critical department, product, or market segment and to work with hard data that can be extrapolated instead of expressing assumptions that are hard to verify.

8

BI and Financial Management

THE 101 ON FINANCIAL BI DELIVERABLES

Financial reporting is pretty straightforward from an analyst's point of view: there are no ambiguities because of legal prescriptions. These prescriptions may differ a bit between the two schools of thought (U.S. GAAP and IFRS) but both organizations, FASB (Financial Accounting Standards Board) and IASB (International Accounting Standards Board), are working on the convergence of their reporting prescriptions. Both organizations recognize the value of high-quality global reporting standards. I refer to both for more information and the latest updates: www.fasb.org and www.iasb.org.

I can hear you think: "Isn't the reporting module included in the accounting software?" Absolutely. But, not many—if not any—accounting software keeps years of history, tracking changes in analytical aspects such as accounts, sales ledgers, and customers and not every accounting software gives you the possibility of linking the operational data with the financial data, so there is a case for the financial data warehouse with a reporting and analysis module on top.

In this section I only deal with financial reports that, to my knowledge, most accounting applications are not capable of providing because of one or more of the following conditions:

- The application allows physical deletes on the database so there is no certainty about the integrity of the data.
- There are several accounting apps in use in the company because of mergers, legacy systems, and so on.
- Management needs "what if" analysis and scenario-based reports.

- Budget systems do not follow the chart of accounts schedule, so a mapping table is needed.
- Sophisticated trend analysis needs daily, weekly, or monthly snapshots of semi-additive data such as inventory, cash, debtors, and creditors.
- A direct link between accounting data and operational data is needed.
- Auditors need full access to all data for ad hoc queries.

In that case, the business analyst has work to do.

KEEP YOUR SOX ON!

Sarbanes–Oxley, or SOX as this U.S. law is commonly known, has affected the business intelligence discipline for financial purposes, even for organizations that are not affected by it. The law was passed on July 30, 2002. It establishes stricter standards for public company boards, management of public companies, and their accounting firms.

From this day on, C-level executives can no longer pretend to be ignorant of a public company's lack of transparency or integrity of the reported financial data. More information on this law can be found on the U.S. government's website: http://www.gao.gov/cghome/2004/amacas/img3.html.

Important for business analysts are the following articles: 302, 404, 409, and 802. Article 302 describes corporate responsibility for financial reporting and asks the following questions, relevant for the data warehouse architecture:

- Are the company's financial data accurate?
- Is transaction-level detail available for audit purposes?
- Are all processes that generate the data documented and understood by management?

Article 404 prescribes an annual management assessment of the internal controls:

- The control structure and its functioning
- The accountability of key persons
- Monitoring and documentation

Article 409 urges management to disclose changes in the financial and operational position of the company as fast as possible in understandable words for the public and Article 802 prescribes archiving the relevant records for later audits.

The impact for data warehouse managers is clear:

- Avoid unauthorized access to or modification of data.
- Make sure all relevant data are available.

But for business analysts, things are a lot trickier. Let us sum up the issues and see how we can deal with them:

- Data lineage consists of tracing the entire life cycle of each data element from its start to its final destination, the data warehouse, its change history, and its consistency in definitions through meta-data management.
- Ensure mutual adjustment between IT and finance produce maximum reporting performance and reduce latency to the minimum.
- Understand the major business process flows to make sure data integrity is if not guaranteed, then it is at least monitored.

Data Lineage

A process analysis of the creation of data in the source systems, the extract, transform, and load of the data warehouse is needed to indicate the various phases through which each data element goes. Booking instructions and source database integrity measures ensure the data are trustworthy from their inception. The rest of the trajectory has to be monitored in the data warehouse environment, using audit keys and other control measures to track changes in bookings after they have been recorded in the data warehouse.

Ralph Kimball's (1996, 1998, 2002, 2004) ideas on compliance-enabled fact and dimension tables in the data warehouse complete the picture by using a SQL registration of the beginVersionDateTime and EndVersionDateTime record combined with ReferenceSource and ChangeReference pointers connecting to the tables that describe the source of the change and explain the change itself. If the database incremental loads only allow inserts of data instead of updates or deletes the organization has a solid data lineage strategy in place. Metadata management completes the picture. More on metadata can be found in Chapter 14, "Mastering Data Management".

Mutual Adjustment

Although this section is not within the scope of the Business Intelligence (BI) department, it is useful to know what is happening between IT and finance in the OLTP (online transaction processing) environment. Most public companies have multiple divisions, from mergers and acquisitions or start-ups that use various accounting or enterprise resource planning (ERP) systems. One of the efforts observed is the consolidation of ERP systems to reduce the complexity of accounting environments together with a reassessment of the security measures and controls needed in complex environments. These organizations often have a compliance committee with members from IT and finance as well as the managers from the business units to facilitate communication and coordination among the users, management, and IT facilitators. It is not uncommon that the committee invites business analysts to express their opinions and ideas on the solution roadmaps under scrutiny. My urgent advice to these analysts is to suppress any urge to position the data warehouse as part of the solution to problems in the sources.

Understanding the Business Process Flows

The Institute of Internal Auditors (IIA) defines internal control as the whole of an organization's plans and measures to achieve its principal goals: to protect the correctness and reliability of financial and operational information. It contains administrative, organization, and control procedures as well as budgets and financial reporting that are affected by SOX.

In a trading company, these are the eight processes that constitute the minimum of any internal control:

- Purchase and reception of the purchased goods
  - Procurement to payables, based on a purchase request, purchase approval, goods reception, conformity check, budget reconciliation, and payment
- Goods reception via a nonpurchase order
- Service purchase via a purchase order
- Service purchase via a nonpurchase order
- Sample goods reception

- Expense reports
- Payments
- Conversion of customer orders to cash
  - Discount approvals, legal and financial management approvals, customer signatures, credit approvals, and accounts receivable validation

Ensure that the four-eyes principle as we call it in Europe is implemented in all of these processes: a separation of duties for all key tasks and compensating controls for the privileged users and managers are to be enforced.

BUSINESS ANALYSIS FOR FINANCIAL REPORTING

Chart of Accounts

The first step is to get a good understanding of the chart of accounts. Have the hierarchies between the various natural accounts explained and map the booking process on the real business processes as in Figure 8.1, illustrating the order and shipment process. It will give you more insight to the timeline, the dependencies, and the reporting dimensions.

The illustration in Figure 8.1 of the accounting process embedded in the physical business process raises a lot of interesting questions, such as:

1. Why is the invoice booked only after the customer has accepted the goods?
2. Why is the inventory adjusted immediately after reception of the sales order?

It pays to get a good look at the ins and outs of the accounting process. In Figure 8.1, the reporting of orders, invoices, and bookings will provide three different figures in what is often called a transaction pipeline. In this organization, revenue recognition happens only when the customer has accepted the delivered goods whereas other organizations take the sales invoice date as the milestone and others the order date. In Figure 8.1, the inventory will never match exactly with the accounting figures unless you make a special note: "Beginning inventory – *Sales Orders* + Purchases = End Inventory."

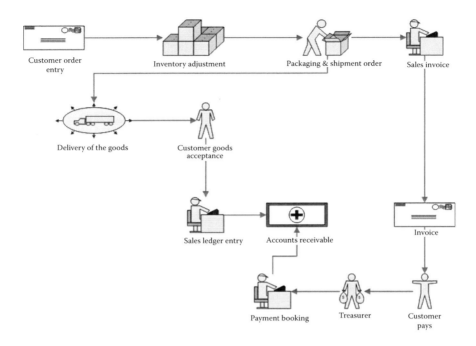

FIGURE 8.1
The accounting process.

Special attention is needed for the treatment of advance payments, subscriptions, service contracts, loyalty stamps, and similar bookings that have effects on revenue recognition, such as a monthly magazine subscription fee invoiced at the beginning of the subscription period but revenue recognition is done pro rata of the actual delivery of the magazine to the customer.

Do the same exercise for the cost of goods sold on the side, operating expenses, capital expenses, and financial cost and revenue and you will get a good picture of how the organization matches its accounting system with real-world activities.

Required Reports

In most financial Business Intelligence projects there are three priority levels that define the project and the analysis approach. The certified reports have the highest priority as they are meant to report to management and shareholders. By "certified" I mean "conform to internal audit principles and procedures," as the external audit only takes place once a year. Then there are the analytical and explorative reports, designed to answer detailed questions from management and stockholders. The third level includes reports that need to link to other subject areas such as marketing, operations, external statistical data, etc. For example, a report that compares your organization's income statement with sector averages and other benchmarks may add great value and insight.

Certified Reports

Determine the set of certified reports with the customer.

Most of the certified reports will deal with revenue, gross margin, and EBIT (earnings before interest and taxes) on a time line with at least two statuses: "invoiced" and "booked." If the customer can add the "Ordered" status to these reports, the connection with the sales pipeline can be made at a later stage of the project. What makes these reports "certified" is not only their conformity with audit principles and procedures but also a feature the BI technicians will have to add: security. Make sure you know, from the outset of the project, who will have access to these reports in case row-level security may be required if the designers choose to develop a financial data mart accessible to other user profiles.

Analytical and Explorative Reports

Auditors like reports with links to all detailed booking lines. They like to analyze them from perspectives the regular business user would not come up with, such as the log files from the accounting software indicating the user who created the booking line, the time of creation, offsetting entries of the booking line, and their authors. They are also very interested in all kinds of balances: payables, receivables, cash, checks to be cashed, and so on. But also the customer, employee, and supplier dimension may be of interest to the auditors as shell companies may send invoices for phantom goods or services or real suppliers' bank account numbers may be altered into the fraudster's bank accounts.

Fraud detection is the main driver of detailed analytical reports and these may require dimensions you won't need for "normal" Business Intelligence.

Finance Reports Connected to Other Subject Areas

Because Finance is at the end of every business process, the demand for these reports is a logical consequence. Have a look at this overview.

The combinations of organization type, other subject area, and finance are great. If you were to add government and its agencies, the combinations would be even bigger. Let me illustrate with a few examples from the synoptic Table 8.1.

Volume and revenue matching for audit and sales
Absenteeism analysis for Human Resources Management (HRM)
Project accounting for R&D

Volume and Revenue Matching for Audit and Sales

In this analysis, the operational systems have to be linked to the accounts receivable journals via the order number. This means that only revenue coming from processed customer orders will come into the picture. If the client organization uses an accrual system for booked orders that have not been billed, the auditor will want to have an idea of the order's "firmness," that is, how certain is the vendor that the order will not be changed, canceled, or postponed. My advice is to leave these probabilities out of the BI system's scope as this is variable contextual knowledge and a forward-looking statement that has to be added after the report has been created. After all, Rule #1 of data warehousing is to record facts that have taken place in the past.

Absenteeism Analysis for HRM

Absenteeism analysis is a tricky one. In some corporate cultures it is not warmheartedly received and both staff and line management may prove unwilling collaborators. The reason? The analysis might reveal some awkward positions for both parties as it correlates job content, employee competencies, employee hierarchy, and geographical and location-based factors with the measures of absences and the cost of these absences.

Project Accounting for R&D

Measuring R&D progress and matching this progress with the budget and the actual spending can be a daunting task. One important factor is hard to cover with a BI system: the percentage of progress in the project toward

TABLE 8.1

Examples of Analyses per Market Organization Type

Subject Area/Organization Type	Industry	B2B Trade	Professional Services	Retail	Not-for-Profit
Marketing	LTV, Direct product profitability (fmcg)	LTV	LTV	LTV, Direct product profitability	LTV
Market Research	•	•	•	•	•
Sales	Volume and revenue matching	Volume and revenue matching	Billable hours per project, customer…	Cash to sales and inventory matching	Membership profit analysis
Sales Promotion	□	Promotion analysis	□	Promotion analysis	□
Customer Service	Cost of defects	Cost of errors	Cost of errors / Timesheet analysis	Warranty costs	
Operations					
Supply chain	Inventory analysis	Inventory analysis	□	Inventory analysis	Inventory analysis
Manufacturing	Accruals/WIP report	□	□	□	□
Asset Management	Maintenance costs and accruals	Maintenance costs and accruals	•	Maintenance costs and accruals	•
HRM					
Recruitment & Selection	Salary comparison	Salary comparison	Salary comparison	Salary comparison	•
Development & Coaching	Training cost analysis / Absenteeism analysis	•	Wage to revenue analysis / Absenteeism analysis	•	•

(Continued)

TABLE 8.1 (CONTINUED)

Examples of Analyses per Market Organization Type

Subject Area/ Organization Type	Industry	B2B Trade	Professional Services	Retail	Not-for-Profit
R&D					
Research	Project accounting	•	Project accounting	•	•
Development	Project accounting Prototype analysis	•	Project accounting Pilot analysis	•	•
Risk Management	Insurance analysis		Insurance analysis	Insurance analysis	•
Quality Management	Cost of quality	Cost of quality	Cost of quality	•	•

Note: • Not commonly used ☐ not applicable.

a solution, a deliverable related to the percentage of the budgeted cost. In other words, if the project has a burn rate of 80%, how do we prove the project is finished for about 80% and the last 20% is not especially more difficult or less feasible than the previous? This solution will have to link activities registered in timesheets, accounting figures for salary costs, purchases, and expenses, and project data such as configuration management data, engineering data, and milestones.

Special Attention for Slowly Changing Dimensions

Most financial systems use all sorts of analytical attributes and groupings reflecting the strategic issues at hand. These can, and will of course, change. Make sure that from the outset of the analysis you get enforce a clear view of management on this issue. In other words: how long and how will they keep track of changes in dimensions such as product, organization, customer, account manager, or analytical account?

Let me give you an example for each of these dimensions:

- Product: Product category management is an art form that evolves quickly as a result of BI analytics. Imagine a chocolate bar with special features such as an embossed car logo. Tests in retail outlets have shown that it sells better in the gift department so this type of chocolate bar will also appear in the "Gifts_Food" category after approval of the category manager.
- Organization: In large organizations cost and revenue centers change to reflect strategic priorities or they simply change because of mergers and acquisitions, new organization theories, or whatever reason management may find appropriate.
- Customer: That is the hardest one because customers also merge or divest parts of their organization. Consider this case: if client organization part A was a customer of department T merges with a larger customer C, who was a customer of department Z; who then inherits the revenue and volume figures? OK, logic may dictate that the smaller customer is absorbed by the larger but maybe the smaller customer's account manager has a better relationship with the larger customer and the latter, customer C, chooses to be handled by department T's account manager. In any case, there will be a rupture in the sales volume reporting between the two departments that

needs explanation. What if these ruptures repeat themselves over a relatively short time period?

- Account manager: They hand over customers, and their client portfolio can be reshuffled now and then.
- Analytical account: In my experience it is not so much a question of change but more of refining existing accounts (which can always be solved through adding grouping levels) but also the creation of new analytical perspectives. If the accounting system allows the creation of new analytical account sets, this is not a big issue, but what if the source system allows only three analytical account columns? Well, you know what happens: either the obsolete column is replaced or (worse) the new system is "interwoven" in the existing columns by adding a special sign or a letter or whatever creativity that the system allows.

Will they simply overwrite it (Type 1 SCD) and only look at the latest reporting version? Will they use a flag Is_Current on all records so the obsolete record's Is_Current status is changed to "N" whether or not combined with the Effective_from_date and Effective_to_date (Type 2 SCD)? Or will they use a Type 3 SCD which keeps the "before" version and the "after" version as well? Whatever the client decides, you will have to assess the impact on the data model, the workload, and the capacity of the data warehouse as with each linear increase of the SCD type number, the workload may double and the capacity of the data warehouse may grow exponentially.

Special Attention for Presentation Options

Financial reports are pretty straightforward but their audience varies from seasoned auditors, accountants, and bookkeepers to junior or assistant managers who specialize in other disciplines such as marketing, operations, sales, or HRM. The presentation should meet their typical requirements. For example, marketing people prefer forward-looking reports so an analytical dashboard allowing them to test scenarios like "increase margin–decrease volume" or "reduce sales force–reduce revenue" are much more interesting than being informed of a YTD gross margin reduction of 0.2%.

Bookkeepers may be satisfied with a PDF document they can file and an Excel file to cook up their own cross-tabulations and salespeople will want detailed revenue levels and volume information per customer. So, you make sure the expectations of each report user type are known well in advance and the report design becomes a powerful weapon for the internal marketing of the BI project.

Business Analysis Issues

To sum up the topics the business analyst should cover when analyzing the finance situation for the BI project:

1. Get a view of the operational process from order to invoice and dunning.
2. Get a good explanation of the audit trails.
3. Look for metadata and, if there are none, start up a metadata track to avoid misconceptions, confusion, and outright chaos in the project.
4. Discuss potential adjacent projects (see Table 8.1) to avoid expensive changes further in the project.
5. Check every major attribute on its persistence; that is, tick all the slowly changing dimension boxes.
6. Manage the various user expectations with regard to presentation, currency of the data, level of detail, and so on.

9

BI and Operations Management

THE 101 ON OPERATIONS MANAGEMENT

A business analyst looking for business cases in logistics doesn't have to look very far: forecasting will be on top of the list and all sorts of optimization strategies of the supply chain will also emerge during a brainstorming session. The operations management scope for Business Intelligence (BI) is so large someone may have to dedicate an entire book to it. I list the frequently asked business questions I have encountered during my practice and work out a few of them to illustrate the added value of BI for operations management.

Customer Order Point

The customer order point (COP) is a very important notion in the supply and manufacturing chain. It depicts the stocks and flows of raw materials, components, and finished goods from the source to the final customer. Figure 9.1 shows the five possible COPs: the arrows represent the movement of raw materials, components, and finished goods and the triangles represent the inventories.

A few conclusions for the analysis of this situation:

1. The COP and a number of intrinsic market and product features interact to influence the organization's approach to forecasting.
2. Only a complete integration of supply chain and sales and marketing data allow the BI system to calculate the optimum COP for the organization.

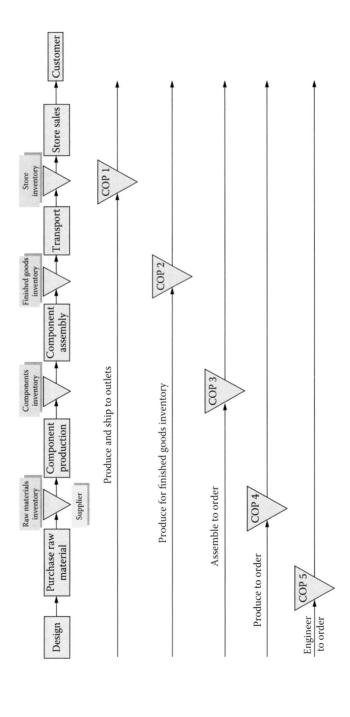

FIGURE 9.1

An example of the customer order points in a production environment. An enlarged version is in the illustrations section.

3. Analyze all levels of complexity in the production process:
   - Material complexity
   - Process complexity
   - Skills complexity

This will give you a clue about the center of gravity of the required analyses.

Forecasting

The IT support for operations management has improved enormously over the last decade. From piecemeal distributed initiatives to integrated sales and order management, production and warehouse management, enterprise resource planning (ERP) has increased the flexibility and cost control, and raised interesting questions about better capacity planning and improved forecasting. This is where statistical techniques (or if you prefer the fancier "data mining") come into the picture. By improving forecasting results, better capacity planning and improved inventory management will result from it.

In this chapter, I do not express any prejudice for or against a particular forecasting technique as I prefer a pragmatic approach to testing, validating, and experiencing what the right forecasting technique is for your organization in a certain development phase, in a certain environment, and with certain IT and statistical skills available. Forecasting yields better results in a context-rich environment. Don't just rely on data! Include forecasting context, procedures, and focus in your everyday marketing and sales activities and ask yourself questions such as:

- Do my salespeople return with enough data from trade shows?
- Do we analyze the clicks on our website?
- Do we make proactive inquiries during service calls or support calls?
- Do we promote transparency and exchange of information with our resellers?
- Do we use account management techniques, drawing up business plans with our customers and resellers?
- Are we willing to pay for market information from external sources?

Every figure your systems register is an abstraction from reality. Make sure you enrich forecasting data with context. This context can be modeled in the data warehouse and comes from sources outside even the most comprehensive ERP system the business community has ever seen. In other words, don't trust your ERP vendor when he says he has a one-size-fits-all forecasting module in his ERP application, not even when it has a data warehouse under the hood.

Optimization of the Supply Chain

Picture the supply chain as a network of goods, information, and services being created, moved, and consumed between agents, ranging in numbers from a few to thousands or millions. Optimizing this network transcends pure mathematics. Again, rich contextual information is needed to improve the organization's operational performance. Let us look at the frequently asked business questions and take a closer look at the setup of a BI system that can answer one or more of these questions.

Business FAQs

Which vendor/supplier performs better than others throughout the entire supply chain?

What is the economic order quantity per vendor in terms of not only profit but also risk?

For international companies:

Which products should be produced in which plants and where should they be stored?

How should the cargo be loaded on the vessel, train, or truck to maximize its utilization?

How do we define delivery territories for optimum staffing and customer satisfaction?

When does our delivery performance hurt our profitability without contributing to higher customer satisfaction?

When and where do we outsource our sales, distribution, or customer service activities?

We work out the analysis example for a part of the last business question: to outsource or not to outsource our distribution activities. This business question—if answered completely—can cover partly or wholly the previous ones.

Quality Management

There are few data warehouse projects known to me where quality management is at the center of attention but almost all data warehouses have implicit quality measures that can deliver interesting results. Managing quality improvement programs is data driven:

1. The organization collects and analyzes quantitative measures such as defects in the process and the end product, throughput times, dead on arrival (DOA) statistics, warranty statistics, lab tests, customer complaints, and so on.
2. The organization develops targets in close collaboration with production engineers and line management and reserves a budget to meet these targets.
3. It develops training and education in all levels of the organization.
4. It uses statistical techniques to monitor the evolution of quality in the processes and products.
5. It clearly demonstrates the interdependency of organizationwide factors and the importance of mutual adjustment between (at first sight) distant factors such as suppliers, workforce, intensity of the lighting, salary and bonus schemes, time of day, and day of week, among others.

Sounds like a BI system, doesn't it? Especially in the service industry, management has to grasp the interdependencies between the employee and his personal management program (PMP), the customer, and contents of the job(s) he has to perform for a particular customer. That way, quality management becomes the wrapper around marketing, operations, and Human Resources Management (HRM).

Setting up Outsourcing Analysis

To answer the business question of which part of the supply chain the organization can outsource, an extensive measurement of time, cost, and risk is needed. The sources are multiple and vary greatly in context and initial purpose. The organization's ERP system has in most cases a purely financial view of the production and warehousing processes. The time perspective is partly present but the risk perspective is absent. Warehouse management systems track time and movements but the cost of inventory resides within the ERP system. Transport and handling tracking systems only measure time and activity type although some of them also register the hourly rate of drivers and handlers to produce a variable cost per weight or volume handled or transported. A business intelligence system can consolidate all these data into one insightful model.

The model will provide context and data for high-level KPI measurements such as cost per ton/km, supplier rating, and risk of overdue, incomplete, or damaged shipping per supplier and per transport mode. It can also evaluate the optimum route in terms of speed, cost, and risk, thus improving the organization's overall management of these three important components.

PRODUCTION MANAGEMENT AND INFORMATION ARCHITECTURE

Manufacturing environments can present complex architectural pictures for the average business analyst. Most business analysts have experience in marketing, finance, HRM, and the like but Business Intelligence analysts with manufacturing experience are relatively scarce. Therefore, it is useful to introduce the main components of an information system (IS) for manufacturing.

There are four types of standard information systems for production management you may come across during the analysis phase:

1. MRP II software or manufacturing resource planning
2. Capacity management software
3. Network planning software
4. Standard software, tuned for manufacturing, for example, spreadsheets, statistical software, linear programming software, and so on.

MRP II Software

Organizations that have mass or series production and assembly of components use MRP II, which is a framework of seven components. MRP II

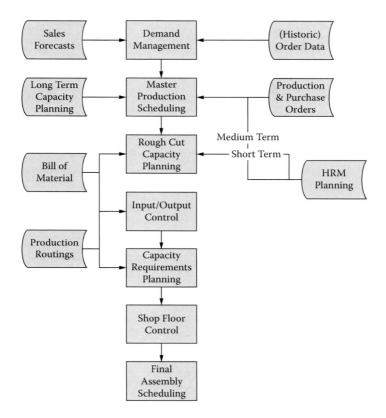

FIGURE 9.2
The information aspects of MRP II.

itself is the next layer on top of MRP I (material requirements planning), which decomposes final products into components, production steps, and raw material in a bill of material. Figure 9.2 shows the flow of data through this planning pipeline.

MRP II makes the choices of the business strategists operable. The question of which products for which markets and in what quantities is translated into production and supply chain schedules. In the execution phase, data of executed steps and their results and other performance measurements such as mean time between failures of machines and absenteeism are registered and may prove valuable Business Intelligence data.

Demand management uses forecasts from sales and marketing and analyzes current and historic order data on seasonality, trend, outliers, and their reasons to come up with a demand curve relevant to the organization's options with regard to flexibility and capacity. It is clear that capacity planning for a shipyard is somewhat more inflexible than for a jeans manufacturer who plans 80% of his production in Chinese sweatshops.

Master production scheduling ends with the agreement between manufacturing and sales about what will be produced when and where in the case where transport costs are determining sales success. Consider a global brick producer such as Wienerberger who knows that brick can't travel farther than 300 kilometers in Europe or they lose their competitive advantage over local producers, with the nonexistent transportation burden for smaller, more glittering stones like diamonds…

Rough cut capacity planning (RCCP) is where the master production schedule is refined and evaluated for feasibility. The potential bottlenecks (i.e., critical components, critical suppliers, critical production steps, etc.) are identified.

Input/output control is also called *order release management* by some authors and software producers and adjusts the input for the production on the output and capacity planning.

Capacity requirements planning is a much finer grain of rough cut capacity planning and uses the bill of material and MRP I data to a greater extent than RCCP.

Shop floor control manages the work in progress per production step, per machine, and per tool; in the case of specialized tools, priorities are determined and work packages are assigned to people, tools, and machines.

Final assembly scheduling translates the production orders of components and parts into an assembly plan, based on customer orders and the priorities indicated by sales and marketing people.

Capacity Management Software

In MRP II the rough cut capacity planning and the capacity requirements planning processes examine the available capacity but the primary focus is on materials for mass and series production. In the case of production of unique products, engineer to order, or small series production, other software is needed. The unique transformation process has to be defined per production run, which immediately affects the machine and staff planning in a less structured way than is the case in MRP II. Meeting the deadlines is the primary focus of this kind of software.

Network Planning Software

When process steps and the tasks transforming raw material into a finished product are at the center of attention, a different type of software is needed. Project production or job shop production does not have capacity or the flow of goods in focus but the skills of people and availabilities of machines determine the planning. The jewelry manufacturing business is a case in point. Some diamond cutters simply cannot be bypassed as the risk of inferior results would cause greater loss than keeping the customer waiting a little longer.

Basic Concept of IS for Production Management

In Figure 9.3 note that I use the term decision support system (DSS) deliberately as this is the classical form of top-down management needed in a production environment. When things are out of control, there is no need for information democracy; swift and disciplined action is needed! Also note that I have placed SCADA (supervisory control and data acquisition)

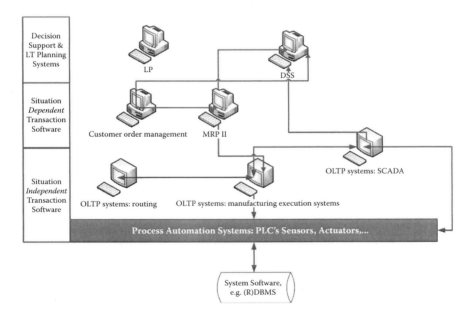

FIGURE 9.3

The basic components of a production environment consisting of the system software (databases, protocols, etc.), the situation-independent transaction software, the situation-dependent software (MRPII or network planning and customer order management), and the decision support and (long-term) planning systems.

in the gray area of situation-dependent and independent software as the control aspect may be both contextual and situational (i.e., the work load dictated by external factors) and out of context because certain production measurements are beyond limits.

WHAT TO MEASURE

First Example: Physical Goods Transport

The first and principal question you will have to answer during the intake is the unit of measure. In an ideal world, the physical and the administrative entities are in sync but I am afraid this is the exception. Take the concept of the consignment of an administrative unit for a shipment versus a unit of transport such as a container or a vessel. The generally accepted definition of consignment is, "A separate identifiable number of goods (available to be) transported from one consignor to one consignee via one or more than one mode of transport and specified in one single transport document." *

A consignment can be divided over various containers but a container can also be divided in many consignments. Analysis of variable costs per consignment may lead to irrelevant information when you look at the administrative costs in the case of many shipping units in a consignment or it may produce irrelevant information when you look at the handling costs per consignment if you have many consignments in one shipping unit. In any case the use of average cost per consignment or per container will yield useless information. So the first analysis step is to determine what measure for what type of customer is dominant and analyze the time, cost, and risk as a function of customer type.

If you are forwarding steel the consignment view may be more relevant than the unit of transport. But if you are in the bulk goods business, the unit of transport may produce better insight. The next step is to chart all possible points of measurement. These points of measurement can be geographically defined but they will also need a legal definition as the inco-terms define the allocation of cost and risk between the buyer and the seller. Table 9.1 makes it clear that cost and risk not only have a logistics aspect but also a commercial one. A clever BI system will enable you to

---

* Source: http://www.geodiswilson.com/en/Global_tools/Logistics_Dictionary/C/.

TABLE 9.1

Table of Incoterms

Incoterm	Loads truck	Pays export duty	Transports to port of destination	Unloads from truck at port of origin	Pays landing charges at port of origin	Transports to port of destination	Pays landing charges at port of destination	Unloads onto trucks from port of destination	Transports to the final destination	Pays insurance	Handles the entry and customs clearance	Pays for the entry duties and taxes
EXW	B	B	B	B	B	B	B	B	B	B	B	B
FCA	S	S	S	B	B	B	B	B	B	B	B	B
FAS	S	S	S	S	B	B	B	B	B	B	B	B
FOB	S	S	S	S	S	B	B	B	B	B	B	B
CFR	S	S	S	S	S	S	B	B	B	B	B	B
CIF	S	S	S	S	S	S	B	B	B	S	B	B
CPT	S	S	S	S	S	S	B	B	B	B	B	B
CIP	S	S	S	S	S	S	B	B	B	S	B	B
DAF	S	S	S	S	S	S	B	B	B	B	B	B
DES	S	S	S	S	S	S	B	B	B	S	B	B
DEQ	S	S	S	S	S	S	S	B	B	S	B	B
DDU	S	S	S	S	S	S	S	S	S	S	B	B
DDP	S	S	S	S	S	S	S	S	S	S	S	S

Note: Who does what for each incoterm: "B" = Buyer "S" = Seller

optimize your pricing tactics, based on your experience with the true cost of the incoterms.

A logistics BI system can capture the most interesting incoterm for the seller or optimize the selling price in case the buyer is adamant about the applicable incoterm. The incoterm, combined with the shipment type, shipper, and shipped goods, will yield insight to the risks and the real costs of the consignment (or the shipping unit). The cost types are well defined: transport, terminal handling costs, insurance, administration, stuffing and stripping from containers, warehouse rent, demurrage (costs for late return of a container), surcharges (express, idle time, night shift, multi-stop, fuel surcharges), and the like.

Time measurement comes in three flavors: the throughput requested by the customer, the throughput time planned by the seller/shipper, and the actual throughput time. Risk is somewhat harder to measure but we can log all incidents that caused an insurance claim or an extra cost or waste of time to one of the parties involved and divide this by the number of shipments to produce a proxy value.

The BI system will have to capture time, cost, and risk on all the segments of the shipping route affected by the incoterms. A list of the major segments for a classical bulk goods supply chain follows:

- Port of origin and quay
- Ocean vessel
- Intermediate port
- Short shipping vessel
- Port of destination and quay
- Barge
- Inner harbor
- Train
- Truck
- Inland terminal
- Trans-shipment terminal
- Warehouse(s): seller, shipper, third-party warehouse, buyer's warehouse

If you can chart all these elements during the analysis phase, you will find yourself (or your colleague) rapidly in the next step: modeling the data warehouse. As this is beyond the scope of this book, I refer to the specialized literature from authors such as Ralph Kimball (Kimball and Ross, 2002), Bill Inmon (1992), Claudia Imhoff (2001), and others.

Once the data warehouse is collecting sufficient data (and I wonder whether you will be able to do an historical load as most systems have very different archiving rules) you will be able to perform analysis about supplier performance, and ultimately a make or buy analysis with potential savings on your logistics costs. Making a business case for this kind of analytical setup is restricted to something ranging from a defensible hypothesis to pure conjecture, namely a percentage savings on your supply chain costs due to optimization that you can only know long after the system is in place. Maybe that is why only the CEO can take this strategic investment decision.

Second Example: Inventory Management Systems

Inventory management systems (IMS) answer three basic questions in various ways:

1. How often do we have to determine the economic* inventory level?
2. When do we place an inventory replenishment or production order?
3. How big does this order have to be?

The answer to the first question determines R (the review interval). Theoretically this could be done on a continuous basis but that would only satisfy math enthusiasts. In real life the review is at regular intervals or it is triggered by a transaction: a shipment to a customer, reception of a production order, or a reservation made by a customer, for example.

When the order is placed it is also at regular intervals or it is triggered by pre-determined stock levels. We indicate the stock level before replenishment with "s" and after replenishment with "S." The order quantity is either fixed or independent of the present stock level or it is dependent on it. We use "Q" as the symbol for the order quantity. The four commonly used inventory management systems are a combination of the aforementioned symbols: s,Q – s,S – R,S and R,s,S.

s,Q or the Two-Bin System

Orders are issued on a continuous basis. As soon as the inventory is at level s a fixed order of Q goes out the door. It is a simple IMS that works well in a stable environment with a fairly even spread in customer order quantities. As soon as unexpected large orders pop up, this system is flawed. To make sure this system works Q has to be sufficiently larger than the average demand during the order lead time.

---

* The economic inventory level is the net inventory (which is physical inventory minus the backorders) plus the stock replenishment orders issued minus reserved stock.

s, S

Orders are made on a continuous basis as soon as the stock level reaches s. The order quantity depends on the inventory at the time of ordering. The main difference with s,Q is the order size, which is variable. In most organizations where there is a lot of implicit knowledge—or call it experience—this intuitive system works well.

R, S

For every R units of time lapsed, an order is placed to replenish the stock until level S. This is a primitive system that only works in cases where there is stable outflow of goods and parts. The inventory cost is relatively high but the order costs may be lower as this system works in cases where many parts and goods come from the same supplier or where the capacity of a transport mode is optimally used.

R, s, S

Most ERP systems offer full functionality to use this system, which is a bit more complicated than the previous systems. R is a calculated optimum order interval. R, s, and S are calculated for the optimum economic order quantity, or EOQ, which is explained in the next chapter. Companies that use this system have the lowest total cost of:

- Ordering
- Inventory risk
- Inventory monetary cost
- Cost of out of stock

BASIC SUPPLY CHAIN REPORT REQUIREMENTS

Introduction

Supply chain managers need to know at least four things to manage their divisions:

1. The cash conversion cycle time per product or the total cycle and optimum variable cost

2. The cost of inventory and therefore the economic order quantity
3. The product analysis in terms of risk
4. The supplier analysis in terms of performance

The following sections describe the basic algorithms a business analyst should know to bridge the gap between management information needs and the source systems. The data warehouse will need to integrate data from the accounting system with inventory and production management systems. So, let's get cracking!

Total Cycle and Optimum Variable Cost

Manufacturing companies need to get a clear view of which products return within which period the cash invested in them. A clear view of four cycles is needed. We take you step by step through the algorithm so you can conduct your analysis focusing on the availability and the sources of the data needed for the algorithm. This algorithm combines the sales effectiveness with production and the policies on accounts receivable and supplier management. It also creates a valuable context for forecasting: each product can be given a sensitivity factor determining the investment in the level of confidence of the forecast. In the case of critical products this factor will be very high and will invite management to follow these products carefully whereas products with a low sensitivity factor enjoy more degrees of freedom so automatic replenishment orders are more appropriate.

Note: The factor 365 indicating the number of days per year in the formulas below can be replaced by 360.

Rotation of Supplies

$$\text{Rotation}_S = 365 \times \text{average inventory}/(\text{beginning inventory} + \text{purchases} - \text{end inventory})$$

Rotation of Production

$$\text{Rotation}_{PR} = 365 \times \text{average inventory of products} \\ \text{in process}/\text{yearly production cost} \\ + \text{end inventory finished goods} \\ - \text{beginning inventory finished goods}$$

Rotation of Customers

$$\text{Rotation}_C = 365 \times \text{average days receivable/sales}$$

Rotation of Purchases and Subcontractors

$$\text{Rotation}_P = 365 \times \text{average days payable outstanding/purchases}$$

Total Cycle = Rotation_S + Rotation_PR + Rotation_C − Rotation_P
Optimum Total Variable Costs

Calculate the optimum economic order quantity using this formula:

$$Q_o = \sqrt{(2DC/rW)}$$

that is, the square root of twice the yearly demand (D) times the order cost (C) over the cost of risk, space, and interest (r) times the purchase cost (W).

If we multiply the EOQ with the cost for interest, space, risk, and purchase we can evaluate the optimum total variable costs per product:

$$TVCo = Qo \times r \times W$$

Reports or cubes for supply chain reporting should indicate the EOQ, the total variable costs, and the total costs both as measures and as dimensions, allowing the business to aggregate on an ad hoc basis.

EOQ with Partial Deliveries

Partial deliveries greatly influence the EOQ. Make sure you also cover this ground by using the following formulas:

U = yearly consumption in units
C = order cost
r = risk, interest, space, and so on
W = total purchases
W/U = cost per unit
N_u = optimum lot in units
x = reception of units per day
y = sales or consumption in units per day

then $(N_u/x) \cdot y$ is the number of units used during the reception period and $N_u - (N_u/x) \cdot y$ is the largest possible cumulative inventory, which makes the average inventory:

$$1/2N_u \cdot (1 - (y/x))$$

and the inventory cost becomes:

$$1/2N_u \cdot (1 - (y/x)) \cdot r \cdot W/U$$

Conclusion: the optimum number of units per order is:

$$N_{uOPT} = \sqrt{((2UC)/(W/U)r(1 - y/x))}$$

Product Analysis

Product analysis reports provide the business with more insight on the importance and risks of each individual product. The previous supply chain reports provide input for a ranking based on total cycle costs and total optimum variable costs. Now we can enhance these reports with the following calculated fields:

Actual total variable costs on a yearly basis
Optimum total variable costs on a yearly basis
Margin for improvement ($TVC - TVC_o$)
Total gross margin on a yearly basis
Contribution to overhead: total gross margin – actual total variable costs
Supplier: name and ID
Supplier: share of Delta Light in the supplier's revenue
Payment terms of the supplier
Supplier evaluation: a composed figure with details in a subreport (see below)

Supplier Analysis

This sub report provides insight to the supplier's performance:

Number of references, delivered by the supplier (split into raw materials, components, and finished goods).
Number of references for which one or more alternative suppliers are in the supplier database.

Total revenue of the references this supplier contributes: double counting is possible (and useful) because one product can have more than one supplier. Make a split for unique products (for which only one supplier is in the picture) and second source options (i.e., products for which one, more than one, or all components have a second source).

Number of orders per year per supplier.

Number of order lines per year per supplier.

Number of orders/order lines within the requested/promised delivery period.

Number of orders/order lines delivered within the requested delivery period or percentage complete deliveries.

Percentage DOA*.

Combining these findings, the supplier evaluation quotation uses two perspectives: the positive perspective:

$$\text{Revenue} \times \text{percentage complete deliveries within requested period} + \text{revenue} \times (1 \text{ percentage DOA})$$

and the negative:

$$\text{Revenue} \times \text{percentage incomplete deliveries within requested period}$$

SETTING UP A FORECASTING SYSTEM USING BI

To set up a forecasting system, you need to take a broad view of the company's activities. I do not go into the details of building an actual forecasting base table, but as a business analyst you should be aware of the various data and information layers available for forecasting and some general recommendations to your client if she considers setting up a forecasting system. Finally, the client has to know the evaluation methods or KPIs to

---

* DOA: defect products at goods reception.

measure the performance of the forecasting system. These are the layers, gradually broadening your view on the subject:

1. Transaction data with history: for example, orders, production runs, warehouse data, invoices, bookings, cancellations, and order alterations
2. Large trend and seasonality patterns and their origins if known: for example, weather, festive periods, or events
3. Marketing budget and the output: for example, campaigns or sales training
4. Market tendencies: for example, consumer indexes
5. Leading indicators: for example, crude oil price, dollar/yen ratio, related consumption indexes
6. Megatrends: for example, smaller households, Asian tigers

General Recommendations

Before you decide on buying software and consultancy, make sure you evaluate both the value and the impact of a professional forecasting system. Use a proof of concept on data from past periods and on products with various seasonality patterns. The data requirements for forecasting are not necessarily good input for the data warehouse data requirements. Some models perform better with aggregated data, therefore this is not necessarily the grain for the data warehouse. Below are a few hints to evaluate the impact and the value.

Forecasting Can Have a Thorough Impact

Professional forecasting may lead to business process re-engineering. Be aware of its impact on your budget and time estimates. Many forecasting projects reveal a lack of communication in the supply chain, in the sales channels, and in management in general. Failing to remedy these communication gaps will severely affect forecasting performance.

Forecasting also leads to new classification schemes. For example, product classifications can originate from an accountant's or a sales channel view but if the supply chain has critical bottlenecks for parts or production steps, a new grouping around these production and supply clusters may prove to be more relevant for forecasting. Forecasting may also lead to advanced marketing research studies such as psychographic segmentation or basket analysis, delivering answers to questions including which products are bought together with other products.

Finally, forecasting may induce organizations to pay more attention to macroeconomic data, such as economic outlooks from national banks, the OECD, the World Bank, and mesoeconomic data such as Gfk* and Nielsen figures for specific markets, as they can affect the trend line.

Forecasting Is a Total Process

Too many organizations consider forecasting as: plug in a tool, feed it with some data, analyze it and . . . done. They forget that measurement itself influences behavior, and that deep knowledge of the context in which the data were produced is needed to challenge the value of the data. Here are just a few examples to illustrate my point.

Sales managers will recognize the end of quarter by two movements in their sales figures: an upswing before or after the end of the quarter. Why before the end of the quarter? Because the company wants to announce positive figures so they come up with all the closing techniques the book allows (and sometimes others like side letters). Why after the end of the quarter? Because the salespeople have already reached their quarterly target and try to optimize their bonus income so they keep the sales orders in their briefcases.

Sales managers will also recognize the fluctuations in buying behavior in large project organizations such as construction companies. When they have excess profits and excess cash, they will purchase consumables and instead of building up inventory they will book them as costs on a project. In the opposite case, they will stop all purchases and reduce their inventory to a minimum.

Defining the KPIs for a Forecasting System

When you start developing a forecasting system, benchmarking the company's results from period n-1 with datasets from period n–2, n–3, and n–4, used to test the algorithms makes sense. But how do you determine the value of the forecasting results?

There are three KPIs that make sense to evaluate the forecasting results, compared with reality. *MAE* (*mean absolute error*) is the average of the

---

* GfK is the abbreviation of Gesellschaft für Kundenforschung, a leading marketing research organization. www.gfk.com

absolute error for every period. It shows the size of the general prediction error and it does not punish extreme prediction errors. Inasmuch as the prediction errors do not neutralize each other because we use the absolute value to calculate the MAE we have no idea of the direction of the errors; that is, we do not know whether the errors were positive or negative, compared to the actual outcome.

Calculation MAE:

$$\mathbf{MAE} = 1/n \sum_{t=1}^{n} |A_t - F_t|$$

where A_t = the actual value and F_t is the forecasted value for a period t.

MAPE (mean absolute percentage error) is the average of the absolute value of the percentage error for every period. The assumption in this KPI is that higher sales figures absorb a higher prediction error. Like the MAE, it does not "punish" extreme prediction errors. MAPE may return bad results when there are zero values in the actuals, which results in a division by zero.

Calculation MAPE:

$$\mathbf{MAPE} = 1/n \sum_{t=1}^{n} |A_t - F_t|/A_t|$$

The difference between actual value A_t and the forecast value F_t, is divided by the actual value A_t again. The absolute value of this calculation is summed for every fitted or forecast point in time and divided again by the number of fitted points n. This makes it a percentage error so one can compare the error of fitted time series that differ in level.

RMSE (root mean squared error) is the root of the sum of all squared errors of every period, also known as the standard deviation. It "punishes" extreme prediction errors that do not neutralize each other because of the squared terms. This measure does not show the direction of the prediction error and is used by most statisticians because the impact of extreme errors should be reduced in the evaluation process.

Calculation RMSE:

$$\mathbf{RMSE} = \sqrt{\sum_{t=1}^{n} (A_t - F_t)^2/n)}$$

Comparing the prediction line in Figure 9.4 with the actual values represented by the circles shows a pretty good seasonal fit in this case.

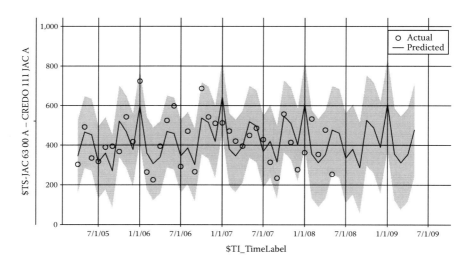

FIGURE 9.4
The prediction line with the actual values.

Cost Justification for Forecasting

This is relatively straightforward: if the extra cost of forecasting can be offset by better results in inventory management or service level then the company should invest. In other words, as soon as one or more of the above KPIs are better for the system than for the "naïve" method (or no method for that matter) the added percentage of improved forecasting should be evaluated on its reduction in costs or increase in revenue.

The model I have set up is just one of the possible approaches a business analyst can take toward evaluating the results.

Step 1: Collect the Data

Take the group of products that represent the bulk of your gross margin (and hope that Pareto's law applies) and test the various forecasting methods with the statistical tool(s) in a proof of concept. You will examine a period prior to last year, for example, as this allows you to compare the forecasted data with the actual data. Make sure you have sufficient historical data, distributed over equal representative periods (i.e., compare Christmas shopping *n*–1 with Christmas shopping *n*–2, etc.). The minimum is sales and revenue volumes per individual product and inventory levels per individual product (and in some cases, per product component) but also macroeconomic data such as market volume, GNP data, and the like.

Step 2: Decide on the Grain

Do we need daily, weekly, or monthly sales data? Do we need the lowest individual product level or will a product group or a basket of interconnected products or a category suffice? The definitions of these three group names vary per organization, so check them!

Step 3: Integrate the Data

In this step, important input can easily be overlooked as not all data will reside in base tables. It is your job as a business analyst to come up with the relevant facts and figures including marketing budgets, competitive counteractions during certain periods, new product launches, or product upgrades.

Step 4: Select the Data

Make sure you have a selection of data that is fit for a forecasting exercise: stable, with repeatable patterns, over a long enough period, and with a future revenue perspective, the latter to avoid forecasting on a sample of obsolete products. A few examples of selection criteria are:

- Products sold within the first six months of 2010
- Products sold within the last six months available in 2011
- Products having a maximum of three months without sales in the complete time series

Step 5: Prepare the Data

This is the data scrubbing phase that makes laymen weary of the forecasting wizards. Make sure you explain why and how you are removing or adding variables and transforming categorical and numerical variables within the forecasting table. Demonstrate why you converted numerical data into strings and vice versa and communicate how you handle missing data, superfluous data, or noise such as outliers or input errors.

Step 6: Choose and Develop the Model

Refer to a good book on statistics. Suffice it to say that there are myriad predictive models available, from the classical and simple models such as (centered) moving average, via time series, to exotic stuff such as projection pursuit regression and neural networks. Try a few of them on a limited dataset and see what works best.

Step 7: Validate the Model

Now check whether the model that came out best also works on the entire dataset; that is, do the predictions on past data concur with the actual sales figures right after the examined period? If this is not the case, examine the second best alternative, as this may give a better fit on a larger dataset. Use the KPIs described on the previous pages.

Step 8: Evaluate the Model in Detail

Calculate the difference between the naïve method and the forecasting method, that is, the deviations from the actuals and the incurred costs such as:

- The opportunity cost of forgoing sales because of a stockout
- The inventory carrying cost because of overoptimistic forecasts

These costs have to match the total cost of ownership of a sophisticated forecasting system. I have broken down this evaluation into a few related steps.

If the outcomes are positive, remember to include the cost of maintaining the forecasting model as it will evolve over time, so don't count on very long payback terms such as five years or more. The more volatile your business is, the higher the internal rate of return for the forecasting infrastructure.

Step 9.1: Evaluate the Results: Improved Delivery Performance

Compare the tool results with the results from your original method and use the three KPIs to evaluate them.

TABLE 9.2

Evaluation Table for the Added Value of Improved Delivery Performance

	Contribution Margin	Tool Method Improvement (%)	Delta (€)
MAE	250,000	55	27,000
MAPE	180,000	61	21,000
RMSE	350,000	42	30,000
Average Gain			**26,000**

How to read Table 9.2? The column "Contribution Margin" is the amount generated by the products actually forecasted and sold during the reference period(s) that have been evaluated. The percentage in the column "Tool Method Improvement" indicates the percentage of the products for which the proof of concept scored better than the old method, based on the chosen KPI. The column "Delta" is the result of a calculation of the additional contribution margin that would have been generated if the company would not have had an out of stock situation for these products.

Step 9.2: Evaluate the Results: Reduction in Inventory Carrying Costs

In Step two we looked at the impact of underestimating demand, now we look at a somewhat more difficult aspect, namely the overestimation of demand and its impact on inventory costs. Should enough evidence have been found for cost justification in the previous step then skip this one because there are discussions on the calculation and appreciation method.

How to read Table 9.3? The column "Inventory Turnover Old" indicates the number of times per year the inventory was replenished. In other

TABLE 9.3

Evaluation for Reduced Inventory Carrying Costs

	Inventory Turnover Old	Inventory Turnover New	Sales (€)	Reduction ICC 8% (€)
MAE	3.2	3.8	3,000,000	11,842
MAPE	3.4	3.9	5,000,000	15,083
RMSE	2	3.6	2,500,000	44,444
Average Gain				**23,790**

words, Sales$_t$/Inventory$_t$ = 3.2. Because of better forecasting the company will be able to reduce the inventory, that is, increase the "Inventory Turnover New," as indicated in the next column. The "Sales" column indicates the amount for which the MAE, MAPE, or RMSE provided these better results. The "Reduction ICC 8%" column indicates the savings on inventory costs based on an inventory cost of 8% per year. But be prepared for discussions on this evaluation. The principal arguments are:

1. The order quantities and order lead times don't allow us to lower the inventory.
2. The sales patterns are too unevenly distributed over time so a gain in one period may cause a stock rupture in another.
3. The cost of losing a customer because of poor delivery performance exceeds the inventory cost manifold.
4. Your calculations do not take products into account that are sold together with other products which were not in the scope of your forecast.

All or some of these arguments may be right and can be verified through further study and investigation. Be wary of these arguments if there is neither time nor budget to perform further investigation.

Step 9.3: Do a Complete Cost of Ownership Analysis

The implementation of a forecasting system requires more than the IT costs of setting up a datamart and implementing a statistical tool such as SAS, Statistica, or SPSS. The process re-engineering and the acquisition costs for contextual data as well as dedicated human resources should also be taken into account. And as the model has to evolve over time to adapt to new long-term trends or short-term ruptures in sales patterns, it does not always evolve for the better.

Step 9.4: Calculate the ROI

Using the net present value (NPV) method for stable, low-risk returns over a longer period or a simple payback analysis for high-risk environments, demanding a rapid payback is all it takes to compare the outgoing with the incoming cash flows.

Business Analysis Issues

General Remarks

Supply chain management is about increasing efficiency, which automatically leads to two conclusions that look contradictory at first sight:

God is in the details. Efficiency is about tweaking every single cost and revenue driver you can come up with, even if it is three decimals after the point because we may be looking at processes that churn out a result every split second, which suddenly makes these small numbers become very big numbers.

Always keep the macroscopic view. Sometimes it is necessary to confront the client who wants to do things right with the question, "But, are you doing the right things?"

So, make sure you get a good view of the customer order point before you start digging for details. The COP will be a leading indicator for the direction of the logistics BI project. A few examples:

1. The farther away the COP is from the customer in a mass production environment, the more need for good forecasting techniques.
2. The more the company relies on project-based revenue, the more need there is for project management analysis tools.

Supply chain management and manufacturing are also about quality management as there is an optimum between the cost and the benefits of quality management. Make sure you are informed about the quality management vision in the organization. It is one of, or a mix of, one or more of these approaches:

1. Philip Crosby's (1967/1990) conformance to requirements
2. Joseph Juran's (2010) fitness for purpose or use
3. Armand Feigenbaum's (1951) meeting the customer's expectations of the total composite product and service characteristics of marketing, engineering, manufacturing, and maintenance throughout its life cycle

Check if there is measurement of the cost of quality.

Questions and Issues to Be Addressed

Make sure you get the ins and outs of the inventory management system (s,Q – s,S – R,S – R,s,S) and how the data are collected. A process description of the IMS can illustrate this.

What quality control points are used and what data are collected about the products, the processes, the goods reception, and the goods shipment?

When and where does management use attribute control (in terms of GO/NO GO) and variable measurement (in terms of deviations from the norm)?

What control statistics does the organization have or wish to have?

10

BI and Marketing Management

INTRODUCTION

Today's marketing management is more and more supported by IT. It started with mail-order companies that were the first to use IT to manage customers and their profiles and it has gradually expanded to all sorts of industries. Yet it is only in the last few years that we can speak of successful marketing automation, or customer relationship management (CRM) systems, as IT vendors have come to understand that marketing and sales are about creativity and the freedom to improvise in the field, which needs quite different IT support than a production system.

Yet, the promise of "CRM/BI in a box" is not fulfilled, despite the CRM analytics claims from tool vendors. Why? Because no tool vendor can anticipate the flexibility needed by a marketing department where there are continuously changing promotions, competitive moves, new product introductions, communication, and so on. Business Intelligence (BI) for marketing is 90% tailormade, based on thorough analysis of the present situation and the (potential) future directions. In this chapter, I try to evoke the major issues to address and questions to ask of your marketing client. But first, let's have a look at the principal sources for marketing analysis.

WHAT DO WE MEAN BY "CRM"?

CRM is an umbrella term for all sorts of process support and process management software in the field of sales, marketing, and customer service, among others. Characteristic modules/sources are:

- Sales management (funnel management/region management/etc.)
- Field sales

- Account management (project sales, industrial sales, fast-moving consumer goods [FMCG] company sales, etc.)
- List management (customer database analysis, geographical information system [GIS] analysis, etc.)
- Quote management (including sales configurator, win–loss analysis)
- Order and fulfillment management
- Aftersales service (including e-service)
- Collateral management (marketing literature, version management, configuration management, etc.)
- Telemarketing (inquiries, tele sales: inbound and outbound, etc.)
- Competitor management
- Campaign management

When the users are trained in obtaining and maintaining high data quality standards, a CRM system can contribute to valuable management information.

Yet many CRM projects have produced nothing else than failure because of unrealistic management expectations, lack of user discipline, an unclear vision and direction of the implementation, and last but not least an insufficient definition and positioning of the return on investment to all parties concerned.

Customer data are a mix of crisp, measured, and recorded data with interpreted information and individual assessments. Managing this mix is a continuous process that is very similar to knowledge management processes. Organizations that fail to understand this will never get the full benefits from a CRM system, let alone from the Business Intelligence system for marketing purposes.

WHAT DO WE MEAN BY BEHAVIOR ANALYSIS?

In the pre-Internet area, behavior observation and analysis was an expensive, resource-intensive activity with a lot of quality issues such as consistency, timeliness, and scalability. Now it still doesn't come cheap but at least the three major issues belong to the past.

Ralph Kimball (2000) was one of the pioneers with his ideas on the data webhouse and Jesus Ména (1999) has made behavior analysis his core business, building on the foundations of the data webhouse and adding text mining and myriad data mining tools, including self-organizing maps to produce clusters of opportunities or churn candidates. Be advised that your client does not necessarily need an E-commerce application; he doesn't even need a website to produce these clusters. There are lots of exciting tools that allow analysis of forums, blogs, social networks, and the like that serve as sources for behavior analysis.

This form of analysis is difficult to perform with the classical online analytical processing (OLAP) and reporting tools. The buzzwords *data mining*, which I consider a fancy name for applied statistics, has been hot in the marketing world for at least a decade. It has often led to expensive one-shot analysis projects, ignoring the potential of the data warehouse architecture. Sure enough, many tools need only one large table with comma-separated values (CSV) but why not make sure the data warehouse can deliver these files on a regular basis and why not feed the results back into the data warehouselike segmentation data whether one-dimensional customer segments or customer–product segments, and other clustering results such as product–channel, product–time, or "aperture"?

CAN WE LEARN FROM PAST FAILURES?

I once had a graduate student in my office who wanted to do a research paper on marketing failures in product launches and the analysis of their causes. I cautioned the student she would have trouble finding interviewees willing to admit any sort of marketing failure, whether in their routine job or in a special project like a new product launch. But being a young student, she did not lack enthusiasm and drive and decided to pursue her quest for at least five product managers in the fast-moving consumer goods market and a couple more in the industrial market.

A few months later, we met again and she told me she had changed her subject as she could not come up with a single interviewee after contacting more than 60 organizations. From the largest household names to the smaller niche marketers, nobody was keen on showing any proof of past failures. I leave the psychoanalytical explanations to the reader but rest assured, during my years as a consultant I have come across a fair amount of failure to produce some interesting insights for the BI aspects of the marketing discipline.

Because I don't want any trouble with sharp lawyers from large companies, I will hide the names and places behind generic labels such as "a large food manufacturer" or "a European logistics company." So here are a few lessons for the business analyst taking on the job of a BI project for the marketing department. Read the cases and look for the symptoms when you make your recommendations and assess the risks of failure.

When Operations Leads the Dance

A large chemical company once contacted us to implement CRM and a data mart for customer analysis. After a week's interviewing and studying the case we stumbled on something too unbelievable to have taken this possibility into account: the IT manager declared that all relevant customer data would reside in the customer order module of the company's enterprise resource planning (ERP) system. Come again? So the entire and important process prior to obtaining a customer's order would remain in the dark? Yes, because this environment was declared the master for all customer data and there could be no exceptions to the rule. We politely excused ourselves and quit the project as this could only lead to disaster. Epilogue: five years later, news reached us that the customer was still struggling with the quality of his marketing analytics.

When Finance Leads the Dance

A financial view of customers that looks farther than the next accounting period is a rare species. On the other hand, once a contact has received an invoice it will always remain a customer for the years to come. Most financial applications use a very narrow definition of "customer," that is, a party that has received an invoice. Yet the notion of customer is a lot larger, as we illustrate in Chapter 1, "Generic Business Object Definitions" section. And this is just the top of the iceberg of potential problems. A marketing and sales analyst needs to support decisions on contribution margins, price elasticities, multilevel pricing, distribution policies, and aftersales service policies. If any of you know of financial software that supports these business questions, let me know as one is never too old to learn.

When Overly Complex Sales Models Are the Rule

In this case, the sales and marketing department was in the lead but not to the benefit of the BI project. The department was loaded with young graduates who never even sold a pack of cigarettes or a newspaper let alone a complex service product in the direct marketing industry. When they were let loose to devise a sales engagement model they tried to foresee a CRM structure and process for every possible case in a multichannel team selling approach.

Team selling implies that more than one account manager and product specialist or technical pre-sales support is linked to the same customer and multichannel means that more than one account team can be linked to the same customer. The combination of the two results in a customer-dependent nested hierarchy. And to make things worse: the client also used a customer hierarchy with the top level being the legal entity, followed by legal daughters, and at the lowest level a physical location where each could have its account manager(s) allocated. Let me try to illustrate this in Figure 10.1 with a diagram of the customer view. Of course, the same can be done for the product view and for the account manager view. In the figure, a customer can have one or more account managers who can have one or more product specialists at their side. The risk of double counting revenue or product volume is imminent.

This sales engagement combination of two already complex approaches led to a very complex (snowflaked) data model, which

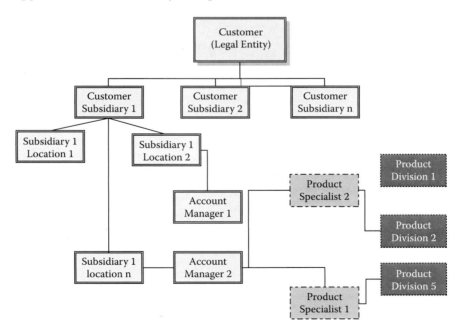

FIGURE 10.1
The complexity of the sales engagement model.

needed monthly snapshots to guarantee some query performance. Even when it is not your job to prescribe instead of describe the business situation you may want to warn the customer in advance of complex sales models like this one.

When BI Is Used for the Wrong Reasons

When I started a new BI project at a logistics company there was an adjacent project already far underway in the wrong direction. The company had set up a data mart to examine data quality issues in the CRM source system. The CRM application was "customized" to allow anybody to do anything on it. Any clerical user could create, read, update, or delete (CRUD) customers, prospects, and other parties, for example, suppliers or competitors. The Soundex algorithm, which prevents the creation of duplicates even in languages other than U.K. or U.S. English was disabled and procedures for CRUD were nonexistent. Obviously the CRM was becoming a serious pain for all parties involved: sales, sales analysts, customer service people, and their managers.

The remedy would have been in the procedures and the setup of the CRM system and, last but not least, creating awareness for customer data quality. Instead, the company decided to analyze the data quality via a data mart using categorical logic. The data mart extracted customer data, order and invoice data, and account manager data, and cross-checked these in reports. Then the reports were used as feedback for cleaning up the source system. Unfortunately, the data quality problems were only about 60% solved and the project was considered a failure.

Why did this project fail? Obviously the project goals were unrealistic and the BI system was the wrong tool for the job. Unrealistic because if a source system has no data quality foundation the BI tool will always remedy the product of a flawed process. First, monitor and adjust the process and then, for safety reasons, check that the product is a simple data quality rule of thumb. It is the wrong tool because a data mart makes pictures of an ongoing process so some of the data quality analysis results may already be obsolete by new entries or deletes. And it is the wrong tool because the SQL used in the data is unfit for probabilistic (or fuzzy) logic to tackle problems such as abbreviations, synonyms, or homonyms in names. Software such as Human Inference® or IBM's InfoSphere® QualityStage, formerly known as Ascential Software, and before that

Vality Technology, can perform this job better as they can cope with unstructured data and fuzzy algorithms.

HOW BI CAN CONTRIBUTE TO MARKETING MANAGEMENT

The benefits of BI in the marketing domain are immense. Where other domains are mainly concerned with efficiency, marketing decision improvement automatically means effectiveness improvement. No other management area has been and is subject to fads, hypes, and sometimes even new insights. But throughout marketing's development over the last century two anchor points have always been there: activities and processes. In the following pages we address the main marketing activities and their typical decision points and how BI can contribute:

- Marketing research
- Affinity analysis
- Direct product profitability
- Product development
- Sales
- Sales promotion
- Customer service
- Channel management

We also take a closer look at typical marketing disciplines, classified by their primary marketing process: the exchange of the seller's promise for the customer's money. I am sure academics may find many different ways of classifying these disciplines but I have warned you: I am not an academic, I look for pragmatic solutions. With this classification it is easy to illustrate how BI delivers a specific contribution to the marketing management areas of:

- Retail marketing
- Industrial marketing
- Professional services marketing
- Fast-moving consumer goods marketing
- Consumer investment goods marketing
- Pharmaceutical marketing

Market Research

Most market research projects look for answers to clearly formulated questions such as:

"In what segment do we have growth opportunities?"
"What is our positioning compared to our major competitors?"

Many of these research issues are managed as a project. With the proper BI infrastructure in place it can become a process, delivering continuous input for marketing decisions. With a data warehouse as a support, the market research efficiency and effectiveness can be increased dramatically.

Here is just one of the many examples of how this can work. One of the greatest difficulties in marketing research is quantifying qualitative research data. The organization may have interesting conclusions on which psychodemographic profile is inclined to become a regular customer of a new product line extension but quantifying this newly discovered segment is another thing. All sorts of proxy methods have been developed to come up with solutions that vary largely in their success ratios but few methods can bridge the gap between these profiles and the customer database. So here are a few questions you can ask your client to attract her attention to this opportunity:

1. Do your Business to Business (B2B) CRM system and your sales approach allow registration of psychodemographic determinants?
2. Does your Business to Consumer (B2C) CRM system track psychodemographic determinants?
3. Have you ever exchanged customer data with other companies?
4. Do you register media consumption patterns of your clients?

Affinity Analysis

The first time I was confronted with affinity analysis was at a time before the concept was cornered by the academic community. My colleagues at the mail-order company were analyzing the sales per catalog page. While comparing the seasonal variances on hardware sales (which have less variation in presentation, product, and pricing than fashion pages) they came up with surprising conclusions: some products sold better in the presence of other products whereas others were unaffected by adjacent products. Affinity analysis has become a major marketing activity for retailers but also for brand owners who seek influence on their product position in the channels. The statistical technique used is often a form of conjoint analysis comparing consumer preferences on all possible combinations.

For example, if a customer buys suntan lotion, there is a probability $P(x)$ that he will put sunglasses in his shopping cart and a probability $P(y)$ that there will be no ice cream. But affinity analysis does not necessarily need to analyze simultaneous purchases. An insurance company can benefit from it as the example shows: a customer who has bought her first car insurance more than four years ago has a higher propensity to buy life insurance today.

Basket analysis is a form of affinity analysis in retail. In its simplest form it is a variation of cross-selling analysis where certain products are chosen as an anchor point and then evaluated on the number and kind of products that are sold together with these products. In its most complex form, basket analysis uses sophisticated algorithms such as k-nearest-neighbor or progression pursuit regression to "discover" spontaneous relationships between products.

Beware of massive redundancy, both in data and in trivial results like "lemonade AND cola" or "oil AND vinegar." There have been many ad hoc solutions for affinity analysis on the market, but I am afraid these quick wins won't win from a sound data warehouse solution as the latter offers more flexibility, more transparency, and scales better than a point solution.

Direct Product Profitability

It is a simple key performance indicator (KPI) that calculates the profit per unit of a physical product earned per square centimeter or meter if you are in the warehousing business. Direct product profitability (DPP) is a common notion for retailers who have to decide on which assortments or which products can take up which space on their floors and shelves but also the FMCG brand. Marketers use it to calculate the tradeoff between buying extra shelf space or spending money on displays and other promotions to get extra space and the extra income earned per square centimeter. I have only come across one business case in a fourth-party logistics service provider who used it to calculate the optimum warehouse rent per product type.

Basically, DPP is a form of activity-based costing marketers use to determine product cost and profitability in areas including manufacturing, distribution, retail, and other businesses. DPP assigns all related direct, indirect, and activity-based costs to products, channels, regions, transportation and handling, customers, and suppliers of raw materials and components. Typical DPP questions for manufacturers are, "Should we increase the production volume to meet increased demand even if this means overtime and more expensive sourcing?" or "Is the surplus we pay to this freight forwarder worth the reduction in inventory throughput and higher customer satisfaction?" DPP also provides input for product development as developers can test scenarios of new product configuration, packaging, and pricing, and their impact on DPP. Finally, DPP influences other KPIs in the operational area as it forces management to develop new processes, sourcing, and other measures of efficiency improvement.

The formula is simple but the data that produce this result present a compelling business case for a data warehouse: the sources are multiple, the granularity is the lowest possible level of detail, and the time horizon can be decades as some brands have been here forever or some customer relationships in the logistics business span decades.

To calculate DPP, multiply the unit sales volume by the profit margin of the product: this is the overall profit for that product. Divide this profit by the shelf space it uses; for example, $6,000 divided by 120 cm equals a contribution of $50 per cm; this contribution is the direct product profitability. One of the problems marketers face in correctly evaluating these DPP results is the influence on DPP of adjacent products on the shelf. Contextual information is equally important. The system should register answers to questions, including:

Is the competition strong, moderate, or weak?
What is their sales surface in the outlets?
What is the influence of promotions: brand, store, and shelf or others?

Product Development

I have not come across a mature business case for a BI system giving full support to product development processes. But the signs are there that BI can contribute significantly to product development. I see two important tracks: the first lies within the value analysis of products that can help to set targets for innovation and the second track contributes by analyzing leading indicators such as:

- Service desk logs of customers asking for products or product features the company has not included in its offer.
- Scanning patent databases.
- Internet research.
- Multi- and interdisciplinary research make a strong case for BI/knowledge management (KM) systems, creating the need for research and development metadata.
- Bridges among fundamental research organizations (universities, research institutes), BI/KM system, and the company's KM or BI system.
- Innovation platforms are stimulated by public authorities allowing better coordination between the business and researchers.

An example of a value analysis report in Q4 2009 is shown in Table 10.1. You don't have to be a brilliant product manager to decide that either the remaining products or new products need to fill the widening gap in the next years. Although this report looks very simple, the underlying data and the algorithms can be pretty complex. Think of forecasting, Chapter 9, "Setting up a Forecasting System Using BI" section, basket analysis,

TABLE 10.1

Value Analysis Example

Product	Widget 1
Added Value in YR	In € (Euro Base YTD)
2006	965,000
2007	945,000
2008	895,000
2009	820,000
Trend	Negative
Prediction	
2010	730,000
2011	630,000
2012	510,000
2013	470,000
2014	320,000

and conjoint analysis, which we described in the previous section. The use of segmentation techniques can also contribute to product development as "unserved audiences" may be detected.

Sales

Most CRM applications, which include salesforce automation (SFA) provide good data on individual customers, customer groups, and segments but most of them lack the long-term perspective and the integration with financial and operational systems. The reason is not always an absence of these features in the application but a happenstance implementation using only 20% of the software's possibilities. A large multinational software vendor used a top CRM package to do no more than capture static customer data and logging the calls. Opportunity management, though supported by the tool, was done in Excel and the contact center module did not provide any management information. The data from the switch was considered a better source.

And then there is a lack of motivation and discipline with the salesforce to feed the system with good data. So, if you embark on a business analysis project for the sales department, make sure you can accommodate them at least for a few basic reports. You will make friends for life.

Make sure your BI project delivers support for the sales budget process with long-term sales data per client. In the case of consumer goods your date and time dimension need the highest level of sophistication to provide reliable forecasting data. If there is some form of sales cost accounting data per customer, make sure you use it to calculate the sales efficiency per customer or prospect type.

Sales Promotion

The basis for sound sales promotion analysis is a good profit and loss report per product. It will show you the cost of rebates and other sales incentives on the product's profitability. But there is a lot more to show. If you really want a sophisticated sales promotion analysis tool, your client will have to create a control group that is not subject to any sales promotion to provide a baseline. In some industries, this is just impossible because all buyers exchange information and in most other markets, there will always be a price comparison tool on the Web that points the consumer to the promotion. Nevertheless, there will always be a segment found that didn't react to the promotion and bought the client's products to give you a clue about the baseline.

To compare the baseline with the sales promotion group, the combination of customer and product on the transactions (orders, shipments, and invoices) needs the finest grain: a line item. Make sure you point this out from the start as this will have an impact on the data volume.

Customer Service

Customer service applications deliver massive amounts of data that can be exploited to enhance the richness of customer contextual data. Combine customer inquiries, whether they are complaints, pre- or aftersales information or other categories, with data such as delivery performance, product, sales rep, channel, supplier, and promotion type and you will learn a lot from your organization's performance, more than any profit and loss statement can tell you.

Channel Management

One of the most difficult marketing decisions lies in the channel management area. Whether you are introducing a new product or optimizing the present channel strategy these decisions can and will heavily influence your product's positioning and its profitability.

I haven't seen the perfect BI solution for channel management decisions but I am convinced that a combination of geographic information systems, product profitability per channel, customer segmentation data, and external data from retail market studies indicating the market shares of the channels per market segment can enhance the quality of decision making. In most smaller BI projects, channel decisions are the result of a study combining ad hoc studies and ad hoc queries with the BI environment where product profitability per channel is a must have.

Retail Marketing

"Retail is detail," as the saying goes, which tells you something about the grain of a BI system: every line item on a cash receipt, every inventory item, every square or cubic meter of space, every employee, every customer, matters. There are two essential problems retailers face: the first is estimating demand per optimum inventory replenishment period and the second is creating optimum cross-selling opportunities. One of the top-performing European retailers, Colruyt, who is active in Belgium and the north of France, has a nonfood inventory turnover of two. Two per business day, that is. It is clear that with such a logistics performance their forecasting is done almost in real-time.

The cross-selling issue deals with category management, displays, promotion management, and affinity analysis: which products are sold together with which other—often unrelated—products? The ABC-based direct product profitability is a major KPI used in retail.

Industrial Marketing

In the last decade the term "Business to Business" (B2B) marketing took the lead but for a few reasons I like to stick with the old term as B2B also incorporates retail and professional services between business organizations, which I consider a totally different discipline and business model. B2B as a pendant of B2C leads to even bigger confusion as in the B2C definition some still use one-to-many marketing as a distinctive trait, which lacks consistency if you look at the B2B retailers, who are also using one-to-many techniques. The term "industrial marketing" defines a more homogeneous business model as it deals with industrial goods, from raw materials to finished products, or projects that are sold one-to-one to other business organizations. Three subtypes narrow the concept a bit further: investment goods, equipment and machines, and consumables.

The BI requirements for these organizations are complex and should be handled with care. What I mean is, there are many "nice to haves" but few of them produce real business value over time. If the organization has a well-implemented CRM tool many of these nice to haves can be provided by operational CRM reports but deeper analytical insight can only be provided by a BI system that crosses many boundaries, including the organization's limits.

As the buying process for investment goods and equipment and machines is a lengthy and complex one, industrial marketers are always on the lookout for leading indicators such as consumer confidence, purchasing managers indices, certain tickers on the stock market, and so on.

Professional Services Marketing

Marketing professional services is the art of managing resources, managing customers, and managing the relationship between resources and customers. This means you need a tight integration of data from CRM, Human Resources Management (HRM), project management, and cost and time registration systems. Only the largest consulting firms can afford these systems but I was lucky to come across a totally different company that used the same management processes in the landscaping business.

The minimum requirements for a professional services organization is detecting relationships between the primary process (tender–pre-calculation–execution–post-calculation) and the two major dimensions: customer and employee. Other aspects such as equipment or methods used will also contribute to a thorough analysis of the company's performance.

Fast-Moving Consumer Goods Marketing

Consider a fast-moving consumer goods company that gathers consumer panel data, Nielsen data, and, of course, its own selling-in (to the channels) and selling-out results (to the final customer). What are the silver bullets they are looking for? Here are a few: affinities, promotion evaluation, account management evaluation, channel evaluation, and market penetration analysis. Also be on the lookout for advertising analysis and the cross-section between marketing and finance: direct product profitability. Here are a few handles that help you detect where your customer focus is

- Affinity analysis: Where and how do we position our product(s) or product range in the channels? This embodies issues including marginal analysis of channel extensions, analysis of the geographical locations of the outlets and within the outlets, shelf management within the outlets, and analysis of the performance of competitive products.
- Promotion evaluation: In an FMCG environment promotion evaluation is no trivial exercise. Establishing a baseline may prove very difficult and getting the competitive Nielsen data on product line level is a costly exercise. Measuring the influence of the account management team beyond their selling-in results and the time spent per location is also difficult but worthwhile pursuing as the cost of sales in FMCG consists largely of staff wages, expenses, and

direct rebates or premiums that are disbursed at the key account manager's discretion.

- Account management evaluation: From key account management to the rack jobbers' performance per outlet, per product, it is a function of market potential. Analyzing the effectiveness of indirect sales is a daunting task. Ask any marketing manager from an fmcg company.
- Channel evaluation: Which channels and which positioning within these channels yields optimum results?
- Market penetration analysis: What is our share of wallet (i.e., percentage purchases of our products divided by the total shopping amount per customer) or our relative market share in a geographical area (i.e., the percentage purchases of our products divided by all product purchases)?
- Advertising analysis: This handles comparisons between the medium's audience and the company's customer database. For example, what is the percentage of PC users a medium reaches compared to the percentage of PC users in our database?
- Direct product profitability: This is explained on the previous pages.

Consumer Investment Goods Marketing

This category contains any durable good from an oven to a car to a house. Investment goods marketing deals with longer sales cycles and comparable to industrial marketing, deals with a decision-making unit (DMU). This DMU can be Dad deciding on the car model and its engine whereas Mom decides on the color and the upholstery and the kids may push for a DVD player and screens in the headrests. Other than that, the product itself determines whether the BI needs are similar to industrial marketing like the housing market or closer to FMCG marketing in the case of branded durable goods such as appliances, sound systems, and so on. The purchase frequency during a consumer's life is the discriminator factor: for a house it may be $f = 2$ whereas for a sound system it may be as high as 10.

Pharmaceutical Marketing

There are two distinct business models: the over-the-counter (OTC) products' marketing, which bears resemblance to FMCG, and the ethical drugs or prescription drugs, which are a very special marketing discipline.

OTC Products Marketing

Although most countries apply some restrictions on advertising and promotion for OTC products, marketing processes resemble the FMCG marketing processes. Some countries also apply distribution regulations, restricting OTC sales to pharmacies that make international sales analysis a complex exercise.

Ethical Drugs Marketing

Prescription drugs cannot be "pushed" like consumer products so they rely heavily on personal visits, one-to-one marketing to the prescribing community, next to logistical efforts to make sure the product is always available in retail and wholesale pharmacies. Linking the efforts of sales and promotion efforts to the indirect sales through prescriptions and via pharmacies poses problems the source systems and business processes should try to mitigate as much as possible.

Answering the question, "Which drug has been sold through which pharmacy via which prescription?" is crucial for this analysis, even when the level of confidence between the connection pharmacist and doctor is lower than 90%.

Business Analysis Issues

Below are the main opening questions for the various marketing situations the analyst may encounter.

Check the CRM Data

Where are the master data located and who has access to them?

What is the possible status of a contact in the CRM system (i.e., inactive, active, reactivated, unassigned, assigned, lost, out of business, etc.)?

Describe the customer creation process and the data quality measures taken.

Describe the customer merge process and the data quality issues that may arise in the case of:

- Legal mergers and the revenue allocation
- Merge–purge process to correct input errors
- Merges with rented commercial databases such as Dun & Bradstreet and the like

Check the Behavioral Analysis Status

Has the organization worked with any of the data mining tools such as
SAS, SPSS, or other proprietary tools?
If so, was this on a project basis or on a continuous process basis?
Has the company acquired all knowledge inhouse or is all knowledge
with external consultants or subcontractors?
How transparent are the models used?
Is there sufficient documentation available?

Market Research

Do you invest in longitudinal studies? If you do qualitative research, how
do you transfer this knowledge to sales reps, sales channels, market analysts, and their target groups?

Affinity Analysis

Do you measure the interaction between products and their effects on
sales, positioning, and buying experience?

Direct Product Profitability

Do you use activity-based costing? (See Chapter 7 on ABC for further in-
depth questions.)

Product Development

How does your client decide on new product development budgets today?
Does he think he can improve this process?
If so, what data does he need to support the investment decision?
Which segmentation techniques do you use?

Sales

What support do you offer your salespeople for their sales budgets
and forecasts?
How do you validate the pipeline input data?
Do you calculate the cost of sales per sales rep, and or per customer?

Sales Promotion

Ask your client whether she wants to see the impact of sales promotions on the sales volume before, during, and after the promotion period.

Customer Service

What customer service data do you record?

Inquiry type, such as:
  Complaint
  General information request
  Delivery information request
  Return information request
  Other
Medium used, such as:
  Letter
  E-mail
  Web posting
  SMS (Short Message Service)
  Phone
Date and time, such as:
  Start and end data
  Start and end time
  Duration of the conversation
Followup type, such as:
  Immediate response and closing
  Escalation
  Suspended
Result, such as:
  Closed
  Open
Audit result: such as:
  Handled to the customer's satisfaction
  Customer rightfully dissatisfied
  Customer wrongfully dissatisfied
  Throughput time
What customer service analyses do you have available today?
How are these results fed back to the organization?

Channel Management

Do you analyze product profitability per channel today?

Do you collect data about your resellers such as accounting and market data?

Retail Marketing

How do you calculate the return per square meter?

Do you have exact figures on the split sales–nonsales surface?

Does this split vary over time?

Do you have data about missed sales opportunities because of out of stock?

Do you record customer backorders in a formal (DIY [do it yourself] stores, brown goods, etc.) or in an informal way (demand logging)?

Do you keep records about your personnel's skills?

How do you trace the various promotion types in your cash register?

- Discounts
- Product plus (i.e., "25% more product at the same price")
- Category promotions
- Volume plus (i.e., "buy two get one free")
- Coupons
- Contests and sweepstakes
- Cash back
- Sampling
- Other

Do you have basket analysis, Pareto analysis?

How do you decide to add or scrap products in an assortment?

How do you forecast demand?

What are the variables you use to decide on category management issues?

Do you benchmark your performance with other retailers?

Industrial Marketing

How do you forecast sales today? What can be improved in the process?

How do you manage your pipeline today?

Which leading indicators do you monitor and by what means?

Professional Services Marketing

How do your HRM, CRM, and financial systems interact/interface with each other?

Do you use personal management plans linked to customers and projects?

Is there a feedback loop between project management registration and marketing analysis, for example, lessons learned and project accounting data and account management data?

Fast-Moving Consumer Goods Marketing

One specific issue to address in this sector is the tight link between the supply chain and the channel management that reflects on the product performance.

Address this complex issue by getting a domain expert from operations and from marketing in one interview session, centered on delivery performance, analysis of stock ruptures, channel contract management, and related topics including demand forecasting and production planning.

Consumer Investment Goods Marketing

Get insight to the purchase frequency and the company's knowledge (or assumptions and hypotheses) about the market drivers and leading indicators such as:

- Innovation cycle length: Compare the rapid introductions in the computer and consumer electronics market with the longer innovation cycles in the automotive or the white goods market and the even slower cycles in the construction market.
- Technology adoption curves: How responsive and how large are the constituencies of techies/innovators, visionaries/early adopters, pragmatists/early majority, late majority, and laggards.
- Exit barriers and switch costs: Many IT gurus have declared the imminent death of the mainframe computer, which is still delivering the goods for almost half a century, from the UNIVAC 1107 in 1962 to the IBM z10 Enterprise Class in 2008.

- Indirect competitors: Many investment goods markets are not characterized by fierce internal competition; completely different investment goods may also compete with the segment: an investment in a new kitchen may clash with the desire to have a swimming pool, or a new flat screen TV may not be compatible with a personal computer.

Pharmaceutical Marketing

OTC Products

OTC product marketing analysis bears resemblance to FMCG marketing analysis with one exception: in most countries, there are no outlet figures comparable to Nielsen figures in FMCG available. In many OTC markets, as in the ethical drugs market, the wholesale intermediary plays an important role but the selling-out data are unreliable in countries where the inventory replenishment is low.

Ethical Drugs

Do you rely on external data to make the link among sales efforts (visits, direct mail, marketing studies, etc.) and the doctor's prescription behavior and the selling-out data from pharmacies linked to the doctor?

What entities and attributes are recorded, linking each pharmacy to a group of doctors: proximity, past transactions, or records of indicators of affinity?

Could you describe these records?

11

BI and Human Resources Management

One of the largest data warehouses in Europe with a focus on Human Resources Management (HRM) was built after the Falkland War. During the voyage to the islands, the British Army had to fly people over by helicopters from one ship to another to compose teams mastering the necessary skills for their designed tasks. HRM has always been the last function to profit from the power of Business Intelligence (BI) systems. But as the other functions become served, HRM will definitely be on the agenda.

WAR FOR TALENT AND HOW TO LOSE IT

Some Western countries and Japan have a rapidly aging workforce. Although at the time of writing of this chapter, the 2008 subprime crisis hasn't been absorbed yet by the real economy, long-term trends clearly indicate that the need for talent will become a leading indicator for which organization will outperform its competitors.

Up to now, HRM and BI didn't go together very well because there were other priorities (finance, operations, and marketing) and because HRM aspects were spread over other BI iterations, mainly financial, and maybe also because HRM never had information and communication technology (ICT) budgets as did the other disciplines. But in the next few years, the HRM BI project will be on top of the agenda of any large organization that wants to stay in business. The sense of urgency will grow. So, based on my very scarce experience with HRM BI projects, here are a few experiences I would like to share with you.

The war for talent is slowly but surely gaining strength and intensity. In the old days, this war was restricted to managerial talent but today, good technicians and skilled professionals who are less interested in a vertical career are very hard to come by, and I submit to my audience that—more than managerial talent—these people can make the difference in the competitive struggle. It is the car designer, not the manufacturer's CFO, who creates value and it is the researcher who finds the highest number of useful molecules per 10,000 trials who creates value for a pharmaceutical company, not the HRM manager.

Recruiting and retaining talent has become an art form and a science using marketing techniques based on data from research in psychology, sociology, and retention economics, in short, anything a good data warehouse should be able to provide. If talent is becoming the only constraint on growth, bigger than capital and brand equity, then the least we can say from a BI point of view is that it is poorly managed and monitored. I have observed the following weaknesses in Belgian, Dutch, German, and French companies:

1. A complete disconnect between the strategic planning process and competence management
2. A lack of employee relationship management (ERM) strategies governing the hiring, developing, and firing of human resources with the same degree of attention CRM is getting.
3. A management of *Kurieren am Symptom*, that is, superficial monitoring and management of HRM, critical success factors (CSFs), and key performance indicators (KPIs).

Let me illustrate these three weaknesses with a few observations.

Disconnect Strategy Planning Process—Competence Management

When in the 1980s the French launched the concept of *banque-assurance* many European banks jumped on the bandwagon. The concept was simple and straightforward: with the coming of ATMs and Minitel (the precursor of the Internet in France), which that allowed electronic banking, the front office should have more opportunities to sell services with a higher added value than paying out checks and counting cash. Selling insurance was one of these services with a higher added value and so large corporate movements were undertaken to merge banks with insurance companies and vice versa, because "merger" is always a euphemism for "takeover," especially in France.

On paper, everything looked promising but in real life the *banque-assurance* companies lost years and millions in lost efficiency, lost customers, and other costs because the workforce was simply not prepared for this complete change in jobs, context, and skills needed to perform as a counselor instead of a teller doing clerical jobs. If the strategy makers would have had an insight in the competence gap, they might have taken things a little bit slower, preparing their workforce better for this new situation.

One of my clients illustrated this point very graphically when he stated, "The last remaining racism is degree racism." What he meant was that a focus on degrees, not competences, masks the lack of organizational focus to measure and manage the development of personal, technical, and organizational or interpersonal skills of the workforce.

A Lack of ERM Strategies

Employees, just as customers, have a lifetime value. It costs money to attract, select, and recruit them. It costs even more money to train and integrate them in the existing team and, in the case of a conflict situation they can cost even more. On the other hand, the employee adds value in return for his salary and bonus scheme. Considering all this money flowing in and out of the company you would think that management would appreciate a BI system that charts and tracks the lifetime value per employee serving as a leading indicator for hidden costs such as reorganization, strategic repositioning, and other employee-related liabilities an ordinary balance sheet doesn't show. Even large professional services organizations who have no other assets than their workforce neglect this aspect.

Treating the Symptoms

Most HRM BI projects I have come across were very concerned with the measurement of symptoms:

- Absenteeism figures
- Descriptive statistics including age, gender, and other characteristics and the wage scale distribution per class
- Contract management data
- Employment history

What I have rarely seen were reports and analyses on deeper causes of absenteeism and employee churn such as the relationship between job contents, competence, direct supervisor, compensation scheme relative to market trends, the image of the company compared to its competitors, and so on.

MANAGING ABSENTEEISM

Introduction

Imagine a company with the following numbers on the dashboard:

- 1,000 employees
- Total employee cost: €50 million
- Absenteeism percentage: 7.8%

This means the total cost of absenteeism in terms of nonproductive use of wage costs equals €3.9 million. Reducing the absenteeism percentage to a more acceptable rate of 4.8 would immediately lower this amount by €1.5 million.

Too anecdotal? Then have a look at these macroeconomic figures:

In the UK absence costs amounted to £666 per employee, being on average eight days absent per year (2008 data from the Chartered Institute of Personnel and Development).

According to a Belgian study from SD Worx, a full-time Belgian worker in 2008 was ill on average 48.5 hours per year. Women were on average absent more hours than men (56.3 hours) and blue collar workers (62.9 hours) more than office workers (40.7 hours). The highest absence figure occurred with people on night shifts (65 hours).

In euros, the cost of absences in a company with 100 employees was €78,426 in 2008.

Senter Novem, a Dutch agency from the Ministry of Economic Affairs, discovered a relationship between energy conservation measures and reduction of absences. Lower office temperatures led to lower absence rates. This proves my point: absenteeism research needs both a broad and thorough approach for BI analysis. Better management understands the underlying causes and focuses its attention on critical employees, teams, and departments and their leaders so the root causes can be avoided, mitigated, or eradicated sooner.

Absenteeism Measures

Too many organizations reduce absence reporting to days lost (i.e., the absence rate) and some exclude long-term absences due to a chronic disease or pregnancy, which leaves calculation of the cost of absences incomplete. Absenteeism has many facets and they should all be presented to provide management with a full picture.

Absence rate: Total absence hours during a fixed period divided by the total available hours in this period. With a fixed period, the first discussion point emerges: if we use a monthly basis this view can be biased in months with a high rate of festive holidays. In Belgium, the month of May can count up to four holidays, pushing the rate up. The rate also fails to explain whether the absence figure is due to one person being ill the entire month or 20 employees being ill for one day. Therefore, the next measure should be added to provide a better insight.

Absence duration: Take the total duration of absences and divide it by the number of absent employees. The system needs to include the ongoing absences and provide them with a temporary end of period closing date to avoid underestimation of the figures.

Absence frequency: This can be either a general figure or an individual number. The general figure is a count of the absence events divided by the number of employees whereas the individual figure counts the employees who had one or more absence reported in the given period divided by the number of employees.

Bradford factor: The University of Bradford combines absence frequency with absence duration to individualize the employee's "contribution" to the overall figures. It severely punishes the short absences that may distort the interpretation of the figures. The formula is simple: $S^2 \times D$ where S is the number of spells of absence of an employee and D is the total number of days the employee was absent in a given period.

How BI Can Lend a Hand

BI and HRM are not as closely tied together as in the finance, operations, or marketing domain. The reason is simple: it is a question of numbers, both quantitative and qualitative. Let me explain. Where do you think number crunching will pay back the efforts in a 200 FTE company with 7,000 clients, producing 300,000 widgets? Well. I am the boss and I know every employee by his or her first name. That should cover the BI and HRM domain, right? Wrong. This particular combination can produce millions of lines of interesting data illustrating hidden relationships between the quality of the widgets, customer satisfaction, employee turnover, and productivity results, to name but a few.

The business case for BI is determined by the following relationships, which can all be plotted on a continuous line:

- Number of staff
- Diversity of skills needed
- Number of products produced
- Diversity of products produced
- Level of customization of the products
- Number of customers served
- Share of direct labor costs in the production costs
- Share of labor costs in the administration and general costs
- Ratio initiation and learning period to average contract duration

I am sure HRM specialists can produce even more meaningful relationships but in my experience, if you can detect these in an early stage of the project definition you will have sufficient data for a business case. Let me give you a few examples to illustrate the value of these figures.

The Shipyard

- Number of staff: high. Even in a well-automated environment, large ships are built by thousands of employees.
- Diversity of skills needed: high. Almost every profile from the building business is needed except bricklayers (although cruise ships may have a fireplace here and there). Carpenters, painters, welders, diesel mechanics, electricians, domotics experts, electronics experts, plumbers: need I go on?

- Number of products produced: low. Some yards produce only two–three ships per year.
- Diversity of products produced: high. One day you are working on a liquefied gas tanker, the next day on a cruise ship or a dredging vessel.
- Level of customization of the products: extremely high. Every ship is a unique product for a unique, and demanding, customer.
- Number of customers served: low in terms of direct customers but it can be high in terms of indirect customers.
- Share of direct labor costs in the production costs: medium. There is also a significant part in plant equipment, depreciation, and material costs as well as supervision costs.
- Share of labor costs in the administration and general costs: medium.
- Ratio initiation and learning period to average contract duration: high. The shipbuilding crafts and trade are highly specialized and the initiation and training period for jobs like welding, plumbing, and electronics can be very long.

So what do we do with these data? We prepare them to answer pressing business questions such as:

1. What skills do we have available to produce successful results for tender xyz?
2. If there are no 100% match skills (competences needed for a successful project), what is the time and money needed to close the gap or to make a documented "buy" decision?
3. What is the optimum mix for the production teams in terms of optimum productivity at lowest absenteeism costs?

The IT Consulting Firm

- Number of staff: medium–high. From the local IT shop with a few dozen employees to mega concerns such as EDS, IBM Consulting, or ATOS Origin.
- Diversity of skills needed: very high. The combination of operating systems, databases, programming languages, specialized software packages, and reporting systems requires a diversified skills palette.
- Number of products produced: from very low to very high. This depends on the focus of the business: tailormade software,

customization of packaged software, or even shrink-wrapped products.

- Diversity of products produced: from low to high. Some companies come up with a product range centered around a certain technology, covering many business domains, whereas others do it the other way around: focus on a business domain using all available tools in the market.
- Level of customization of the products: medium to high. The added value of an IT consulting firm lies exactly in the skills to adapt or create software that fits the unique needs of the client.
- Number of customers served: medium to high.
- Share of direct labor costs in the production costs: high to very high. In the case of bespoke work it can be extremely high compared to customization of packaged software.
- Share of labor costs in the administration and general costs: low. Most IT consulting firms strive to achieve the lowest possible overhead automating time registration and billing.
- Ratio initiation and learning period: low to high. This aspect depends on the market segment served. If you are a system engineer outsourcing company you may hire only MCSE profiles that can be immediately billable. But if you're in exotic market segments such as MUMS programming, you may need to train your new hires for weeks and weeks before they produce anything worth selling.

The business questions worth considering are at the cross-section of HRM, operations, and CRM and cover issues such as:

1. What is the level of customer satisfaction correlated with the employee satisfaction level?
2. Can we produce long-term trends translating the above correlation in customer and employee churn?
3. What are the relations among job requirements and skills, competences, and absenteeism?

The Fast-Food Company

- Number of staff: high to very high. Lots of part-time employees to provide flexible service to the customers.
- Diversity of skills needed: low. Every worker does relatively simple and well-prescribed manipulations.

- Number of products produced: low to medium.
- Diversity of products produced: low to medium. It's about chicken, beef, bacon, and buns.
- Level of customization of the products: low. Although Checkers may be the exception, most fast food places (I abhor the use of the term "restaurant" in these cases) have a small assortment.
- Number of customers served: very high.
- Share of direct labor costs in the production costs: low to medium. Wages are low and there is a high level of industrialized pre-processing of the food and automation in the fast-food place itself.
- Share of labor costs in the administration and general costs: low to medium.
- Ratio initiation and learning period to average contract duration: low to medium.

The business questions worth considering are at the cross-section of HRM and operations to cover issues such as:

1. Who serves what number of customers per hour?
2. Who works which hours?
3. What are the absence patterns per business day?

Business Analysis Issues

Security

Make sure you raise the security issue. HRM matters in most cultures have serious inhibitions when it comes to disclosing salary figures, birth dates, and other private information. In many cases this asks for strict security policies on the database level: row- or column-level security comes into the picture. Be aware that row-level security is a no-brainer for some and a complex subproject for other database brands.

"Hard" KPIs

Make sure you get all the hard data such as hours or dollars spent on:

- Position inventory: who occupies which position
- Salary surveys

- Employee selection data
- Performance evaluation: the marks
- Training, certification, coaching, and human resources development

"Soft" KPIs

Although harder to manage in most BI systems, these soft data can bring context to the measures:

- Performance evaluation: the text files.
- Employee survey data: employee satisfaction can provide a hint.

Questions for the HRM Department

The business analyst needs to check if these steps are taken to make sure she can produce valid absenteeism reporting:

1. Check the procedures and the business processes for measuring absenteeism:
   a. Is there a dark number and if so, what does the company do about it? In the case where there is no generally applied time registration system, chances are that employees and managers fail to report their absence to the HR department.
   b. Are there false positives due to managers forgetting to close absences?
2. Check what contextual data are registered to add meaning to the figures.
   a. Working out a solid employee dimension will certainly add context. Data such as job title, salary level, age, gender, direct supervisor, business unit, and hire date will all be used as independent variables in the analysis.
   b. The absence registration itself should contain at least the following data: date of absence reporting, start date of the absence, expected return date, reported cause of absence, involvement of a doctor, hospital, or other medical authority (i.e., self-diagnosis should also be registered).

3. Check if there is a feedback procedure for employees returning to work.

   a.   Is there an intake if the sickness or injury was work-related?
4. Is all collected information coded or do you use free text fields?
5. How do you record absenteeism: in hours, days in absolute, or relative figures? For example, an hour absence for a part-time employee hits harder than for a full-time employee.

12

Starting a BI Project

OVERVIEW

The illustration in Figure 12.1 shows the necessary steps to introduce Business Intelligence (BI) to the organization. It is an attempt to marry business analysis with project management techniques. Some will argue that these functions should be separated. Whatever your point of view is, you cannot refute the argument for better communication between these two disciplines that share great responsibilities for making the BI introduction a success. Do not underestimate the challenges ahead: missing data, resistance to change, blatant ignorance, and jamming stations inside and outside the organization; these require a *patterned plan of attack* to deal with them, such as that shown in the figure.

The blue process steps in the figure illustrate the flow of the project initiation; the three underlying perspectives (scope, conceptual, and logical) constitute the patterns that a good BI business analyst has to recognize at all times. This is your challenge: to be the *trait d'union* between all these aspects, the users in general, IT technicians, C-level management, and the budget, quality, time, and other project management aspects and yet produce the foundations for a working solution.

An Iterative Process

The high-level process diagram and the sequence of the following chapters may give the reader the impression that every step is conclusive and precedes the next one without ever returning to examine the premises and the analyses done. By no means are we dealing with a

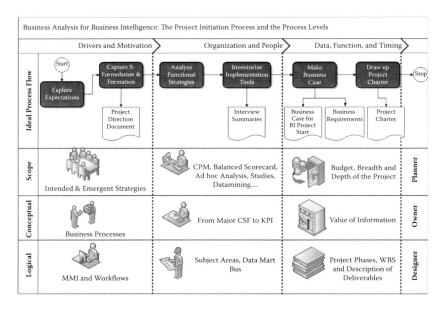

FIGURE 12.1

A patterned plan of attack: The blue process steps illustrate the flow of the project initiation.

waterfall-like method. The analysis process for BI is a constant balancing act between:

- The expectations from the business and the hidden potential in the data, in the early stages of the analysis
- The answers given by the BI system and the new questions that rise from this information in the later stages of the BI process

Always be prepared to return to the interviewees with feedback based on information gathered from other interviewees and from source data analysis.

To make things a bit more clear, the scheme in Table 12.1, guiding a business analyst through the BI introduction phase, maps the process steps in the following chapters. It immediately becomes clear that all process steps need many reiterations to make sure the analyst has covered all grounds.

Mapping the Process Stages on the Business Analysis Issues

You will have noticed that the approach to business analysis (BA) for BI is a holistic one: there is no room for easy takeaways. On the contrary, BA

TABLE 12.1

The Stage–Activity Matrix

	Explore Expectations	Capture S-Formulation and Formation	Analyze Functional Strategies	Inventory Implementation Tools	Make Business Case	Draw up Project Charter
Creating the Need	Scout	Scout	Scout	Scout	Initiate	
Gathering the Information	Update and Check	Check	Check	Check	Develop	
Analyzing the Decision-Making Process	Check	Check	Check	Check		
Developing the Project Charter	Confirm Feedback	Record	Record	Record Feedback	Finish Check	Finish Project Closure
Validating the Results						
Support and Maintenance	Scout, Update, Check, Confirm, Feedback	Scout, Check, Record	Scout, Check, Record	Scout, Check, Record, Feedback	Extend, Check	Process, Phase, Closure

for BI is a constant process of zooming in and out between macro concepts of the organization's economics and the strategy process managed on one side and microscopic analysis of source data, low-level create, read, update or delete (CRUD) processes, report requirements, and other detailed analysis to cross-check the consistency and feasibility of the organization's BI needs. In addition, your client expects you to follow a step-by-step process that demonstrates you are (a) leading the project and (b) decreasing the project risk by reducing all sorts of uncertainties. To make sure you don't get lost, I have mapped the chapters and sections dealing with the business analysis issues for the six process stages in Table 12.2.

For the deliverables I refer to the templates at the end of the book and the section "Producing the Documents."

CREATING THE NEED

Managers have the information and the authority; analysts have the time and the technology

Henry Mintzberg
1990

TABLE 12.2
Recommended Reading per BI Analysis Process Step

Process Step	Recommended Reading
Explore Expectations	What I Mean by "Business Intelligence"
	The Increasing Cycle Speed of Growth and Its Laws
	Creating the Need
Capture S-Formulation and Formation	Balancing the 5 Ps of Strategic Management
	Adapting BI to the Organization
	Understanding the 4 Cs
Analyze Functional Strategies	BI and Cost Accounting
	BI and Financial Management
	BI and Operations Management
	BI and Marketing Management
	BI and Human Resources Management
Inventorize Implementation Tools	Dimensional Modeling
	BI Application Specification
Make Business Case	The Business Case for Business Intelligence
	Business Requirements Gathering
Draw up Project Charter	Producing the Documents

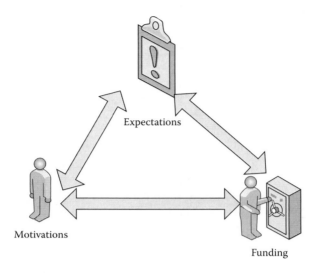

FIGURE 12.2
The three issues you have to explore to determine the settings of the project.

This is where we start to explore the expectations from the C-level executives. There is a constant interaction among the motivations, the expectations, and the funding of the project. The business analyst who wants to
start the project on the right foot had better check these three aspects.
As Figure 12.2 shows, you start with exploring the expectations but these
cannot be disconnected from the motivational aspects and the budget.

Expectations: In Search of the Business Value

A company who initiates a Business Intelligence project "because everybody
is doing it" is of a rare species. If you want the project to become a success,
make sure you have inventoried all the expectations, and more! I believe it
is the duty of a good business analyst to point out possibilities unknown to
the customer to make sure the project is embedded in the strategy process
and to prevent the competition from interfering in this early stage when the
contract for the entire project is probably not signed yet.

When I hear a prospect mutter things such as, "My consultant never told
me this," I know that I can leave the table with a contract or at least I did
some damage to the relationship between my competitor and his client.
Don't let this happen to you!

Check the expectations shown in Table 12.3 and try to translate them
into performance criteria during the project.

TABLE 12.3

BI Expectations Checklist

Expectations	Performance Criteria	Example	Put It Forward
Query performance	Query response times	Refresh: max 10" New query: max 15"	What are reasonable response times in your daily practice?
Relevance	Unequivocal reports	Separate definitions for objects as function of the perspective	Does your department use specific definitions for items such as customer order, etc.?
Currency	"Freshness" of the last update	2′ for fraud detection, 1 week for financial reports	How current does your information have to be?
Availability of the data	Uptime of the system	24/7 for fraud detection 20/5 for marketing analysis	When do you need to dispose of which information?
Navigation possibilities	Meaningful aggregates	Product by time by geography	Three-way aggregation needed among all hierarchy levels?
Granularity of the data	Level of detail	Every written line of each insurance policy	What is the level of detail you need for further analysis of your reports?
Backup frequency	Maximum loss of loaded data	1 day for financial transactions, 1 week for customer data	What backup frequency is needed?
Data quality	Level of accuracy	All numeric data are cross-checked All customer data are 99% correct	What is the cost of incorrect data for your department?
SCD strategy	Appropriate handling of changes in perspective	Type 1: overwrite Type 2: create a new record Type 3: current status record	Do you often change aspects such as sales regions, divisions, or packaging? Do you keep a history of these aspects?

Historic staging	Audit trail for changes in the source system	Switch from Debit to Credit bookings after discovering a booking error	Do you want to track changes in the source data and the reason?
Change request handling	Flexibility of the system	Minor changes to existing reports: 2 days New iterations: 3 weeks	What response times for change requests do you consider reasonable?
Security	Access to sensitive data	Role-based security plan	What security base is preferable? Data? Roles? A combination?
Support response times	Service-level agreement	1 hour response for front-end problems and 1 day response for back-end problems	What response times for support requests do you consider reasonable?

Funding the Business Intelligence Project

Who is going to pay the bill? The IT department? The business? The answer to this question may remain of utmost importance throughout the project. Make sure you get the right answer as deception on this issue for obvious reasons is not uncommon in larger organizations. Although I have not often come across the ideal funding principle for a BI project, my experience with mixed funding is not at all negative. Figure 12.3 illustrates an infrastructure based on two online transaction processing (OLTP) systems such as enterprise resource planning (ERP) and computer integrated manufacturing (CIM) systems, accompanied by the inevitable spreadsheets used for anything that is not accepted by the OLTP systems, like budgets or market data, for example.

The ideal mix is IT funding the back-end infrastructure, which fits perfectly in an asset-based IT strategy, and the business users providing the money for the front-end tools and the applications. Thus, IT can guarantee the necessary technical performance, integrity, and quality and the business can feel free to use the tools they deem fit for their job and their department, regardless of technical issues. There is some discussion over whether the business users should have a say in the choice of tools as some

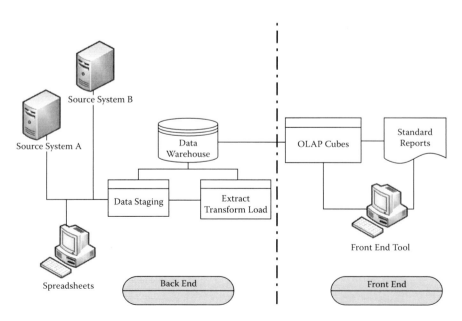

FIGURE 12.3
A very simple Business Intelligence infrastructure scheme.

IT managers consider the front-end tool as part of the infrastructure. I prefer user buy-in for the front-end tool as sometimes tools and applications are inseparable in the perception of the users.

I have been involved in more than 15 front-end tool selection projects and in all these cases human, organizational, and man–machine interaction aspects were far more important than the aggregation algorithms and the index structures of the online analytical processing (OLAP) cube or the programming language used. In other words: better a technically inferior product that is used 100% by motivated users than a technically superior product—which is often more expensive—used sporadically by only half the potential user community.

Probing for the Motivation

Don't be alarmed if you can't come up with crisp answers, especially if you put a straightforward question to your interviewee. Organizational motivations are often well concealed behind mission statements, which you should read because they can provide you with arguments for the business case. As for the private motivations of your BI project sponsor, these are even harder to detect. These are the questions you shouldn't ask but to which you need to get an answer:

- Is there a bonus plan for management, sales execs, operations, and so on?
- What are the mechanics of this (these) bonus plan(s)?
- Where was the project initiated: in this business unit or somewhere else? On this management level or higher up in the food chain?
- How long has the initiator of the BI project been with the company?
- What is her attitude toward IT and new technologies in general?

Focus on the Expectations through the Entire Project

Make sure you have the set of expectations, expressed by the C-level executives, on your mental radar while interviewing the managers, the source data owners, and the users in general. At a minimum, you should monitor the interaction among the completeness, accuracy, and currency of the data and the budget. The latter is fixed as you will appreciate but the other three may cause scope creep (see Figure 12.4).

As soon as you are called in by the customer, your most important task starts. From day one, you will be managing expectations. The

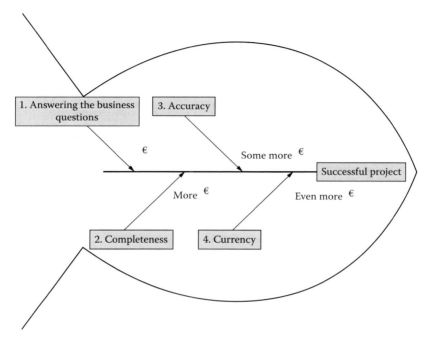

FIGURE 12.4
The project definition and budget exercise have to be constantly synchronized.

customer has contacted you because he assumes you have been there before and know the road ahead toward a more intelligent enterprise. He expects you to evaluate his wishes and dreams and shape them into a project definition.

Why is this aspect one of utmost importance for a business analyst? The answer is simple and fact-based: many projects that deliver exactly what was promised fail in the perception of the customer. And where does that mismatch of reality and perception originate? No, don't pass the buck. It stops at your desk! A business analyst should at all times be aware of what the customer wants and close all doors to misperceptions. So here is some empiric knowledge I have collected during my business analysis projects:

- Formal things customers want
- Informal things customers want
- Handle queues
- Close loops

Formal Things Customers Want

With regard to the analysis and requirements-gathering process, custom-ers are very reasonable in their wishes; they want efficient service and they want you to anticipate their needs. Keep them informed about the options and give them feedback after each conversation. In short, customers want professional service.

With regard to the product and its specifications, customers want clear contract terms describing what they will get for their money and efforts. These are the "must haves." As you know, there are also "nice to haves," or wishes that need to be examined for their feasibility within the confines of the contract.

But there are two other "haves" that are sometimes forgotten: the "should haves," such as generally accepted practices and last but not least "can haves," which is the ambition to exceed the customer's expectations. This is where your added value as an analyst is clearly demonstrated. If, for example, a customer points out she wishes for a report on the internal efficiency of a manufacturing process and you can produce a second version (often with little extra effort) that illustrates the relationship among optimum through-put time per machine, mean time between failures (MTBF), and fixed cost absorption, this customer will adore you.

Informal Things Customers Want

Although this is not a book on relationship management or DIY psy-chology, I can assure my audience the atmosphere in which the analysis process takes place contributes to the quality of its outcome. What my customers always told me (luckily most of the time implicitly) was:

- "Take me seriously!" It wouldn't be the first analyst eagerly showing how much smarter and informed he is than the interviewee on the subject of BI, resulting in a loss of information as the interviewee turns into "sabotage mode."
- "Use my vocabulary!" Refrain from technical mumbo jumbo. Which one do you prefer: an engineer who explains the boiling of an egg using the laws of thermodynamics or an engineer who makes the laws of thermodynamics as simple as boiling an egg?
- "Don't do the relay thing!" Make sure you are the single point of contact, even when the customer's question is not in your knowl-edge domain.

- Finally, be empathetic, honest, friendly, courteous, and pay attention; even if you hear something for the nth time, the client may discover this for the first time.

Handle Queues

A requirements gathering and analysis process is not a trivial exercise, especially in large organizations. Sometimes waiting queues will emerge because a management decision is needed or important information cannot be divulged before a certain date. Meanwhile, the customer asks the most asked question in any project: "When?" There are two things you can do about this: one before the "When?" question emerges and one when it does. Make sure you define a few simple service-level agreements with your client before the project starts and define response times for e-mail, voice mail, and feedback on interviews.

But when there is missing information or when things are held up by causes out of your control do the Century 21 thing. The what, I hear you say. I call it the Century 21 thing because I discovered a long time ago that the U.S. real estate franchisor distinguishes itself from the competition by delivering excellent service, justifying a higher commission than the market average. And one of the crucial elements in delivering this service is handling waiting queues. Imagine you have entrusted the sales of your house to a person in a golden, or rather a yellowish, jacket and now you're waiting for the first candidate. You are not giving away the property as you have worked hard to pay the mortgage, so the candidates are not pouring in.

What does the Century 21 agent do? Does he wait for the first caller to inform you? Of course not. Every week you receive a report of the actions Century 21 has taken to draw the market's attention to your house: the ads your property appeared in, the number of inbound calls, the verbatim information if relevant, and so on. In short, the Century 21 client's perception of an active partner doing his job is managed perfectly. So this is the Century 21 lesson: don't wait to inform your customer about the output when you have news to tell about the input and the process leading to the expected output.

Close Loops

Customer: "I want software that registers all cell phone calls."

Analyst: "Do you mean a central repository to monitor inbound and outbound calls for policing purposes?"

Customer: "No, I just want to register outbound calls for cost analysis."

Analyst: "Do you mean cost analysis for managing expense accounts?"

Customer: "No, I want to use the data for better contract negotiation with the provider."

Analyst: "You mean data on the call volumes as a function of time and local or long distance to find better tariff plans?"

Customer: "Yes."

This dialogue illustrates how you should close all doors to make sure that misunderstanding on essential requirements is out of the question.

Conclusion: Even if you have no formal management role, you are managing one of the most important aspects of the BI project: the customer's expectations. Make sure you are giving it your best shot.

GATHERING THE INFORMATION

This phase should not be confused with business requirements gathering to develop the Business Intelligence product; it is rather a phase to facilitate the Business Intelligence process by creating awareness, translating this awareness into critical success factors and key performance indicators (KPIs) for the project. This awareness creation should be handled carefully as you are on untrodden paths. There may be ambushes, pitfalls, and other unknown obstacles that may lead you to defeat before you even start the project. So, therefore, here is some advice to prevent this from happening.

Study the Terrain

I haven't come across an organization that is free of politics. As soon as I hired my second employee in my company, politics came into the picture. I stopped counting at 80 highly skilled and well-trained professionals and many times the expression "herding cats" came to my mind. Compare this to a multimillion dollar global company with many brands, departments, production units, countries, and cultures and you have some homework to do. Are politics a bad thing? No, they are just a means to obtain ends. And as long as these ends are to the benefit of the organization (and probably also to the people using politics) I don't see the problem. It is normal that there is internal competition for resources such as money and talent, time and commitment. So, be aware that your project competes with not just another information and communication technology (ICT) project but also with less related or even unrelated projects, like building a new HQ.

From the less related projects competing with BI, I remember market surveys and studies, audits of all sorts: finance, quality, Human Resources Management (HRM), and so on. Make sure you chart the (im)balance of power between the involved departments and map the people with authority or influence on the organization chart.

Who You Need to Know

First and foremost you have to detect, identify, and connect with the formal and informal business leaders and sponsors of the project. Identifying the informal leaders may take more time than you expect but here are a few tips:

- If your formal partner needs time to make a decision, who is he asking for advice?
- Who is the person always in cc when important information is passed on to you?
- Whose name appears in all major project steering committees?
- Study the history of the organization: when it underwent important changes, what happened? Who was in favor? Who was resistant to change?
- Who can deviate from corporate standards or take shortcuts in lengthy procedures, even if she doesn't have the authority?

But don't just look for leaders and managers. All too often analysts only speak to the managers, thereby underestimating the clout of profiles such as application source owners, present report developers and report users, and database administrators, among others. Maybe they don't have the power to drive your project forward but they certainly have the power and the means to thwart it.

What You Need to Know

Nothing speaks louder than an analysis of the income statement and the balance sheet of the last three years before you talk to management.

Make sure you get answers from the figures to very simple but important questions including:

- Is the company growing or shrinking slowly or rapidly?
- What is the evolution of:
  - The cash position
  - The gross margin
  - The assets (watch out for the immaterial assets' evolution!)
  - The liabilities: long- versus short-term financing, stock versus loans?
- How stable is the management team?
- Has the company taken new large shareholders on board and does this reflect in the composition of the board of directors?

As soon as you have the answers to those questions, it is time to check the grounds:

- What are the unofficial vision and mission statements in the organization and who is champion of which version?
- Do you have the curriculum vitaes (CVs) of the decision makers in the organization?
  - Do their backgrounds affect their vision on the business questions?
- Are they looking for options, solutions only in their comfort zone? That is, is a CEO with a financial background willing to admit that the most pressing issues are other than financial ones?

Now it is time to zoom in a bit further on the ICT aspects and check the organization's capability maturity level and ambitions for the future. We can use the U.S. Air Force's capability maturity model (CMM) and adapt it for BI environments. As shown in Table 12.4, the BI version of the capability maturity model helps the BA with identifying broad project management issues.

ANALYZING THE DECISION-MAKING PROCESSES

Introduction

This chapter has to be read on two levels: the first as an aid for business analysts to help the customer reach a decision about the BI investment and the second level is for the BI project itself: the more and

TABLE 12.4

BI Version of the Capability Maturity Model

CMM Level	BI Symptoms	Principal Risks
Initial	A serious case of "spreadsheetitis:" every decision maker has his own set of spreadsheet files to support him in his battles with the other owners of spreadsheets. Everyday tugs of war over who has the correct figures.	Your project may never take off because of political infighting and if it does, there will be a pressing need for change in management of the highest quality and huge efforts will have to be invested in adoption tracks.
Repeatable	The organization uses some form of project management, in most cases inherited, or even a carbon copy of systems or application development.	The project management method may be totally inadequate for a BI project, leading to expensive rework and potential project failure in the case where everybody remains in his position.
Defined	The organization has a standard procedure for the production of certified reports. These can connect with one or more source systems in a standardized way: direct connection to the source tables, import of flat files, or some form of data warehouse.	Resistance to change. This depends on the way the organization has implemented the data warehouse concept and how reversible the previous efforts are in a migration scenario.
Managed	The development processes are standardized and monitored using key performance indicators and a Plan-Do-Check-Act (PDCA) cycle.	The iterative and explorative approach of BI project management may frighten the waterfall and rapid application development (RAD) fans in the organization. Make sure you communicate well about the specifics of a BI development track.
Optimizing	The development processes only need finetuning.	Analysis paralysis and infighting over details may hamper the project's progress.

better information you have about the way decisions are made in the organization, the better you will tailor your analysis and advice to the organization's needs.

The part about organizational configurations should be used as a background for this chapter as it largely influences the decision-making process.

Decisions, Teams, and Groups at Work

Classification of Decision-Making Environments

This matrix illustrated in Figure 12.5 covers all decision-making situations or environments based on two pertinent factors: how certain are we about the causality between events and to what extent does everybody on the decision-making team share the organizational goals? Anyone who has worked in a political organization will recognize the lower right quadrant as, more than any other organizational form, the political one is used as a vehicle for a number of individual ambitions. The judgmental environment bears a strong resemblance to the missionary and the entrepreneurial organization. The other two environments may be found in any of the other organizational configurations.

Process View

Too many management professionals consider decision making as a rational process to obtain an optimum result. Linear programming, queueing techniques, and other nice algorithms require the right input to produce the right output. It is as simple as that. I agree, as long as you can exclude the human factor, which is not obvious in managing an organization. Maximizing rationality in decision making is often not congruent with the subjective expected utility (SEU) of some or most parties involved. *Maximizing*, the search for maximum gain, is often replaced by *satisficing*, the search for an alternative that

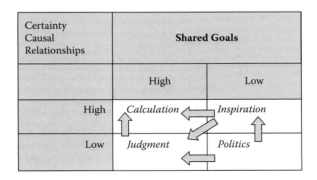

FIGURE 12.5
Decision-making environments provide context for the BI project.

one or more parties consider good enough. There are three types of decision- making processes:

1. Consequentialism: A process on the basis of expected personal consequences. I won't bother with stories of CEOs who initiated takeover bids because this would increase their bonuses; there are plenty of newspaper stories to go by. But also on a lower level does this play an important role. A successful manager has enough empathy to get the picture of the SEU of each person involved in the decision-making process.
2. Thorough structuring: More than one option must be considered and the outcome will have to be communicated to third parties who might want to audit the process in case something goes wrong afterward. Typical tools are multicriteria selection with all its flaws if used in an unprofessional way.
3. Compensation: Most decisions in strategy formulation and implementation are tradeoffs of one benefit against another. Especially when strategy formulation is left to functional managers, there will be a lot of tradeoffs to be made. Consider the marketing manager who wants a service level of 98.5% and the logistics manager who wants to reduce the cost of inventory with 15%.

What Drives the Decision-Making Process

The following mechanisms, inhibitors, or bias (whichever you prefer) can play an important role in the decision-making process:

- Certainty versus uncertainty
- Gains versus losses
- Framing
- Escalation of commitment
- Heuristics
- Anchoring bias

Let us look into them inasmuch as they are serious barriers for efficient BI implementation. Daniel Kahneman (1974, 1979, 1981, 2002), Amos Tversky (1974, 1979, 1981), and others deserve full credit for this section.

Certainty versus Uncertainty

Research has shown that we tend to find highly likely pleasant outcomes less attractive than we should. We are inclined to find a highly unlikely pleasant outcome more attractive than we should. People are more inclined to bet on a long shot.

Gains versus Losses

The attractiveness of a possible gain is less than the aversion to a loss of the same amount. Firms in financial difficulties may take more risks, because they are trying to eliminate losses, than firms doing well.

Framing

The same information can be presented in different ways that can affect decisions made on the basis of that information. Consider the same information:

Now! Early Bird discount of 20%! Compare this with:

Next week, 25% price increase!

Escalation of Commitment

If a decision is made freely and explicitly, the person making it feels a need to justify it to self and others. The person is committed to it and seeks retrospectively to find reasons why he or she "did the right thing." The Bush administration's communication between 2003 and 2008 about the invasion of Iraq is already a classical example. And stockbrokers see it all the time: people throwing good money after bad when their favorite stock goes down the tank. The classical rationalization is: "I want to average out the losses per share."

Decision makers who specify the expected outcome of their decision before choosing the best decision are more likely to abort when things are not going well. They reduce their escalation of commitment. Another way to reduce this is to evaluate the quality of the decision-making process, not the outcomes.

Heuristics

These are "rules of thumb" that people use to simplify information processing and decision making.

Social Heuristics

"I will ignore information from Mr. A."

Representativeness

This is how representative is phenomenon x belonging to a category and ignoring the naturally occurring probability of this phenomenon to occur. This so-called base rate ignorance leads to tragic miscalculations.

Anchoring Bias

This is our failure to change our views as much as we should in the light of new information, because we are "anchored" by our starting point. The only thing we do is adjust or correct the initial value. Anyone who has been part of or observed a budget exercise will know exactly what I mean.

Availability Heuristic

This is our tendency to consider an event more probable if we can imagine it than if our fantasy can't deliver the image. It is also cleverly exploited by marketers, making sure their products are "top of mind" when the generic need emerges.

Attribute Substitution

> A judgment is said to be mediated by a heuristic when the individual assesses a specified target attribute of a judgment object by substituting a related heuristic attribute that comes more readily to mind. This definition elaborates a theme of the early research, that people who are confronted with a difficult question sometimes answer an easier one instead. Thus, a person who is asked "What proportion of long-distance relationships break up within a year?" may answer as if she had been asked "Do instances of swift breakups of long-distance relationships come readily to mind?" (Kahneman and Frederick, 2002)

Control

Managers tend to act as if they can have influence on situations over which they have no control whatsoever. Especially in forecasting situations they will overestimate probabilities of favorable events.

Stereotyping, the Dark Force

Whatever Business Intelligence system you develop, always be on the lookout for stereotypes that, at best, lead the BI project and at worst nullify its results. Social psychology practitioners have observed over and over that stereotypes justify the social roles of the various member types in groups or justify our actions toward them. Who has never heard expressions such as:

"Accountants can only look backwards and they are only concerned with cost reduction as they have no clue about realizing the top line."
"Sales people are an uncontrolled bunch of winers and diners and even worse."
"Is there any creature on earth more rigid than a production manager?"
"IT buffs haven't got a clue about the business; they are only interested in their toys."

Or more subtle:

"Neglect older customers; they won't even consider buying this product."
"We have done an advance-warning mailing before sending out the catalog in 1999 and it was a failure, so I don't think we will do this again."

The only remedy to this kind of stereotyping is to analyze case by case and element by element what led to this stereotype. There are multiple sources of information supporting a stereotype. They can be personal or interpersonal. Let us illustrate this with a common stereotype: "Neglect older customers; they won't even consider buying this product."

Personal Sources of Stereotypes
- Overreaction to extreme observations: I know of a customer over 50 who has never bought a single item from this product line.
- Mixing up correlation with causality: All older customers in our database buy less of this product line than the younger. (Yes, but is your customer database representative of the entire market potential? Or, do you communicate adequately with this target group?)
- Interactions shaped by social roles: I observe that in my family, people over 50 are not interested in this product line.
- Emotions mixing with the observation: I hear a lot of negative remarks from people over 50 about our company and that really bothers me.

Social Learning

- We can learn from others: My marketing professor always told me that the younger the public, the easier it is to introduce new products, so why bother about the over-50?
- We can learn from media: I see nobody over 50 advertising this product line and in films, nobody over 50 is seen using it.

These sources lead to the above-mentioned stereotype and it justifies our neglect of this group in our marketing plans. Once established, a stereotype can be activated by obvious cues, use of group labels, or even the presence of a group member! Some stereotypes are learned so well and used so often that their content comes to mind automatically. When a stereotype is activated, it often causes us to treat experience, cases, people, and groups as interchangeable members of a stereotype concept than as individual phenomena.

Group Decision Making

Business Intelligence can contribute, for better or for worse, to group decision making. It is important that a business analyst be aware of the basic group decision-making aspects. We live in a world of organizations where group decision making is the norm or rapidly becoming it. The intensity and the frequency may vary depending on aspects such as culture and type of leadership (i.e., in an entrepreneurial organization, group decision making has more to do with the leader convincing the group of his decision). Psychologists confirm that if handled the right way, group decisions create greater commitment than decisions made by individuals, because people have more sense of involvement as they were able to contribute to the process. Needless to say that group decision making is more costly so the issue of cost justification is often raised in organizations.

Whether the quality of group decisions is better remains open for debate but in the case of idea generation tests have clearly shown that the group loses to the individual. The principal mechanisms responsible for lower output are inhibitions caused by the fear of what others may think and social loafing. The response to this behavior by active members of the group is reducing their own output. And last but not least, the simple fact that one group member is talking while the others are listening may make them forget or suppress their ideas because they consider them inferior.

Key Learning Points

- Groups linked by a computer produce more ideas than groups meeting face to face, as an experiment by Hollingshead and McGrath proved in 1995.
- Status has an influence on the decision making: even when people of a lower status are correct, they have less influence on the group than the higher status ones, although I find evidence in the works of Geert Hofman (1991, 2004) (and my business analysis practice in the Netherlands) that this is also culture dependent.
- Even when one person in the group knew the correct answer to a problem, the group decision was not always correct.
- Group decisions make people more convinced that the group's decision was more correct but it didn't make a correct decision more likely.
- On average, the group is as good as its second best member because you need two people who know the correct answer to convince the rest of the group.
- Groups, confronted with complex decisions to make, will look for the easy way out and go for acceptable, but not necessarily optimum, solutions.
- Some authors believe that discussing and agreeing on the decision-making strategy before discussing the actual decision helps to improve the quality of the decision.

The General Group Problem-Solving Model from Aldag and Fuller

Relevant aspects for BI are (see Figure 12.6):

- The structure of the decision at hand and the procedural demands (decision characteristics)
- Treatment of dissenters (emergent group characteristics)
- Problem identification, generation and analysis of alternatives, evaluation, choice of implementation, source of solution, and decision control (decision process characteristics)
- Quality of decision (outcome)

Effective BI takes all relevant perspectives for analysis into account. As a business analyst you should explore all possible dimensions, even those that are not even tracked let alone registered. The business analysis process is more than a descriptive effort; real added value is to be found in the prescriptive part of your work.

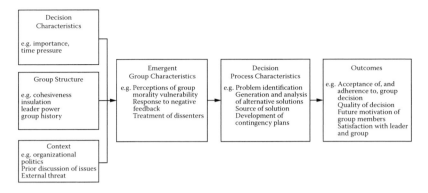

FIGURE 12.6
An abbreviated version of the model. (Reprinted from: Ramon J. Aldag and Sally Riggs Fuller, *Psychological Bulletin* 113: 533–552.)

This framework provides an interesting approach to decision making and Business Intelligence on two levels. First, the acceptance of BI as an aid for decision making and second the output of the BI system as trustworthy input for the decision-making process.

Creating Acceptance for BI

The importance of a BI system has to be demonstrated in the project charter, but that is not enough. A good analyst creates a sense of urgency: every day without BI is a day lost forever. Leadership and corporate sponsorship are crucial for the acceptance process. More on this in the next section.

BI's Input for Decision Making

I often hear this one-liner in my practice: from data to information to knowledge. When I ask people what they mean by that, many seem to struggle with a coherent explanation. Yet this one-liner touches the very essence of Business Intelligence. I often use the metaphor of a bus timetable. Imagine you are a consultant who has just completed your mission in Segovia, near Madrid, and you want to go back to the office in Brussels.

The schedule in Figure 12.7 represents data about departure times for buses to the subway station Principe Pio in Madrid, where you can take the subway to Madrid Barajas airport. In Barajas you can take a regular Iberia or Brussels Airways flight to Zaventem Airport. If you want to consider the cheap alternative Ryanair offers, then you consult the other bus schedule (Figure 12.8), which takes you from Segovia to Valladolid, which

⑤ LA SEPULVEDANA, S.A.

SERVICIO PUBLICO REGULAR DE TRANSPORTE DE VIAJEROS POR CARRETERA ENTRE

MADRID Y SEGOVIA

| HORARIOS | A PARTIR DEL 1 DE OCTUBRE DE 2004 |

SALIDAS DE MADRID			SALIDAS DE SEGOVIA		
LUNES A VIERNES LABORABLES	SABADOS LABORABLES	DOMINGOS Y FESTIVOS	LUNES A VIERNES LABORABLES	SABADOS LABORABLES	DOMINGOS Y FESTIVOS
6.30 D	8.00 S	8.00 S	6.00 D	7.30 D	8.30 S
7.00 D	8.30 D	9.00 D	6.15 S	8.00 D	9.30 O
7.30 D	9.00 D	10.00 D	6.30 D	8.30 S	10.30 D
8.00 R	9.30 D	11.00 S	6.45 S	9.00 D	11.30 D
8.30 D	10.00 D	12.00 D	7.00 S	9.30 D	12.30 D
9.00 D	10.30 D	13.00 D	7.15 S	10.00 D	13.30 D
9.30 D	11.00 S	14.00 D	7.30 D	10.30 R	14.30 S
10.00 D	11.30 D	15.00 R	7.45 D	11.00 D	15.30 D
10.30 O	12.00 D	15.30 O	8.00 S	11.30 D	16.00 D
11.00 S	13.00 D	16.00 D	8.30 S	12.30 S	16.30 R
11.30 D	14.00 D	17.00 S	9.00 D	13.30 O	17.00 D
12.00 D	15.00 R	18.00 D	9.30 S	14.30 S	17.30 D
12.30 D	15.30 D	18.30 D	10.00 D	15.30 D	18.00 O
13.00 D	16.00 D	19.00 D	10.30 R	16.00 D	18.30 D
13.30 S	17.00 S	19.30 D	11.00 D	16.30 R	19.00 D
14.00 O	18.00 D	20.00 R	11.30 D	17.00 D	19.30 D
14.30 D	19.00 D	20.30 D	12.00 D	17.30 D	20.00 R
15.00 R	19.30 D	21.00 D	12.30 S	18.00 D	20.30 D
15.30 D	20.00 R	21.30 D	13.00 D	18.30 D	21.00 D
16.00 S	20.30 D	22.00 D	13.30 D	19.00 D	21.30 S
16.30 D	21.00 S	22.30 S	14.00 D	19.30 D	22.30 O
17.00 S	21.30 O		14.30 S	20.00 R	
17.30 D	22.00 D		15.00 D	21.00 D	
18.00 D	22.30 S		15.30 D	21.30 S	
18.15 S			16.00 R		
18.30 D			16.30 D		
19.00 D			17.00 D		
19.30 D			17.30 D		
19.45 S			18.00 S		
20.00 D			18.30 D		
20.30 D			19.00 D		
20.45 R			19.30 D		
21.00 D			20.00 R		
21.30 S			20.30 D		
22.00 D			21.00 D		
22.30 S			21.30 S		

D.- Expediciones DIRECTAS   R.- Expediciones RUTA
S.- Expediciones SEMIDIRECTAS con parada en: SAN RAFAEL (Estación), OTERO y REVENGA

INFORMACIÓN Y VENTA DE BILLETES

| MADRID | PASEO DE LA FLORIDA, 11 | Tfno.: 91 559 89 55 |
| SEGOVIA | ESTACIÓN DE AUTOBUSES (Pº. DE EZEQUIEL GONZÁLEZ) | Tfno.- 921 42 77 07 |

ABONOS MENSUALES CON UTILIZACIÓN EN TODAS LAS EXPEDICIONES DEL SERVICIO

FIGURE 12.7
A timetable: data or information?

is not quite Madrid and from there you fly to Brussels South, (actually it's Charleroi) which is not quite Brussels.

So there are your data. Now you make your first decision based on the lowest cost to fly and you choose Ryanair. By making a choice of which airport you are going to use, one of these data sources becomes information, especially at the moment when you know your check-in time so you choose the best departure hour for your bus. The next level, though, is

FIGURE 12.8
A timetable: data or information (bis).

not to be found in the data, nor in the information. It is a form of enrichment via third-party sources or proper experience, which tells you there are roadworks on the road between Segovia and Valladolid causing possible delays of more than two hours. This is knowledge. Now you have to reiterate: will you stick to your initial decision, causing you twice as much (not-billable) travel time for a low price or will you take the short trip via Barajas and gain at least six billable hours?

This process illustrates clearly that you should be able to go back to the lowest level of detail in the case where you need to substantiate or reconsider the decision. In general terms, BI systems should always keep detailed information such as line items on an invoice, an order, call data records, measurements of process steps, and so on. Only then will you be able to create acceptance for the data validity and avoid discussions about the BI output itself. To go back to our consultant in Segovia: wouldn't she have a hard time explaining to her boss why she chose the expensive scheduled flight with Iberia or Brussels without the bus and airline timetables at hand?

Some practitioners and academics argue that this data-to-information-to-knowledge chain is too simple in a complex world. They postulate context as the determining factor to define data, information, or knowledge. It is possible that someone's knowledge is another one's data but in the context of a BI project where you organize knowledge on the group and organizational levels, this interesting perspective does not help in defining a BI project. Unless someone can point me to software or a toolbox that enables an individual user to re-evaluate, regroup, and reorder the knowledge, information, and data from a BI or a KM system I will keep the simple and pragmatic approach to the data to knowledge "D2K" issue.

Organizational Change

The introduction of BI causes a change in the way people communicate, gather and exchange information, and how they make decisions. Part of this change will be planned but an important part may be emergent and better not pass by undetected by management. Many fine books on change management have been written, from Kurt Lewin (1947), Tom Peters (1997), Rosabeth Moss Kanter (1983), and Charles Handy (1978) among others, so I will not repeat their theories. This section is only a plea to be aware of the change in management aspects that come along with more democratization of faster and more reliable management information. The "information is power" culture has to shift toward "knowledge is the only asset you can develop by sharing it" and that may take all the tricks of the trade to make it happen. Let me give you a few tips from my practice.

Make the Trade Profitable

In other words, when you ask for information from your colleagues or employees, make sure they get something in return: information they would never have known without sharing theirs. Picture the classic example of a sales rep who has to file visit reports and never gets any information in return. How motivating is that, you think? Now imagine this rep getting an analysis of his time consumption compared to best practices, a simulation of what extra income he might gain from better time management, win–loss analysis, and tips for better closing techniques used in other sales situations, and he will be glad to share his visit reports.

Make Them Dream

Everyone wants to perform better in his or her job. Make an inventory of what the ideal job is and you will come up with wishes such as:

- I wish to get better information, and I want it more quickly and more accurate.
- I want feedback that helps me improve my work.
- I want to know the relative position of....
- I don't want to waste time on making reports while I have so many important and urgent tasks waiting for me.

Your job is to help management to create a vision of better performance through better information. If you can position BI as a (partial) solution for their wishes, you have won the first heat of the race. What race? The race against prejudice, fear of change, and immobility.

Use Positive Feedback

Claim every success to which the BI system contributed. Make sure that users are aware of these contributions. Create ambition for more information using a simple sentence such as, "Now that we know x, wouldn't we want to know y and z?" Make users aware that BI is an ongoing management improvement process and not a project with a start and an end.

Phase Out the Old Systems, Fast

You can't prevent spreadsheet junkies from fiddling with figures but you can kill or block the SQL statements they fire off to get their data. Once you have demonstrated that the data from the BI system is just as useful—or preferably more useful—there is no reason for maintaining the old information management processes. The spreadsheet junkies will still use the syringe but at least the drugs they inject are clean and safe and the data in the BI system has a clear audit trail.

Form a Coalition of the Willing

We have just learned that a group is as good as its second-best member because you need two people who know the correct answer to convince the rest of the group. Why not stimulate this mechanism actively by demonstrating in meetings that the BI users are gaining more clout because they have the correct answers, on time?

Adapt to the Organization's Risk Profile

Are we dealing with innovators, early adaptors, early majority, late majority, or laggards? Each risk profile has its own set of arguments, for example:

- Innovators: This will change the way of doing business.
- Early majority: Leave your competitors behind you.

- Late majority: Everyone is using it.
- Laggards: The competition will put you out of business if you do not change your way of managing information.

Prepare for Setbacks

You will meet people who are not welcoming your gospel, which requires them to challenge their beliefs and values especially if they cannot reconcile the new approach with what works for them and they will be ready to manipulate whatever has to be manipulated to prove you are wrong. It is often easier to change a company's logo than its behavior. To use Kanter's often quoted words: introducing BI in an organization may be a combination of "bold strokes" and "long marches." Be prepared for both.

Mintzberg's Management Myths

In his book *Mintzberg on Management*, Henry Mintzberg (1989) debunks four myths (or "folklores" as he calls them) about managerial work. Let us have a closer look at these myths and see what we can learn from them in our business analysis practice.

1. Folklore: The manager is a reflective systematic planner.

   Fact: Study after study has shown that managers work at an unrelenting pace, that their activities are characterized by brevity, variety, and discontinuity, and that they are strongly oriented to action and dislike reflective activities.

2. Folklore: The effective manager has no regular duties to perform.

   Fact: In addition to handling exceptions, managerial work involves performing a number of regular duties, including ritual and ceremony, negotiations, and processing of soft information that links the organization with its environment.

3. Folklore: The senior manager needs aggregated information, which a formal management information system best provides.

   Fact: Managers strongly favor oral media, namely telephone calls and meetings.

4. Folklore: Management is, or at least is quickly becoming, a science and a profession.

   Fact: The managers' programs, to schedule time, process information, make decisions, and so on, remain locked deep inside their brains. Thus, to describe those programs, we rely on words such as judgment and intuition, seldom stopping to realize that they are merely labels for our ignorance.

What Do We Learn from This for Our BI Projects?

1. BI systems should present information on all possible levels between the highest aggregated level and microscopic detail. Considering today's extract, transform, load (ETL) performance, the price of disk space discussions on granularity should take less time than in the previous century. Always go for the lowest level of detail even if you have no clue today about the added value of microscopic data.
2. BI systems should allow for feedback from the users as idea generation via a computer network is an efficient and manageable process.
3. BI systems increase their effectiveness with interpreters and storytellers to convey meaningful and context-rich information for managers but also for everyone else in the organization, as our findings confirm that stories containing images, metaphors, comparisons, and other style figures are more easily assimilated than rows of numbers, even when they are accompanied by graphs. Compare the two presentations of the same information shown in Table 12.5. Which do you prefer, the story or the numbers?

   The story: Overall, our customers prefer product B, especially those in the + €50,000 income class. *Yet considering there are more potential consumers in the lower income class we shouldn't neglect these consumers and we should examine the possibilities for better product positioning in this segment.* The italics in this story add context and invoke discussion. It is clear that although the

TABLE 12.5

Results of a Customer Survey: The Numbers

	Total	M	F	< €50 k	> €50 k
Total Customers	5,000	2,390	2,610	2,890	2,110
	100%	100%	100%	100%	100%
Prefer product A	2,010	1,120	890	1,470	540
	40.2%	46.9%	34.1%	50.9%	25.6%
Prefer product B	2,990	1,270	1,720	1,420	1,570
	59.8%	53.1%	65.9%	49.1%	74.4%

report should contain both, the latter will last longer in the minds of the users.

4. BI systems must create a mix of regularly scheduled standard reports and ad hoc exception reports and analyses, and studies leading to a call for action.

5. BI systems should have feedback possibilities for all users to make soft information available for everyone in the user group. I have found a strong correlation between managers' willingness to delegate and their willingness to share soft information with their colleagues and coworkers.

Conclusion

Kahneman (2002) postulates the concept of accessibility, expressed on a continuum among rapid, automatic, and effortless presentations and slow, serial, and effortful presentations. He adds that perception is a choice of which we are not aware, and we perceive what has been chosen. Perception is also reference dependent. The illustration in Figure 12.9 illustrates this: the central square seems lighter in the left drawing as the contrast is greater, yet it has the same color as the central square in the right drawing. So the caveat for a truthful BI presentation layer is: "Be aware of rigid presentations based on minimal efforts on the information aggregation and grouping issues as they will impoverish instead of enrich the BI experience.

Business Analysis Issues

Make sure you get a clear picture of one of the central questions for the positioning of a BI project: Is the future BI system intended only for

 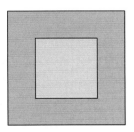

FIGURE 12.9
Context can change the perception of identical phenomena.

formal information and negative feedback loops or does it encourage exploration and positive feedback loops? In other words, what are the underlying assumptions for the BI project in the sponsor's mind? Is it control, centralization of information, and keeping the execution of the strategic plan within predefined boundaries? Or does it allow some form of dissidence enabled by a democratization of information, learning processes, and some form of decentralized decision making? Finding this out may take you more time than just interviewing the people in the organization. Often, it is a matter of "Don't listen to my words, look at my actions."

PRODUCING THE DOCUMENTS

Starting a BI project means charting existing but also uncharted areas in the organization and documenting these to produce a level of understanding between all parties concerned that builds trust and confidence the project will yield a useful product.

Consider a project as the gray area between routine work and improvisation and you will agree that a step-by-step iteration and reiteration of a few key issues, questions, and decisions need to be accomplished successfully before the sponsor is ready to put money and reputation on the line. This step-by-step approach is documented in a project direction document, interview summaries, business requirements, a business case, and in the project charter that binds it all together. The project charter is to a BI project what the Ten Commandments are to Judeo-Christian religions except that it is drawn up in a number of group decision-making processes whereas the latter was more of a unilateral kind. A good project charter covers all important areas of the project but leaves enough room for adaptations as the project is under way. We refer to the templates in Chapter 16 for an in-depth discussion of the contents.

Project Direction Document

Whether you have a small or a large project ahead, you cannot skip this phase as it does not take too much of everybody's time and from the outset draws everybody's attention to the issues at hand. All important aspects are (superficially) covered except one: how the strategy process (formation and formulation) is done in the organization and how information sources play their role "as is" and how management would like it "to be."

The only purpose of the document is to receive a GO or NO GO for further study and a commitment of the people to be interviewed that they will cooperate to produce the requirements.

Interview Summaries

These documents will hold detailed information about business processes, functional areas, and their information needs. They will link them to persons and profiles in the organization, which is crucial for the implementation phase. Without figureheads responsible for information domains or subsets of these domains, the BI system cannot survive in the long run. No matter who is responsible for writing up the business requirements, these summaries will provide context and content for the BI project and will help you to identify your allies and your troublemakers for the future course of events.

Business Requirements

Your client will probably have a good idea of what he wants. Now you have the choice: do you act as a notary, taking in these requirements or do you see your role as coach, challenging him in this early phase of the project. The answer is not unambiguously clear: in some organizations you are not the person to make this choice and the client will tell you what role to play. In some cases it is better not to intervene too much at an early stage as this may cause delays, take away the momentum, and even create confusion in the project team. I leave it to your ad hoc, case-by-case judgment as to what is the best way to move the project forward.

Business Case

Although every project methodology known to me puts this at the heart of the project, I have come across too many BI projects where the requirements were either on a basis of "I need this information no matter what the cost" or "This is my budget, now get me as much as possible." This is correlated with the role you are allowed to play in the organization. If the client is dumb enough to treat you as the errand boy then you may skip this section but if you have the chance to work with grownups, they will appreciate your input for the business case even if it challenges their assumptions and it forces them to reduce (or to expand) the business requirements.

Project Charter

This is the final deliverable to produce all the necessary information for the project sponsor to make an informed decision about the project's GO or NO GO. All other documents contribute to this final deliverable so my first advice here is: don't lose your audience. Make sure they can follow the conversion from the initial documents to this final foundation for the BI project.

VALIDATING THE RESULTS

After each phase, after each interview, you will have to validate the results. Never take anything for granted, as the following real-life examples display.

"I Wanted Performance!"

Some managers confuse lists with reports. They want to see 200,000 order lines in a report and be able to filter them ad lib to produce the needed information. Normally the OLTP system should be able to produce a straightforward list. But some lists can produce large result sets: "All products that were sold to all customers via all channels in the last three years, by all account managers." This looks more like an OLAP cube* than a report.

At the beginning of the analysis in this introduction phase, you may not be aware of the volume and the performance of this "report." So either you give your client advance warning about the performance or you examine the potential result of this report in terms of query response time and refresh time to provide feedback in an early as possible stage. Then your client has the choice: go through with it and accept the performance

---

* OLAP: Online analytical processing as opposed to OLTP (online transaction processing) was introduced by Chris Date in the 1980s. A "cube" is a metaphor for the way OLAP data are accessible for querying and "slicing and dicing" to rearrange the data for analytical purposes.

issues, use OLAP technology to provide better performance, or split up the "report" into manageable chunks.

"Why Do I Need the Full Client?"

Some functionality desired by the users may not correspond with their user profile. The user may not have the technical knowledge or the access rights to produce the desired report results; for example, the majority of BI users are report consumers. The tool may provide simple access via a Web interface or push out pdf or spreadsheet files. Avoid frustration by checking the consistency between user profile–user requirements and tool functionality so corrective measures can be taken in an early stage.

"Now That I See the Results..."

That is a classic one-liner that you will not always be able to avoid: the user knows what he wants when he sees the first results of his initial requirements. A seasoned business analyst can foresee extra functionality on the basis of these initial requirements by suggesting the lowest grain for the facts and proposing additional dimensions that may add extra context to the measures. It may be smarter to ask for extra budget at the beginning of the project than risking disappointed users and expensive rework after delivering the first reports.

Check the Business Case

The business case has to be under continuous development, refinement, and extension as requirements grow and users express new wishes. Whenever new functionality is asked, you will make sure there is a cost–benefit analysis to provide input for the decision maker.

SUPPORT AND MAINTENANCE

As soon as the project charter is finished and the project budget is approved, we move to the next level: the project life cycle. In some cases there may be a need for a more specialized business analyst but even when you stay on the team you will have to foresee some time and effort to transfer your knowledge to other roles in the project team. The project charter should speak for itself but the process preceding the final deliverable may need some further clarification.

Validation

The project charter's first objective is to communicate clearly the boundaries, the risks, the opportunities, and the impact for the organization to the project sponsor and the steering committee. Communication means adapting the message to the audience that is not preoccupied with details. Consider the project charter as an abstraction of a wealth of information and you see the task: convey the details and the context of the project charter to the project team and make them validate your observations, assumptions, and analysis as soon as possible. Misjudgments or plain errors are better detected in an early stage when corrective action is still feasible.

Vision Support

The sponsor's response to the project charter presupposes her acceptance of the vision expressed in the charter. When you remain part of the project team it will be your task to keep the project's vision intact. And don't think this is a walk in the park! The project may suffer benevolent and malignant attacks from well-meaning and not so well-meaning people in the project team who are mainly interested in optimizing their performance in their domain. Designing and building a BI system requires a multidisciplinary task force where you run the risk that the buck is passed on to the wrong person.

A database administrator (DBA) will see the project differently from an extract, transform, load (ETL*) developer and the ETL developer will have quarrels with the report developer. Within the ETL development team there will be tugs of war on the methodology, and so on. Your role is to make sure the deliverables supporting the project's vision will be there at the end of the project.

---

* ETL: Extract, transform, load: the basic operations for getting the data from the source system(s), cleaning them, and turning them into useful chunks of queryable datasets to be loaded in the target system, which is a data warehouse or a data mart.

13

Managing the Project Life Cycle

The Business Intelligence (BI) project life cycle, illustrated in Figure 13.1, needs interventions from the business analyst in varying intensity, depending on the phase and exogenous factors we discuss in this chapter.

Project planning: The book does not provide answers to the question, "How do I plan a BI project, step by step," but it offers valuable input for planners.

Business requirements definition: The book provides tools, concepts, and straightforward questions to enhance the quality of the requirements. This is the central point of gravity of the book.

Dimensional modeling: There are many fine books on dimensional modeling but it may help here and there to link business analysis issues to modeling issues.

BI application specification: Again, authors such as Kimball, Pendse, and many others have extensively published on this aspect. I restrict my contribution to high-level positioning of BI tool types.

Growth: As the growth phase is—from a methodological point of view—a new analysis iteration, I only address the events that signal the analyst to take an initiative even before the business users are aware there is a need for a new iteration.

The book presents best practices in business analysis for Business Intelligence with much emphasis on the project startup, as this is the main issue in many BI projects: how to overcome the inertia and gain momentum so the BI project becomes a BI process.

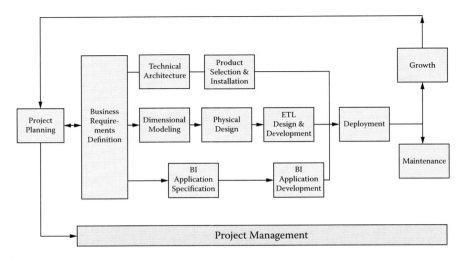

FIGURE 13.1
Kimball's data warehouse project life cycle.

BUSINESS ANALYSIS AND PROJECT PLANNING

Input from the business analyst will serve as a basis for a solid project plan. Below are the high-level project steps for which the business analyst can provide input. For more in-depth information we gladly refer to *The Data Warehouse Lifecycle Toolkit* from Kimball et al. (1998).

- Business requirements: More on this subject on the next pages.
- Application landscape: While analyzing the existing application landscape or city plan the analyst can detect inconsistencies in the use of data and data definitions. As each application has its own specific purpose and context, the risk of "narrowcasting" data definitions is imminent.
- Data modeling: The analyst can contribute to design choices and to the design itself.
- Building the data warehouse or data mart: A good analysis provides input for the order of the iterations that will be based on feasibility and business value. If the analysis has been done thoroughly, an analyst can calculate fairly accurately the workload and cost of the building phase.

- Loading the data warehouse or data mart: In the perfect world, everything should go smoothly now. But in many cases some in-depth analysis will be needed when loads fail. Although this analysis is mainly technical and deals with issues such as timestamps or database COMMIT procedures, the business analyst can look for improvements in business procedures that affect these issues positively.
- Developing a layer in the report server: The business analyst can keep the team's focus on the business needs and context to provide a semantic layer that is clear, appeals to the users, and remains stable whatever later additions are needed.
- Building the reports: This is where the final reality check by the analyst happens. "Does the system provide the desired reports?" is the question to be monitored.
- Testing end to end: The analyst is familiar with the data lineage aspects and can therefore interact with the technicians performing the unit tests and the end-to-end tests.
- User training: User acceptance is quintessential in BI. Any contribution the analyst can make to improve the training's effectiveness enhances the effect of all previous investments in time and equipment.

BUSINESS REQUIREMENTS GATHERING

Making the transition from probing for the expectations to capturing the ways and means of strategy formation and formulation can be difficult. But the hardest part is to systematize it so the information is accessible to a data modeler and if the modeler is the same person as the business analyst, then the need for a systematic approach is even greater to guarantee a smooth transition of the data models to the technicians.

The reason is simple: a conceptual data model is still close to the contextual information gathered and the knowledge of the organization's strategy process. As soon as the logical, the physical modeling, and the extract, transform, load (ETL) priorities come into the project, a poorly documented analysis and modeling phase may cause disruptions in the process. But before we get to any data modeling we examine the BI requirements gathering cycle for large projects to make sure we cover all areas; see Figure 13.2. Let's assume we start with a blank page.

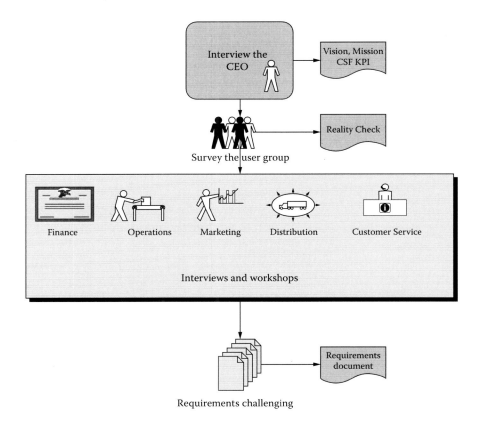

FIGURE 13.2
A schematic overview of a requirements gathering process for a complex BI project.

Interview the CEO

You have done your homework, studied the figures, and reconnoitered the terrain so you are ready to meet the Man with a Plan (or Person with a Plan to make this pc).

What Are Your Objectives?

Build trust: Make sure that at the end of the conversation the CEO is convinced you're the right person at the right place. You don't get this by reciting from your curriculum vitae (CV); showing you understand her strategic priorities and how BI can help her achieve her objectives is the better way. I hope you are now convinced that the previous pages served a purpose.

Obtain backing: You will be confronted with people who are less willing to cooperate than expected. Via various levels of C-level backing,
ranging from a subtle communication, "This project is important
and we expect all of you to contribute," up to a "Do as you're told or
else," you will overcome these resistance pockets.

Chart the organization: The CEO can give you hints which persons in
the organization he trusts. Be alert for remarks such as: "You should
talk to Jim, our marketing manager but you should also see Jack
who's head of the market research department."

Formal deliverable: An interview summary capturing the strategic priorities, the mission, the vision statement with personal comments
from the CEO and a list of critical success factors and key performance indicators (KPIs) the CEO uses to gauge the organization.

Survey the User Group

Some critics will find this over the top but in large projects a survey can
uncover a lot of obstacles below the waterline.

What Are Your Objectives?

Do a reality check: Are the mission and vision statements and their
expression into critical success factors:
a) Known
b) Integrated in the daily routine
c) Operable
d) Translated into KPIs on a personal level
e) Integrated in a personal development program

Detect potential contributors: A survey can be the combination of a
few discreet questions and a blank space with "Your comments"
or "Please specify." Make sure you test the survey for clarity and
unambiguity before you launch it companywide. An example of a
survey can be found in "Appendix D: Survey for a BI Project for the
Purchasing Department."

Formal deliverable: This is the survey results with descriptive statistics
if this should yield added value. By "descriptive statistics" I mean
crossing the results with age groups, function levels, departments,
and what have you to describe the organization's population without
violating the privacy of the respondents.

Interviews and Workshops

As you have the general directions from the CEO and a companywide superficial view of how management's vision is adopted, it is time to do in-depth interviews with functional managers, key users, and analysts to get to the bottom of the required information. Notice that I put "interviews" and "workshops" in one section as they are interchangeable: in some cases the interview yields better results but in others you need the interaction between colleagues a workshop can offer.

Interviews can be conducted quickly and easily and require less preparation than a workshop. But if you have to interview a large number of people, a workshop might take less time, especially if there are inconsistencies or diverging opinions between the interviewees.

After 20 years of interviewing and workshopping I still don't know where the best starting point is. Sometimes you need workshops to cover as many aspects, perspectives, and opinions on the matter at hand to elucidate them in detail, interviewing the opinion leaders of the workshop afterwards, and sometimes you need to work the other way around as you experience smoldering conflicts that might break out during a workshop, which you want to avoid. In that case, interviews may become more of two-way communication where the business analyst tries to reconcile diverging opinions on the subject. But be advised, you are stepping out of your role and are taking serious risks. The choice is very uncomfortable: either you remain neutral and risk seeing the project slip out of your hands because the client clearly demonstrates he is not yet ready to demonstrate a coherent vision of where the BI project will be heading or you are seen as a member of one of the opposing factions, and then you'd better have chosen the right one. Even then you will need eyes on your back because sabotaging a BI project is easier than you think.

What Are Your Objectives?

Get an in-depth understanding of:

- The business processes and the capturing, storing, updating, and deleting of process data
- The flow of data between business processes
- Master data and their use in the departments and the business processes

- The dimensions (or perspectives) used to evaluate the business process' performance. Think in terms of:
  - Generic dimensions such as CALENDAR, TIME, GEOGRAPHIC REGION
  - Contextual dimensions such as BATCH_SOURCE, ORDER_TYPE, NATURAL_ACCOUNT
  - Decision dimensions such as CUSTOMER, PRODUCT, EMPLOYEE, and all other dimensions you can influence with management decisions
- The meaning and grain of measured facts such as SALES_AMOUNT, SALES_VOLUME, COMPLAINTS_COUNT, and what have you
- Analysis and report requirements: analysis methods, drilldown paths, presentation methods, refresh rates
- Validation procedures and sources of the truth

Provide input for:

- The bus matrices
- The dimensional model
- The use and type choice of slowly changing dimensions
- The next phase: the business requirements challenge

Formal deliverable:

- Business requirements (see template)
- Bus matrix: [business process] × [dimensions and facts]
- Bus matrix: [report] × [dimensions and facts]

Requirements Challenging

I plead guilty and if you are honest you will too: this is the most overlooked phase in the requirements gathering. Every person involved has given you his wish list and the customer-friendly person you are has accepted them. OK, done? Wrong answer. Your client has the right to be challenged; it is your duty to identify potential problems down the road and help your client to make an informed decision. Now you should evaluate the impact of these requirements on the feasibility, data quality issues, total cost of ownership, and the business case, initially developed in the project charter, which can now be refined to attribute level.

How to Challenge the Requirements

The requirements reality check will be in the data. Only a check on the source data combined with interviews of the source data owners can bring about the truth. The "truth" being the answer to two questions: are the requirements feasible and are the requirements robust to allow future enhancements or do they commit us too much to an inflexible solution?

Profiling checklist

Check the following points in the source data:

- Environment: This is not a trivial element. Did you do the profiling on the development, test, acceptance, or production data? Each environment may determine a specific outcome. Because latency is different, the data model may have been altered.
- Database schema, for example:
  - Table.
  - Column.
  - Number distinct records: the size of the source data may give you a clue about future load performance.
  - Domain: what are the allowed data values? List of values? A range?
  - MAX and MIN Value.
  - Index, index type.
  - NULLS%: how well is the column used by the application? If there are a great deal of null values, what is the probable cause?
  - Foreign Key to [Table Name]: check constraint violations.
  - Number orphans: are there child records without a parent? This may testify to a database update by the database administrator (DBA) instead of the application owner.
  - Unique pattern: some input fields enforce unique patterns such as DD/MM/YYYY for a date or AA9999 for an article code. If there are violations to that rule in the data, you may, again, suspect the DBA.
  - Irregular pattern(s): examples.
  - Start and end dates: if you want to track changes, does the source support this feature?

- Conclusions/Remarks: Choose one of the three possible conclusions:
  - The data are OK for extraction, analysis, and reporting.
  - The data are not OK and should be fixed in the source system.
  - We need further investigation of a number of issues namely . . .

Source Owner Checklist

The source owner in my vocabulary comes in many flavors. It can be the IT technician responsible for the application, the analyst who maintains the system from a business point of view, the DBA, or the senior user who is involved in the development team. Sometimes you may need to see all of these people to get a complete view of what happens to the data.

Make sure you come up with answers to the following questions:

- Are batch inserts, updates, or deletes of data directly on the database possible and have there been such cases in the past?
- Have the data domains been unaltered since their first use?
- Can there be retroactive changes to start and end dates of records?
- Are cascading deletes possible in the system?
- If there is more than one source for a record, which version of the truth do we allow in the data warehouse?
- How do you handle obsolete data: with a physical delete or do you change the Active_Flag from 'Y' to 'N', that is, a logical delete?
- How do you handle merged data:
  - Create a new record and (logical or physical) delete of the merged records?
  - Create a new "merger" record and add a column to the old records "IsMergedInto" with the ID of the newly created record?
- Relationships with a start and end date require special attention: can these dates change or is a new relationship created?
- How are hierarchies modeled? And how does this affect the ETL's complexity?

Figure 13.3 shows hierarchy models where the self-join is more complex to handle and keeping track of changes in the hierarchy is not a trivial challenge. The hierarchy bridge table offers more flexibility and keeps track of historical changes very well where it is important to compare year

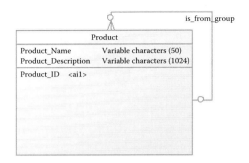

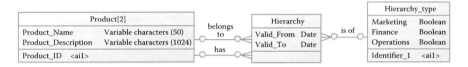

FIGURE 13.3
Two examples of modeling a hierarchy in the source system.

to date figures when hierarchies are volatile, such as sales regions, product hierarchies, staff hierarchies, and so on.

Testing the Robustness of the Requirements

While examining the source data within the scope of the requirements, you can do some extra useful work: check for candidate entities and attributes for facts and dimensions you may not need today but in case of future requirements would demand a re-engineering or reload of your data warehouse.

A simple example: FACT_INVOICES is necessary for a project to analyze the revenue per customer and per account manager. If you check all attributes in the source data (most of the time INVOICE_HEADERS containing general data and INVOICE_LINES containing the product, unit price, and quantity) and find there is a contract number in the header record, you may attract your client's attention to this useful attribute, which can easily be added to the FACT_INVOICES even when there is no requirement for this attribute. Adding it later would probably need an INSERT in a multigigabyte table at a far greater cost than offering it a piggyback ride in this iteration.

Formal deliverable: At the end of the process, you should be able to indicate where issues, risks, and impossibilities lurk. The client must be made aware of technical constraints on the business requirements in such a way that:

a)   The client understands the technical mumbo jumbo.

b)   New issues may emerge further down the road.

c)   The client is ready to refine the business case to make an informed decision on whether to keep, postpone, or drop the requirements that may cause problems.

d)   The client sees opportunities in enhancing the requirements for future growth.

Making It Stick

I often hear the remark that it is so hard to foresee the future information needs of an organization and that BI systems regularly need revision and sometimes even complete re-engineering to meet the new business requirements. This was true in the pioneer years but if you have followed the approach of this book you will have covered 99.9% of all future requirements even when the client is unaware of them! The business analysis method for business intelligence offers you three solid, persistent building blocks and three auxiliary analysis areas.

Solid Building Blocks

The strategy process: If you have analyzed this using the models and information of the first three chapters you will have a solid foundation to understand the way the organization works with data and information.

The 4 Cs: All Business Intelligence requirements can be abstracted to four knowledge domains from now on known as the 4 Cs: customer, cost, competition, and competences. If you can scope these fundamental knowledge domains and map all your requirements on them you will see the future development path sooner than your client.

Master data: From the first iteration and onwards master data should be your guide on the path to an upgradeable BI system. Master data indicate immediately what the organization is interested in as it takes special care of these objects throughout all source systems.

You either take all of them into the scope of your solution or, if this is too much of a burden for the project's budget and time constraints, foresee graceful update possibilities for future developments.

Auxiliary Analysis Areas

Business Processes: The more you go into detail, the more chance there is that business processes may change. But if you can match the high-level processes with master data and the 4 Cs you will make your analysis resilient for future adaptations.

Functional areas: These may also change as responsibilities are reshuffled, new disciplines emerge, or functional areas are merged. If you consider functions as a grouping of processes then they are merely adding context and shouldn't distract you from the essence: the data necessary to produce the required analysis.

Available data: The source data analysis can reveal the volatility of the record keeping. Columns are added to tables, attribute values are changed or redefined, and so on. In some business domains such as retail or wholesale the volatility can be high whereas in government or insurance domains the essential records are pretty stable. Make sure you get an idea of this rate of change as it may be the start of a separate track to improve overall data management in the organization.

DIMENSIONAL MODELING

As indicated in the introduction, this is not a course on dimensional modeling, although the concept is introduced in "Appendix C: The 101 on Data Warehousing." I prefer to have a discussion on the three major modeling approaches and how they can affect your job as a business analyst in keeping the information infrastructure aligned with the strategy process. A very simple diagram points out the issue:

1. The organization picks up signals from competitors, government, consumer trends, and other external influence and...
2. ...Adapts its strategic priorities, processes, ploys, and so on...which...

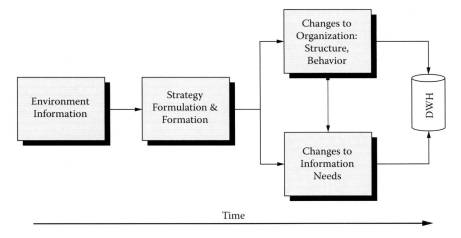

FIGURE 13.4
The strategy process and information feedback to the data warehouse.

3. …Causes changes to the organization's structure, behavior, and its information needs which…
4. …Interact with each other and in their turn affect…
5. …The data warehouse

So here's the decision to make: do we choose the Inmon, Kimball, or Linstedt architectural approach? And how irreversible is each choice? And can we mix these design choices? See Figure 13.4.

Data Warehousing 2.0 from Bill Inmon

The "Father of Data Warehousing" launched his concept a few years ago, stressing the need for data life cycle management and incorporating unstructured data in the data warehouse. I leave it to the data warehouse diehards to determine whether this is the next thing or old wine in a new barrel. In simple terms, the Inmon approach is a top-down one. The starting point is an enterprise data model designed, built, and loaded and data marts as derived subsets of the corporate data warehouse. The data warehouse contains the lowest level of detail whereas the data marts are purpose-built for a subject or functional area and may contain higher levels of granularity, summary data, and accumulating snapshots.

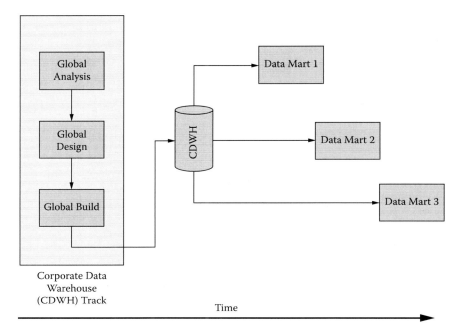

FIGURE 13.5
A graphical representation of the Inmon approach to dimensional modeling.

The Inmon approach (Figure 13.5) works in a stable environment where there is plenty of time to stay away from the user community and deliver the comprehensive basis for subject-oriented data marts. It is no coincidence that Inmon has launched his Government Information Factory and it is no coincidence that I have never come across the Inmon method in organizations operating in a turbulent, rapidly changing environment.

Conformed Dimensions of Ralph Kimball

If Bill Inmon is to be called the "Father," then Ralph Kimball is the data warehouse doctor. His bottom-up method offers quick relief for information pains without jeopardizing the future by creating new stove-pipes. By scoping the conformed dimensions from the very beginning on a corporate level the data warehouse grows as it becomes the sum of all data marts. A data mart is built around a business process or a source and delivers rapid (but sometimes only in part) information to the user community. The main worry of this approach is to prevent the data marts from "continental drift:" a slow but sure diverging of dimensions as new attributes, new hierarchies, snapshots, and aggregates are added. The business analysis role is pivotal in this modeling strategy. See Figure 13.6.

My advice is to think ahead about the granularity of the facts, allowing drill-through in a later phase when more data marts are operational. The Kimball method has followers in all corners of the organization ecosystem: government, high-tech companies, pharmaceutical companies, multinational companies but also medium-sized and even small businesses. The STAR schema is an easy communication platform for the business and IT communities whereas the 3NF, which is often used in Inmon's corporate data warehouse, is a lot more difficult to explain to business users. But there has been a new kid on the block for a few years claiming to combine the comprehensive Inmon approach with the flexibility of Kimball's method: the data vault.

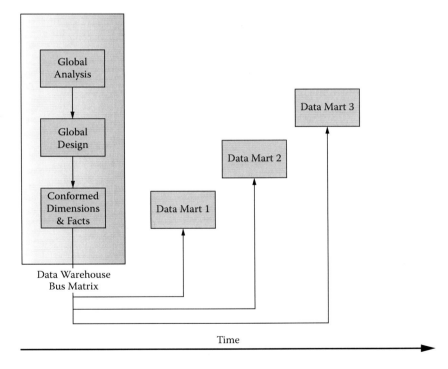

FIGURE 13.6
A graphical representation of the Kimball approach to dimensional modeling.

The Hubs, Links, and Satellites of Dan Linstedt

Dan Linstedt published his first article on the data vault in *The Data Administrator Newsletter* in July 2002 and since then his method has gained credibility in the BI community. See Figure 13.7.

Data vaults are conceived to design, build, and exploit corporate data warehouses

The data are distributed over three entity types: hubs, links, and satellites.

Hubs represent the basic concepts of the business, which are almost always master data such as employee, customer, product, geographical location, and so on.

Links are positioned between hubs and represent transactions or relationships. The links hold the keys from the hubs.

Satellites store the contextual information for hubs. They are very similar to dimensions and contain a Valid from–Valid to indication.

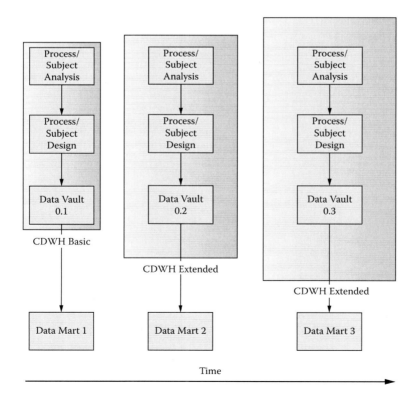

FIGURE 13.7
A graphical representation of the Linstedt approach to dimensional modeling.

Attributes are distributed over satellites according to their frequency of change.

Data vaults are found in fast-moving organizations that need to combine massive amounts of detailed data that have a high rate of change. Think of telecom operators and some fast-moving consumer goods companies.

Mixed Design Choices

There is a mixed design choice, combining the top-down approach of the corporate information warehouse with the conformed dimensions approach of Kimball. The flowchart in Figure 13.8 illustrates this approach.

The advantages are only realized when the corporate data warehouse evolves toward 100% completeness. Then economies of scale help the organization to build new data marts rapidly. But as long as we are still under 50% the disadvantages have the upper hand: twice the amount of work, the risk of having to rework the corporate model when new insights are discovered, and possibly new initial loads of historical data. My advice: think twice and choose one distinct approach.

Conclusions

In the quest for one version of the truth, there are many versions of the truth about the dimensional modeling approach. The opponents of Inmon state you can lose a lot of time and money while waiting for the ultimate data warehouse. Those attacking the star schema approach from Kimball develop the argument that it is not built for growth, is inflexible to changing business requirements, and will lead to new stovepipes. The Linstedt opponents refute the data vault argument of flexibility, considering it a carbon copy of the operational systems, forcing you to create an extra layer between the corporate data warehouse and the data marts. Whatever your choice, you will always have to perform the following tasks at the outset of your business analysis:

1. Get a high-level view of the entire scope, even if the client is not interested.
2. Examine the basic building blocks that will always appear in some form in the requirements, namely: customer, cost, competitor, and competences.

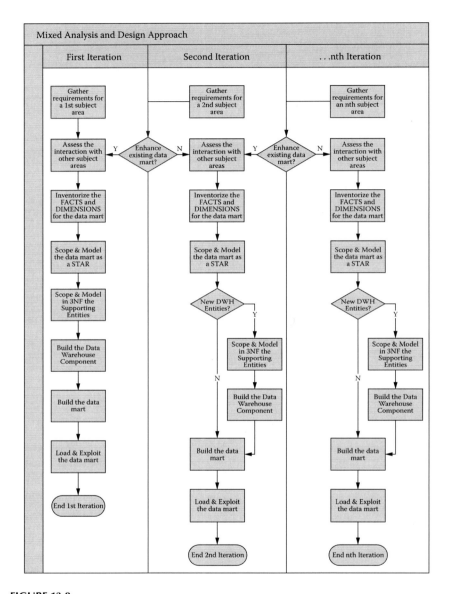

FIGURE 13.8
The corporate data warehouse is developed in parallel mode with the various data marts.

3. Check all attributes of the fact table candidates: this analysis will give you a hint of future dimensions even when no one is considering them as a candidate.

4. Analyze the tradeoff between delivering rapid functionality to the (always demanding) business and being the best-in-class pupil,

TABLE 13.1

Modeling Approaches and Data Model Types

Modeling Framework	Tick Box
The top-down approach from the corporate data warehouse to subject-oriented data marts from Bill Inmon	☐
The bottom-up approach from the conformed dimensional data marts from Ralph Kimball	☐
The flexible but deferred modeling choice from Dan Linstedt's data vault method	☐
Data modeling in the third normal form (3NF)	☐
Data modeling in the denormalized form (STAR)	☐
Data modeling in the sixth normal form (anchor modeling)	☐
Other (please specify):	☐

adhering to the corporate architectural standards demanding a global data warehouse standard, built to last.

5. Follow the money: your sponsor will have to make the final decision. Make sure it is an informed decision and you are all set.

Maybe we should let the market judge. So I have conducted a small survey among 29 BI specialists and managers, representing 29 organizations with a total of half a million employees. The survey question grid is shown in Table 13.1. Respondents could tick more than one box as this could reveal interesting facts. And it did! Although a large majority embraces the Kimball method, not every Kimball fan takes it all the way as no less than six BI specialists use other data models than the STAR schema.

The Linstedt method is fairly new to the community as is anchor modeling, which explains the low figures. The lower number of STAR models than there are Kimball followers has a simple explanation: some respondents use a third normal form staging area before they start building the data marts. At the time of the survey, these data marts were not yet in production. The survey results are shown in Table 13.2.

TABLE 13.2

The Survey Results

Modeling Approach	Inmon	Kimball	Linstedt	Other
No. of respondents	4	22	1	
Data model method	3NF	STAR	Data Vault	Anchor
No. of respondents	9	16	1	1

BI APPLICATION SPECIFICATION

The market for BI tools is continuously changing, so this section cannot compete with Web publications on timeliness and accuracy about the technical features of, say 10 market leaders; at least that is what they all call themselves. For a business analyst, there is no need to have in-depth knowledge of all these tools and I doubt if such a person exists on this planet. You only need to deliver a structured and verifiable tool selection requirements document that can help the technicians to base their choice not just on a performance and total cost of ownership basis but to include the fit with the organization.

I learned this years ago when a large U.S. multinational directed its European HQ to do a proof of concept with the high ticket/top performance BI tool they had bought. The proof of concept went well, that is, from a technical point of view, but the users revolted. "We have no DBAs available to keep this system running," someone said. Another one added, "This interface is gruesomely difficult for our user profiles." That is when I started thinking of a checklist beyond the technical specifications.

So, leave the discussions about load balancing, fail-over, 64-bit architectures, and in-memory or caching support to the technicians. Don't bother them with your concerns about AJAX or SDK choices but make sure you include technical choices that have an impact on user experience, such as single sign-on or support for enterprise directories.

If you can prioritize the list, based on the input from all parties concerned, you will secure an informed choice for that important part, which can determine whether your BI project succeeds or fails: user acceptance. Without this no BI project, no matter how great the technical achievements are, can survive. And after all, who pays the salaries and fees of the tech people? Right, so now you are motivated to take this list into account.

Feel free to add your specifications, refine the existing ones, or remove some of them, which may have become obsolete or are replaced by a new architectural approach by the time you read this book. An example is shown in Table 13.3. Make sure you include all user profiles in your survey and ask your user group to give each criterion a Likert value between one and seven. Afterwards, and in total agreement with the business sponsor, rank your users in descending order of importance to add an additional weight to the criterion. That is, if the DBA is

TABLE 13.3

High-Level Criterion List with BI Usability Criteria

Criterion	Source/ DWH/DM DBA	Analyst	Report Designer	Key User	BI Application Manager	Other Users
Zero-footprint viewer						
Zero-footprint definer						
Zero-footprint portlets						
Dashboards						
Single sign-on support						
Row level security						
Column level security						
Criterion (Ctd)						
Active directory support						
Data lineage						
Metadata access						
Checkout and lock reports						
Query analyzer						
Query optimizer						
Drill across						
Statistical analysis						
Query response						
User-defined calculations						

(Continued)

TABLE 13.3 (CONTINUED)

High-Level Criterion List with BI Usability Criteria

Criterion (Ctd)	Source/ DWH/DM DBA	Analyst	Report Designer	Key User	BI Application Manager	Other Users
User-defined results publishing						
Export to broadly accepted formats (.xls,.pdf, etc.)						
User-defined grouping and hierarchies						
Integration with unified messaging						
Thin- and rich-client options						
RSS compatible						

considered the main decision maker then all her scores will be multiplied by 1 whereas the lowest form of life in the user food chain will see his score multiplied by 0.1.

BUSINESS ANALYSIS AND GROWTH—MAINTENANCE

Once the first reports are being used, the maintenance phase will demand the BA's attention. Requests for changes will pour in, new reports as a variation on existing ones will be asked for, source systems will change and affect the BI environment, and tool upgrades will affect the possibilities of the BI exploitation, so what once started as a project will become a process for you to monitor and provide with enhancements and updates to the analysis documents.

This section discusses a few major maintenance issues you should discuss with the business client(s) and the IT people to come up with a coherent modus operandi, preventing hiccups in the BI process and unnecessary frustration for both parties. New requirements cause a reiteration of the analysis track and should not cause too many problems. Let us focus on what can cause a pain: source changes and lack of user support. But on the plus side, the sharing of knowledge from the project team to the organization can mitigate these risks. Finally we make the case for a Business Intelligence Competence Center (BICC) to institutionalize the transfer from BI project to BI process.

Source Changes

There are two types of changes to the source data: explicit and implicit changes.

> *Explicit changes:* New tables, new relationships, new attributes are added, tables are renamed, and so on. All these changes are clear, identifiable, and should trigger a briefing to the BI maintenance team.
> *Implicit changes:* Ay, there's the rub.

A memo field is used to record a new value that wasn't in the list of values so reports will be incomplete without anyone knowing unless someone from the data entry people sees one and asks, "Why isn't type XYZ not included in the report?" Or what about a change in meaning of existing lists of value or measurements? A large logistics company used weight category labels (ranging from AA to GG) for palletized shipments. These labels referred to 49 categories ranging from 25 kg to 450 kg. Years later, a new division started operating in the bulk market, using the same category labels but for different weight classes: from 5 tonnes to 60 tonnes. And instead of using all 49 combinations, only 10 were used. Needless to say there was some pollution in the revenue and cost analysis.

So how do we prevent this from happening? The solution lies in the organization, not in the technology. Some organizations propose 100% technical solutions such as grants on tables or—worse—views for the BI people so any time things change the developer and the DBA are alerted. Others rely on metadata managers and data lineage tools but these tools do not always offer a proactive view on what happens if the data sources undergo changes. In the section on data quality, I refer to data ownership and data stewardship. Only when these concepts are well embedded in the organization and in every data "consumer's" practice can technology become effective.

Smaller organizations may not be able to fund a Business Intelligence Competence Center, but they have no excuse for not appointing data stewards monitoring their key dimensions and measures on a regular basis with the source data owners. In a small business it can be the business process owner who has a complete view of what happens with the key data from registration in the source system to the end user report whereas in larger organizations with similar business processes, data stewards will monitor these data across the processes.

Dwindling User Support

I have seen it happen at many sites and I admit some of my projects underwent the same fate: users lost interest and appetite for the Business Intelligence environment. Not that they stopped using the reports. But they stopped giving suggestions, criticism, reviews, alternatives, and the like. What this means is that the BI system is narrowed down to delivering the specified products instead of creating a knowledge enhancement process to fuel strategic initiatives.

Let me give you a metaphor I use in my classes. "How do you explain what a palm tree is to an Inuit?" (or an igloo to a member of the San people, for that matter). You build the concept step by step, looking for connection points with the Inuit's environment and context. This is where most business analysts (including myself) fail miserably: consultants are off to their new client and leave the organization behind, happy in their snowy landscape (or under their palm tree if you prefer the other metaphor), ignorant of other realities, possibilities, and opportunities a BI system can provide.

Sharing Project Knowledge

This section is based on an article by Luc Bouquet from TEKA Info Pilots (2010).

1. Were there during the project processes, procedures or ideas and insights that need sharing with the rest of the entire organization, or specific departments?
2. Can you describe the shareable object in a structured way so others can take in the knowledge?

If both questions yield a "yes," there is room for knowledge sharing.

All project methodologies have a "lessons learned" phase but this method takes it a little bit farther. In short, the method suggests a central approach, provides a checklist to identify knowledge worth reproducing and where to reproduce it, tips for the interview, and publication suggestions. A template for reproducing a best practice (which we have expanded to other knowledge objects) concludes the method. It makes sense that the business analyst and the project manager manage the knowledge objects centrally: the project manager will do this according to his PMI BOK or PRINCE 2 method, recording issues, risks, and lessons learned and so on, but he needs the business analyst (BA) to provide context. And when things get purely technical, the BA will call in the help of developers and DBAs.

The method suggests using a dedicated communication specialist to record, describe, and publish the knowledge objects. Before you start thinking, "'I can do this myself," try to remember the last time you gave a recipe or driving instructions to someone and what he or she made of it. Structured writing is an art and a craft requiring specialized skills and by using a counterpart (completely ignorant about the project, BI, or information technology for all I care), decomposing your knowledge object into reproducible information bits and pieces, you make sure nothing gets forgotten or remains ambiguous. And, believe it or not, it will save you time and effort you can better spend elsewhere.

Knowledge Objects

Number one on the list are best practices. Nothing is more valuable, more direct, and hands-on than sharing time and money saving processes with the organization.

Number two is a lower-level version of, sometimes very short, procedures, which are a combination of instructions.

Number three is the lowest level: tips and tricks aimed at getting one thing at a time straight such as, "How to copy an entity to a new diagram."

You can consider levels two and three as a reduced version of the more complex best practice for which TEKA Info Pilots have developed a template that is in the template section of Chapter 16 and adapted for BI purposes. Working with the template has the advantage that you will cover all aspects of the best practice in consistent descriptions, even the ones you may not need afterwards.

Interview

Make sure you are present at the interview with the best practice owner to guard the scope. In my opinion this is not always easy for an outsider to do. The interviewer will explain the goal of the communication exercise and keep the owner to the subject. In the case where there is more than one owner, you will need to get them in the same room at the time of the interview to avoid contradictions or noise when launching the best practice. Gather hardcopies of documents, pictures, schemas, and anything else that can illustrate or support the best practice description.

Publication Platform

There are three publication platforms, each with its own pros and cons:

A *content management system* (*CMS*) which provides good functionality for maintenance of intranets but the technology may allow too much freedom, permitting the breakup of the best practice into reusable objects, which in most cases are not reusable. On the plus side a CMS is cheap compared to the latter two, and a clever setup of user roles may mitigate the risks of creating information chaos.

A *document management system* (*DMS*) provides good versioning and search functionalities, using sophisticated indexing (although some CMS have pretty good search algorithms too) and handles metadata very well. It also manages the life cycle of documents with regard to fast retrievability and near line storage and archiving for less frequently used documents. Security and workflow management functionality make it more manageable in a large organization than a CMS. A good DMS integrates easily with other applications such as customer relationship management (CRM) or enterprise resource planning (ERP) systems. To make the description complete with some less relevant features in this context: a DMS allows rapid entry of large volumes of forms and printed and even written material using optical character recognition (OCR).

An *enterprise repository* (*ER*) manages all artifacts, their relationships with each other, and objects outside the repository in a meta model that can present the organization's activities on various levels (or "layers" if you prefer that term):

- The business process layers from high-level value chains via process levels one, two, and three to microscopic procedures (and "how to's"). The levels include category, process, subprocess, activity, task, and work instruction, to be more precise.
- The business requirements, use cases, and other graphical and verbal exchange methods between business and IT.
- The functional descriptions of existing and future applications supporting the business processes.
- The enterprise architecture or "application landscape," a high-level description of which application does what with which data.
- The information layers from a business glossary to high-level entities including PARTY and LOCATION to lower-level entities used by transaction applications and by the data warehouse, the data marts, online analytical processing (OLAP) cubes, and the reports.

The ER offers possibilities for consistency checks between the layers, creates views, and even generates database schemas such as CASE tools. Does this long description mean I am in favor of the enterprise repository? By no means. But if your organization has the budget, the culture of knowledge sharing, and is a complex structure in a dynamic environment, this may be the tool you need.

Preparing a BI Competence Center

"Competence" is a wonderful word. It means both "authority" and "ability," which is what an organization needs to manage the transformation from a BI project to a BI process. Most BI projects see the light in a department and, at best, are the first iteration after an organizationwide scoping of the BI potential has been undertaken. In both cases you will need some form of a BICC to coordinate the BI efforts between departments, users, and source owners. This section deals with the introduction of a BICC, shown in Figure 13.9: a readiness assessment and the team setup.

Assess Readiness

Most organizations are very much aware of what a BICC should manage:

- Data quality
- Master data
- Total cost of ownership of the BI system
- Architecture of the BI system
- Best practices management and methodology
- Alignment between strategy and information management

Fewer organizations have given good thought to how a BICC should manage all this. Although it is not always easy to quantify the added value

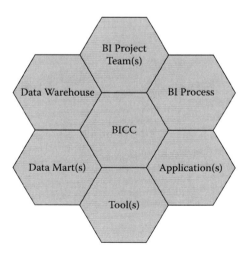

FIGURE 13.9
The BICC is at the heart of the BI system.

of a BICC for an organization, there are arguments for "administering the right dose of BICC" to an organization. A theoretical model multiplies three basic factors (scale, scope, and level of heterogeneity) on a five-point Likert scale, where the governance score plays a key role and therefore uses a different scale:

$$S \times Sc \times Gov \times H = x$$

and

$$0 < x < 5^4$$

The input for the calculation model is:

- (*S*) Scale of the organization: the number of BI users. Take 50 on the lower side scoring 1 and 2,000+ on the higher side scoring 5.
- (*Sc*) Scope of the decisions taken with help from the system: take 1 for operational reporting, 3 for tactical analysis and reporting, and 5 for strategic and forward-looking analysis.
- (*Gov*) Level of IT governance, preferably an IT–business duopoly and certainly not a feudal environment. To make the impact of the governance a little more graphic, here are the scores I would use:
  - Anarchy: zero, as it ensures a 100% certain dead on arrival of your BICC.
  - Feudal: 0.1, indicating you will have a long way to go if this is the ecosystem of your BICC.
  - Business monarchy: 1. You will have a hard time finding experienced candidates as they will see a steep learning curve.
  - IT monarchy: 2. At least you can enforce some of the important standards via your systems management.
  - IT duopoly: 5. Yep, only the balance between the business needs and the IT constraints can produce a workable, viable, and successful BICC.
- (*H*) Level of heterogeneity of the online transaction processing (OLTP) and BI systems used in the organization: use 1 if there are more than five platforms (databases, operating systems, etc.), 3 if there are three to four platforms, and 5 if there is only one platform.

So, the closer your calculation comes to 5^4, the more chances of producing an added value the BICC will have.

Build the Team

A BICC team needs to fill in at least five roles at the start:

- Source systems application architect: He knows how the source systems interact and how they exchange which data via which interface. He is preferably also a member of the enterprise architecture board.
- BI architect: She manages the ETL schemas, the BI application architecture, the data architecture, and the interfaces with other systems inside and outside the organization and with the enterprise architecture board.
- Data modeler: He is responsible for a coherent and consistent modeling approach that provides rapid functionality without reducing future growth opportunities.
- Data manager: She manages the content, quality, and life cycle of data on the enterprise level.
- BI leader: He is the figurehead, the evangelizer, and conflict solver. He interfaces with C-level management to ensure that the strategy process is adequately supported by the BI system and thereby he provides input for the strategy process.

Larger organizations may split up these roles even further; for example, the data modeler role in larger organizations may be split up into:

- Conceptual data modeler
- Logical data modeler
- Physical data modeler

Or a data manager may become a master data manager and a data quality manager (who in turn can split into an OLTP data quality manager and BI data quality manager).

Business Analysis Issues

The main question that remains is a chicken and egg one: what comes first in a BI life cycle: the architectural decisions before the project gets a "Go" or incorporating the project's results in the architecture framework? The architectural decisions cover four domains: the business architecture, the data architecture, application, and the technology architecture. I have observed both approaches and they both knew success and failure.

If you follow the book's approach to business analysis you will observe a preference for developing the architectural aspects as the project gets defined and the requirements become clear.

The business architecture should be clear at the outset of the project. You may need to clarify some points here and there but the major decisions should have been taken:

- Business vision and business drivers
- Prioritized information needs to support decisions on the strategic, tactical, and operational levels

The data architecture is obviously clear for the source systems and for your part of the deal, the data warehouse or the data mart(s), this will develop organically during the business analysis process. It concerns decisions on:

- The modeling method
- The grain of the fact tables
- The lookup tables and mappings

The application architecture in terms of what the BI system will provide (i.e., churn analysis, fraud detection, financial reporting, etc.) becomes clear during the requirements gathering process.

For the technology architecture in a greenfield environment, this decision should be taken as late as possible to make sure you have maximum input of users' requirements and the complexity and performance levels of the desired applications. In a mature BI environment the technology may be a given before the start of your project but don't be afraid to challenge the status quo if the client appreciates a sound business case.

Conclusion

A BI project has fewer architectural constraints than an OLTP project for a few simple reasons:

- A BI system is basically a "read only, clean and prepare data for analysis and interpretation" operation. This is less radical in its effect on the primary processes than a transaction system. Architectural flaws in transaction systems may affect the way the organization treats its customers, suppliers, and staff; it may, as a client once said, "Speed up the rate at which we are going bankrupt."

- BI architecture decisions on business, technology, and application level have lower exit thresholds than OLTP decisions. What needs utmost attention is the data architecture. Wrong decisions in that area may lead to expensive rework and reloading the entire data warehouse.
- Try to cover architectural issues as early as possible: in the project initiation phase, the project charter includes a section on the architecture. In the project life-cycle phase, the technical architecture comes in the picture as early as possible.

My advice is: consult the enterprise architect in an early phase to check if he or she is on the same page with you about BI. If the architecture board transplants its OLTP standards on the BI project you may have to add up to 50% overhead to your project budget to produce the necessary red tape, convince the organization of your view, and work on a business case with an abnormal level of detail in this early initiation phase or at the beginning of the project life cycle.

14

Mastering Data Management

Note that I do not use the term "master data management." Not that I don't like the concept but I am afraid it will go the same route as the corporate data warehouse in the pre-Kimball era: a nice idea but extremely hard to realize in everyday business practice. Again the tension between providing the business with rapid response to their demands and maintaining a well-architected master data management may push the choice to an imperfect but useful environment instead of the perfect solution, which is never going to come out of the planning room. The true value of Ralph Kimball's work to the development of working corporate data warehouses, emerging from hands-on data marts, is rapidly delivering business value, but using conformed dimensions to facilitate large integrated warehouses addressing all the subject areas cannot be underestimated. Yet, data management in any of the projects approached (whether the old top-down from Bill Inmon or the bottom-up approach from Kimball) is often an orphan in the process. Just like documenting the project and its deliverables, it is regarded a tedious and superfluous extra on which neither the technicians nor the analysts like to spend their time.

Data management in a Business Intelligence (BI) project is like the blood circulation in an organism: it is needed everywhere but appears in various doses and throughput levels through various blood vessels from the aorta of the extract, transform, load (ETL) process to the capillaries of everyday atomic data capture on the shop floor. The following sections intend to create awareness for clarity and understanding of uniform master data such as "product" or "party" (internal and external, such as supplier and customer) during the business analysis process.

MAJOR COMPONENTS OF DATA MANAGEMENT

Overview

Data management with regard to BI and your role as a business analyst reflects on the following aspects:

- Managing master data and the system of record
- Source analysis
- Data profiling
- Source-to-target mapping
- Metadata
- Data management architecture
- Business analysis issues

Master Data

Data management for Business Intelligence requires time and effort to gather and unite every department in the organization around the major entities:

- *Party* which is a generalization of:
    - Internal party, which in its turn can be a:
        - Person, that is, DIM_EMPLOYEE or DIM_PARTNER
        - Organization, that is, DIM_ORGANIZATION or DIM_BUSINESS_UNIT
    - External party, which can also be a:
        - Person, that is, DIM_CUSTOMER
        - Organization, that is, DIM_CUSTOMER or DIM_CHANNEL
- *Product* describes the physical or service delivery to internal and external customers. It can comprise purchase items, saleables, or consumables but not gross plant addition (GPA).
- *Geography* is the territory or region that can be strongly determined by the type of operation or the department looking at it.
- *Time* can be trickier than one may think at first sight: business hours may vary in full continuous operations like the process industry or logistics and in a global or multicultural environment an eight-hour workday may be distributed over eight, ten, or even twelve hours. "Siesta" ring a bell?

- Time can be registered from three viewpoints:
  - The *happening time:* which represents when the event actually happened or "will happen" as in budgeted events.
  - The *valid time:* this can be both a point in time and a period when an event or a status was valid. It is a derived value from a slowly changing dimension type 2 or type 3.
  - The *system time:* also known as "SYSDATE," or the time when the event was recorded.
- *Calendar* where the business days vary over time and per country or even per region may also require a little bit more attention than expected.

More on these concepts in the section on generic definitions.

In complex IT architectures, it can be useful to construct an extended CRUD matrix, superseding the level of one system or database. This high-level matrix shows the relationships between (master) data needed for BI and the applications where the data are created (C), read (R), updated (U), or deleted (D). Potential inconsistencies are easier to trace in a CRUD matrix. Don't expect to do this in a one-off process.

Table 14.1 tells us immediately where the master data's system of record resides: for customer, order, and territory it is the customer relationship management (CRM) system, for product it is the inventory system, and for the Human Resources (HR) member, the Human Resources Management (HRM) system. But the U's here and there point to applications that add data to the master data such as accounts receivable adding a customer contact responsible for the accounts payable at the customer site or the territory specification for staff members other than sales and marketing people in the HRM application.

TABLE 14.1

Example of an Extended CRUD Matrix Type[a]

	CRM	Accts Receivable	Inventory	HRM	Accts Payable
Customer	CRUD	RU	R	R	R
Product	R	R	CRUD	–	R
Order	CRUD	R	R	–	R
HR Member	R	R	R	CRUD	R
Territory	CRUD	–	–	RU	–

[a] Application *x* target data element.

Extended CRUD matrices can be constructed in various flavors depending on the viewpoint:

- [Application x target data element] as in the example above
- [Application x source data element], which produces a much more refined view as each source record's life cycle is mapped in the matrix
- [User x source data element], which is only relevant in the case where one user has CRUD access to many applications. In that case a drill-down of "applications per user" will be necessary.

Source Analysis

The source analysis should yield the following information per entity and its attributes:

- Entity name, definition, source application, table with the master file, and the data definition owner.
- Attribute name, definition, datatype, domain (the list of values for discrete values and the data range for continuous values).
- Physical data model.
- Access and security methods (rules, passwords, etc.).
- Check how the data are used by business processes and complete the extended CRUD matrix in complex environments.
- Check how the data are used by applications and complete the extended CRUD matrix.
- Check for gaps in data domains such as: insufficient data currency, availability, or relationship gaps.
- Assess a rough approach to the necessary transformations for BI purposes.

Data Profiling

Some practitioners exclude this exercise from the business analyst's responsibilities. I tend to disagree as data profiling can provide the acid test for the assumptions made during the analysis. Sometimes the business user (or even the source IT specialist) has spent less time with the company than the specific tables he is talking about. It wouldn't be the first time the client tells you he has 78,000 clients, which a simple count rejects with the proof of the existence of half a million customer records!

TABLE 14.2

Simple Data Profiling Analysis

Record	# of Instances	# Nulls	Datatype Not Conform
FLEX_VALUE	300,895,742	5,894,755	215
DESCRIPTION	300,895,700	42	0
ATTRIBUTE_7	300,895,645	107	0
PARENT_FLEX_VALUE	56,800	0	0
CHILD_FLEX_VALUE_LOW	89,478,484	58,7999	0
CHILD_FLEX_VALUE_HIGH	12,874,595	450,022	0

Table 14.2 teaches us that a large proportion of values is missing and the source system does not support data consistency.

Data profiling comes in two flavors: business or contextual data profiling and technical or out of context profiling. The first checks the assumptions from the business community: that is, "Every employee has a manager," or, "Every active customer has received at least one invoice in the last three years," and so on. The technical profiling checks the feasibility for ETL and answers all the necessary questions to scope the complexity and workload of the ETL.

Before you start the business profiling, you should ask yourself (and your customer) about her expectations about the quality of this job. The higher the quality requirement, the more thorough work is needed and the larger the sample size is required, up to profiling large tables entirely. Don't underestimate the time and resources needed for this job. The sample may be random using SQL functionality to pick every nth record for profiling or it may be a stratified sample using an important decision variable to spread the sampling in a meaningful way. Common strata are "Product," "Customer," "Employee," and "Time."

Unless you are asked to estimate the end-to-end project workload you needn't be involved in the technical data-profiling exercise. Nevertheless, don't take on this job without the involvement of the technician(s) who will actually do the ETL design and build the data warehouse. Ignore this rule and you may find yourself in big trouble as soon as the builders come in.

Source-to-Target Mapping

Some practitioners also exclude this exercise from the business analyst's responsibilities and here I tend to agree. Nevertheless, one should be aware of this exercise and consult the results as this may prove to be a reality check for the assumptions made during the analysis. Make sure you and the ETL designer have an exchange of ideas and information about this stage. In Table 14.3 the transformation column at least will certainly be of interest to the analyst.

Metadata Management for Business Analysts

I couldn't agree more with Kimball (2004) who says the following about metadata tools in his book, *The Data Warehouse ETL Toolkit*:

> Metadata is an interesting topic because every tool space in the data warehouse arena including business intelligence (BI) tools, ETL tools, databases, and dedicated repositories claims to have a metadata solution, and many books are available to advise you on the best metadata strategies. Yet, after years of implementing and reviewing data warehouses, we've yet to encounter a true end-to-end metadata solution. Instead, most data warehouses have manually maintained pieces of metadata that separately exist across their components.

Kimball's description of metadata structures is complete and serves a basis for any business analyst who wants to get deeper into the subject. Let me pick out the metadata questions about metadata the business analyst should ask before, during, and after the project.

Before the Project

These questions are mainly about the front room metadata that describe the source data from a business point of view as well as the dimensions and their attributes and the measures in the fact tables. These are to be found in the report requirements or in the business requirements. In complex environments, an application landscape can provide a high-level lineage view on crucial data such as customers and employees. For example, an organization may have different input possibilities like a checkout and a call center, and external customer data sources that need to be reconciled in a customer master data repository.

In this phase, a first estimate of data volumes may be useful to determine the technical scope of the project. In the case of heavy security demands (e.g., HRM analytics or BI for legal or policing purposes) the metadata should also include which profiles (or even persons) have access rights to

TABLE 14.3

Example of a Mapping Table

Target Table	Target Column	Source Table	Source Column	Transformation Rule
GL ACCOUNT	GL ACCOUNT NUMBER	FND_FLEX_VALUES	FLEX_VALUE	
GL ACCOUNT	DESCRIPTION_UK	FND_FLEX_VALUES_TL	DESCRIPTION	
GL ACCOUNT	DESCRIPTION_GE	FND_FLEX_VALUES	ATTRIBUTE_7	If empty THEN take same as DESCRIPTION_UK
GL ACCOUNT CHILDREN	GL_PARENT_ ACCOUNT_NUMBER	FND_FLEX_VALUE_ NORM_HIERARCHY	PARENT_FLEX_ VALUE	
GL ACCOUNT CHILDREN	GL_CHILD_ACCOUNT_ NUMBER_MIN	FND_FLEX_VALUE_ NORM_HIERARCHY	CHILD_FLEX_ VALUE_LOW	
GL ACCOUNT CHILDREN	GL_CHILD_ACCOUNT_ NUMBER_MAX	FND_FLEX_VALUE_ NORM_HIERARCHY	CHILD_FLEX_ VALUE_HIGH	Replace 'Z' by '9' e.g., 7070ZZZZ becomes 70709999

which data. Finally, a conceptual or logical data model of the data warehouse or the data mart is both the result and the documentation of the business analysis process. This should provide enough input for the project definition and the project charter.

During the Project

As the business analyst delves deeper into the analysis levels and the metadata are well documented from a business context perspective, the source metadata are described in technical terms: for example, datatypes, record lengths, source to target lineage, results from data profiling, default values, null values, and missing data handling, mandatory flags, slowly changing dimension attribute handling, data quality policies and strategies, business rules on the source systems, and so on. During the project, the physical data model serves as a guide and is also used for technical documentation purposes.

After the Project

I advise the business analyst to play more of a documentalist role as this third layer of metadata is mostly about the ETL process, a further refining of data lineage and a description of the business translations of technical row and column headers. This is the realm of the developers.

A FRAMEWORK FOR DATA MANAGEMENT

The following recommendations are not the gospel. Whatever classification and representation framework you choose, as long as they are consistent, practical, and first and foremost manageable, you are avoiding the two major pitfalls of data management: getting bogged down in unworkable procedures on the one hand or creating data chaos leading to new stovepipes of "Never-mind-I'll-do-it-myself" solutions. I combine the elegance of the Dublin Core's metadata catalog with the complexity-reducing Zachman framework and deliver this blend with the usability of the structured writing approach. Before you get too mixed up by all this, let us describe the three building blocks.

> 4: Description Set Profile Interoperability
> • Shared formal vocabularies and constraints in record
> 3: Description Set syntactic interoperability
> • Shared formal vocabularies in exchangeable records
> 2: Formal semantic interoperability
> • Shared formal vocabularies based on formal semantics
> 1: Shared term definitions
> • Shared formal vocabularies denied in natural language

FIGURE 14.1
The Dublin Core and other comparable ontologies.

Dublin Core

This open source glossary (http://dublincore.org/) provides the BI architect with a set of metadata constructs to promote interoperability between internal and external systems but also between people and systems and this is where our interest lies: to translate natural language into interoperable information objects. Figure 14.1 poses a compelling question about priorities to the Business Intelligence community: is master data management (MDM) about implementing an MDM tool or developing an MDM language before there is any business case for a tool?

The Dublin Core comes in two flavors: Simple and Qualified. The Simple Dublin Core Metadata Element Set has (on the day of publication) 22 data elements that can be used for large documents as well as for entities and attributes. For BI purposes we subtract two elements from this set as they are irrelevant for BI.

In the next schema, Table 14.4, the original Dublin Core definitions are, where necessary, adapted for BI purposes. To keep the link with the original some constituents including "resource" (data object) and "collection" (database) are kept in their original form. As the Dublin Core is a living organism we advise to check regularly for updates and changes on their website. The Dublin Core can be easily made user friendly by translating the elements to the classical search entries such as WHO–WHAT–WHERE–WHEN–HOW, as shown in Table 14.5.

So there you have it: the link with an architectural framework like the Zachman Framework can be made. And what's more if you make good use of clear encoding schemes, both machine and human readers will be able to interpret the metadata.

TABLE 14.4

Dublin Core Elements

Simple Dublin Core Element	Description
Title	The name given to the object, for example, DIM_CALENDAR.
Creator	The responsible(s) for the content of the resource: Is Source Owner = "John Doe".
Subject	Keywords or key phrases to express the topic of the resource.
Description	The content of the resource: abstract, free text.
Contributor	Should always be used when the primary responsible is unknown. The entity can make contributions to the resource.
Date	An entity with many subtypes: StartDate, EndDate, ValidToDate, ValidFromDate.
Type	The genre of the resource based on BI categories: measure, dimension.
Format	The digital manifestation of the resource. Format = TABLE.
Identifier	Unambiguous reference to the resource: URI, URL, DOI or file path.
Source	A reference to the source represented by a string: Is Source Of datamarttablename.
Language	The language of the content of the resource.
Relation	A reference to a related resource represented by a string: Is Source Of sourceApplication.tablename.
Coverage	The extent or the scope of the resource: space, time.
Rights	Narrowed to access rights as the original IPR concept from DC is irrelevant for BI. In the shape of: dc.creator HasRights; dc.contributor HasRights.
Publisher	The entity responsible for making the resource available. It can be the source owner or the DBA.
Audience	A class of entity for whom the resource is intended or useful.
Accrual Method	The method by which items are added to a source or target application, using controlled vocabularies, for example, Target Accrual Method = SCD Type1.
Accrual Periodicity	The frequency with which items are added to a collection.
Accrual Policy	The policy governing the addition of items to a collection using controlled vocabularies, for example, Accrual Policy = "D + 1".

TABLE 14.5

Search Entries in the Dublin Core

Search Entry	DC Element
WHO	dc.creator, dc.contributor, dc.publisher
WHAT	dc.title, dc.title.alternative, dc.description, dc.subject
WHERE	dc.coverage, dc.coverage.spatial, dc.date
WHEN	dc.coverage.temporal, dc.date
HOW	dc.type, dc.format

Zachman Framework

As the BI discipline evolved from a purely technical exercise to a full-blown companywide business and information and communication techonology (ICT) process with a methodology and quality standards, it became harder and harder to define interfaces between the parties involved. Séan Kelly was the first practitioner who in his seminars in the early 1990s pointed to the Zachman Framework as a cupboard with all the necessary drawers and compartments on which to map the major BI processes.

Figure 14.2 illustrates my interpretation of the Zachman Framework for 13 major processes that lead to the delivery of a data warehouse or a data mart. As far as I am concerned, the more you want a BI project to be successful, the better your homework on the scope, business, and system level has to be. John A. Zachman's (1997) framework is of great help in aligning C-level management with the IT architecture. It is also a helpful tool for improving IT governance processes. The framework can be used as a domain ontology that helps us define the BI domain and the BI enterprise architecture by mapping the construction phases of a data warehouse on the related components.

In Figure 14.2, the numbers refer to the following phases:

1. Commitment to proceed (project charter approved)
2. Draft conceptual data model (first business analysis iteration completed)
3. Decisions on granularity, data mart bus (second business analysis iteration completed)
4. Assessment of the technology environment
5. Prepare the technology environment

	What	How	Where	Who	When	Why	
SCOPE	1		1		1		STRATEGISTS
BUSINESS	2						EXECUTIVE LEADERS
SYSTEM	2,3,4,6	3,4	3,4	13		2,3,4,6	ARCHITECTS
TECHNOLOGY	5,7,8,9	5,7,8,9	5,7,8,9	13			ENGINEERS
COMPONENTS	5,10	5.10	5.10	13			TECHNICIANS
OPERATIONS	11,12	11,12	11,12	13		13	WORKERS
	Business Intelligence	Process	Network	Organization	Timing	Motivation	

FIGURE 14.2
Zachman Framework and the BI process.

6. In-depth subject area analysis and logical data model (third business analysis iteration completed)
7. In-depth source analysis: source-to-target mapping
8. Physical data modeling and data warehouse design complete
9. Specifications for build complete
10. Building the data warehouse, end to end
11. Populating the data warehouse: initial load
12. Populating the data warehouse: incremental load(s)
13. Transfer the data warehouse to monitoring, maintenance, and minor updates, documentation complete.

Needless to say the notions "data warehouse" and "data mart" are interchangeable.

Structured Writing

An accessible methodology for exchanging knowledge is any good methodology for structured writing. With Darwin information typing architecture (DITA) or information mapping (IMAP), a structured exchange of knowledge becomes feasible through the use of strict information typing, applying some simple guiding principles for copywriting and information presentation. The IMAP methodology was developed by Robert E. Horn,* and the DITA methodology stems from IBM's Standard Generalized Markup Language (SGML).

Structured Writing and Data Management

If the Dublin Core bridges the gap between machine and human interaction with metadata and the Zachman Framework neatly classifies all metadata from high-level business knowledge elements via process metadata to the lowest level attribute descriptions, then a structured writing method helps us to repackage this for help files, user manuals, and conceptual descriptions of the Business Intelligence system. Information mapping uses seven information types, which are:

- Fact
- Procedure
- Process

---

* For more on Information Mapping go to www.infomap.com

- Structure
- Classification
- Principle
- Concept

DITA has a different approach using:

- Concept information types
- Task information types
- Reference information types

The DITA markup language saves time and effort for multilingual documentation that needs regular updating.

How the Three Components Interact

Very simple: you have your intrinsic encoding and description of master data with the Dublin Core approach and a structured engineering framework that links the master data to strategic and executive management, to information architecture and the application landscape with the Zachman approach. Last but not least you can document and communicate with all stakeholders in the organization via the documentation method in a structured and modular way.

Whereas the Dublin Core and the Zachman Framework offer clarity and direct a multidisciplinary BI team to the issues at hand for each specialist, the structured writing method helps us better communicate to and with the business users. It is an illusion to think that data management can be left to applications and application engineers. Only via adequate communication of relevant business information extracted from the master data development and maintenance process can we keep the business users on board. And remember, we have very diverse interactions with data entry coworkers, via call center agents, sales reps, product, sales, marketing, finance, and other managers to external data sources who will all exert influence on the use and recording of data. Let us make sure they understand the structure, the definitions, the classifications, the processes, and the procedures of the master data.

Figure 14.3 shows an example of a framework. On the left side are the repositories serving as the only version of the truth and keepers of the core attributes, which values need to be adhered to and used throughout

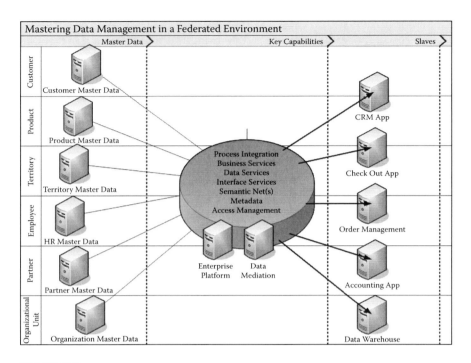

FIGURE 14.3
Example of a master data management architecture.

the organization. On the right side are the online transaction processing (OLTP) applications, which add domain specific attributes to the core. In fact, mastering the core attributes of key dimensions is the best support you can give to Ralph Kimball's conformed dimension approach to data warehousing. At the center, seven core processes are represented by two application platforms:

Process Integration: The hub provides the exchange platform for process integration as the umbrella over different applications supporting specific business processes.

Business Services: This helps the user to make an abstraction from the application and approach IT as a provider of business services supporting the value chain. If we want all parties in the value chain to be aligned with shared concepts such as master data, this aspect cannot be underestimated. The IT components support the goals of the business much more effectively as the business gets a better

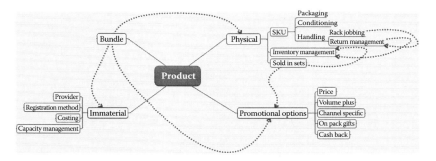

FIGURE 14.4
A simple example of a product ontology using a mind mapping tool to illustrate the relationships between aspects of "Product."

understanding of the opportunities business services offer and the technology people get a clearer view of how the business demand impacts future IT developments.

Data Services: Monitoring new data sources, cleansing input data, and other data governance tasks belong to the hub's task list.

Interface Services: It serves as a reference aid, pointing to the appropriate sources for the correct version of the truth.

Semantic Net(s): This is the cherry on top of plain vanilla data management. It links data elements into concepts and adds meaning and structure to the corporate knowledge elements.

Metadata: Both technical and business metadata need to be available and up to date, to provide business intelligence users with support information to get a complete view on the data lineage.

Access Management: Some data, for example, employee or partner data, segments of customer data, and the like may need secure access in a consistent cross-application security framework.

Figure 14.4 shows a product ontology example and there is more about the master data definitions in the section, "Generic Business Object Definitions" in Chapter 16.

15

Mastering Data Quality

This section focuses only on your tasks as a business analyst being confronted with data quality as defined in terms of "fit for BI purposes." For a comprehensive view on this important subject we refer to authors, including Larry English (1999), Thomas Redman (2001), and others. Your task is to interview two major players in data quality management of the organization: the owner and the data steward.

The owner may be the buyer of external data, the creator of company-owned data, the sponsor, or the user; whoever the organization has decided can play this role, make sure you get in touch with this person or persons. The owner is responsible for the definitions and decides who has access or who may grant access to data. The larger the organization, the more you will have to make sure they are all on the same page with regard to policies and responsibilities and there are no territorial battles between them. The data stewards manage data sets with a special focus on integrity, privacy, and data quality.

WHICH QUALITY?

The data quality issue is an orphan in many Business Intelligence (BI) projects. It is often addressed when the embarrassing results of the first reports have come to the attention of the business sponsor. One of the reasons is the lack of understanding what data quality for Business Intelligence implies. From a transaction point of view, 99% of the data may be correct but from an analyst's point of view these same data may be useless. So, how do we address the issue before the data warehouse is built and before the business sponsor becomes annoyed?

When we are talking data quality, what are we really talking about? Is it product quality? Is it user-defined quality? Production-oriented data quality? Value-based quality or even transcendental quality? The quality perspective for data quality is Joseph Juran's (2010) "fitness-for-use" approach. Data quality for BI purposes is defined and gauged with reference to fitness for purpose as defined by the analytical use of the data and complying with three levels of data quality, as defined by:

[Level 1] database administrators
[Level 2] data warehouse architects
[Level 3] business intelligence analysts

On level 1, data quality is narrowed down to data integrity or the degree to which the attributes of an instance describe the instance accurately and whether the attributes are valid, that is, comply with defined ranges or definitions managed by the business users. This definition remains very close to the transaction view.

On level 2, data quality is expressed as the percentage completeness and correctness of the analytical perspectives. In other words, to what degree is each dimension, each fact table, complete enough to produce significant information for analytical purposes? Issues such as sparsity and spreads in the data values are harder to tackle. Timeliness and consistency need to be controlled and managed on the data warehouse level.

On level 3, data quality is the measure in which the available data are capable of adequately answering the business questions. Some use the criterion of accessibility with regard to the usability and clarity of the data. Although this seems a somewhat vague definition, it is most relevant to anyone with some analytical mileage on his odometer. I remember a vast data-mining project in a mail-order company producing the following astonishing result: 99.9% of all dresses sold were bought by women!

Although there is no 100% data quality possible on this planet and although we defined the fit-for-purpose quality approach as the leading criterion, this does not dismiss us from striving toward the optimum solution, namely the breakeven point between data quality prevention costs and the cost of poor data quality.

ROI APPROACH TO DATA QUALITY

Data quality does not come cheap. Assuring integrity and providing validation costs time, uses resources, requires skills, everyday attention and discipline, and creates extra overhead for IT systems, people, and procedures. So we'd better make a good business case for data quality in the BI project. We can do this by referring to literature such as Larry English (1999), who makes an alarming statement on page 12: ". . . costs of non-quality data, including irrecoverable costs, rework of products and services, workarounds and lost and missed revenue may be as high as 10 to 25 percent of revenue or total budget of an organisation." Although it is very hard to quantify something that does not happen due to bad data, I fundamentally agree with Larry English on the urgency and the importance of good data quality management.

But better than referring to literature is the creation of a personal experience of the benefits of good data to your business sponsor. Only then can you launch a wakeup call in the organization by crossing the boundaries of the analytical and transactional ecosystems. This is quintessential during this wakeup call. What does a salesperson care about data quality as long as he can register a sales order? Maybe he will create a "new" customer if it is beneficial to his bonus. What does a customer service agent care about a customer's address change as long as she has the customer's ID and she can close the support ticket as fast as possible? There are examples enough of poor data quality being induced by processes that do not take the final use and value of data for BI into account.

If you want to play your role as business analyst in this tug of war between the world of transactions and your world, you have to make not one, but two business cases: one for the source owners to make them aware of the cost of poor data quality and one for the data warehouse users to make them aware of the opportunities of good data quality. I hope the following examples will give you some inspiration because every data quality process management case may be similar in its use of best practices but the context is always unique.

Data Quality for Source Systems

Let me give you three possible business cases which may all occur at the same time in the organization: a marketing, finance, and operations case.

Marketing Aspects

Any experience with direct mail? It is a costly but intense way of communicating with your customers and prospective customers. So, you don't want to send:

a) Two or more of the same mailing pieces to the same addressee.
b) Send the wrong offer to the right person.
c) Send the right offer to the wrong person.
d) Any combination of the above.

Ever worked in call center? This is an even more costly and more intense way of communicating with your market. Data quality is even more imperative there as you don't want to:

a) Waste valuable time looking up who the caller exactly is (even the best computer telephone integration [CTI] system won't give you too many clues in a business-to-business market).
b) Waste valuable time correcting the spelling of the client's name, gender, age, or other characteristics.
c) Waste even more valuable time handling service calls from customers who were wrongly billed (not to count those whose bill was lower than it should be and who don't call).

The examples above are operational aspects that are easy to measure and do the math with to produce the cost of errors and consequently a budget for prevention and quality management. To produce a figure for the BI consequences is a lot harder. What is the cost of a wrong decision as it was based on low-quality data? What is the cost of employees and managers losing faith in their company as they are confronted with unreliable information?

Finance Aspects

Errors in billing do not only cause extra work for the customer service people; they may end with loss of revenue and errors in the bookings, resulting in inappropriate decision making about cost and revenue allocation. If the company is listed on the stock market this could even lead to damages to its reputation and loss of market value.

Operational Aspects

How are your inventory writeoffs? I hope they are better than a retail client who discovered he had a stock of carnival wigs worth $95,000 but his inventory list didn't mention its existence. In the inventory system, the carnival wigs had a special prefix to indicate this was a product with a short shelf life. A new clerk merged the inventory code with the normal assortment of wigs causing a lower inventory turnover for the entire assortment. Only a visual control by management brought about the truth.

Watch out for conversion errors like these or imperial to metric and vice versa, package-type conversions like 40-ft bulk container to big bags, and watch out for fraudulent inventory writeoffs to scrap or past the sell-by date, to name but a few.

Data Quality for Data Warehouse Systems

In my experience as a business analyst, I have come across three interesting business cases, but I am aware there may be more and better ones.

Customer Segmentation

Customer segmentation from a marketing point of view can be done in many ways (geographic, demographic, psychographic, etc.) but one aspect will always play a role: the financial perspective. The relevance of any customer segmentation method can only be validated by examining its correlation with revenue, contribution margin, or variable costs. So if your data warehouse does not allocate these figures correctly to the right client, your segmentation will go out on a limb. Revenue allocation to customers is a BI-related discipline that combines customer relationship management (CRM) data, order data, contract data, sales engagement data, financial data, and management judgment to produce the correct figures. Sounds like the integration of multiple sources into a data warehouse or data mart, right? If the quality of one or more of these sources is substandard, your segmentation will be flawed and your account managers or resellers will cause trouble.

Customer Credit Analysis

Bad credit strategies can chase your customers to the competition before assigning a credit rating, during the delivery of the goods and invoice, and after, when expecting payment or after payment processing.

> Before: Credit rating is based on transaction data such as order and payment behavior, customer service data, and other sources including external credit rating data from companies like Dun & Bradstreet worldwide, CIBIL in India, SCHUFA in Germany, and Graydon in the Benelux. It wouldn't be the first time a person with a common name like Smith in the Anglo-Saxon world is denied credit because the system has recorded a large number of Mr. Smiths with a bad credit rating.
>
> During: When there are false negatives as described above, there will also be false positives. The mail-order company I worked for in the 1980s identified a number of mail fraud addresses that consistently ordered expensive products via different names and never paid the bill. The cost for this "empiric mail fraud detection system" could have been lower if we would have matched our data with the competition's data. Of course, European privacy laws forbid this so every mail-order company's credit analyst had to find this out for himself.
>
> After: Badly targeted dunning actions may also annoy customers and chase them to the competition.

Fraud Prevention and Detection

Fraud detection is almost always done using more or less sophisticated algorithms ranging from regression analysis via k-nearest neighbor and projection pursuit regression to more exotic constructs such as multivariate adaptive regression splines (MARS), generalized additive model (GAM), and genetic algorithms. What they all have in common from a BI point of view is the search for the optimum between robustness and sensitivity. This can only be achieved if the data quality reaches the highest levels of accuracy, timeliness, completeness, and every data item is well defined and understood by all parties concerned. A simple attribute like "gender" that does not match with the title of the contact can wreak havoc in a less sophisticated analysis setup or produce error files to be checked manually by the data owner.

Building the Business Case

What you need to calculate the upper limits of data quality management budgets is not a lot: the prevention-appraisal-failure (PAF) model from Lesser, Feigenbaum, and Juran (1951/2010), which postulated the optimum below 100% error-free products. See Figures 15.1 and 15.2. Later the PAF model pushed the envelope to 100% quality (Schiffauerova and Thomson, 2006), which is totally understandable if you consider the cost of a lost customer due to a defective product can be enormous. When applied to data quality, the tradeoff between the prevention and appraisal costs on one side and the failure costs need a nuanced and balanced approach.

In some cases 100% quality may be necessary but unattainable, in others it may be possible but not necessary and I leave the other two combinations to the reader. Data quality may have analogies with product quality but the processes leading to data capturing are quite different from an industrial manufacturing process.

In a production environment the raw materials are specified so the supplier knows exactly what to deliver. With data, the supplier may have diverging

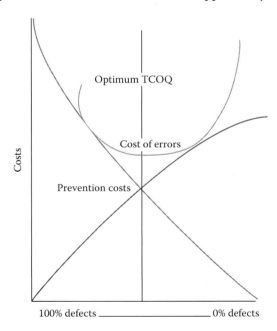

FIGURE 15.1
The classical PAF model where the total cost of quality (TCOQ) may yield substandard products.

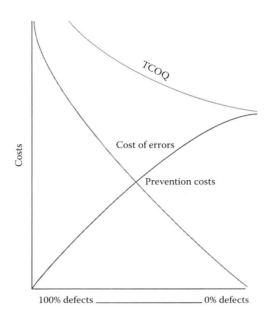

FIGURE 15.2
The modern version of the PAF model where no quality concessions are allowed.

intentions: a sales rep who wants to claim his commission or a customer who wants to collect more than once on a promotional offer, for example. The production process is a chain of well-described conversions from raw materials to finished goods. The data production chain can bear resemblance to this process in very controlled environments such as accounting (for VAT numbers and bill to addresses) or inventory management (for product codes and descriptions), but in CRM this process sometimes looks more like musical chairs: data are added and changed to prospective customers until someone, or some system, collects an order and the data are frozen.

Typical short-term quick wins are: aligning definitions, data domains, and cleaning records in the source systems. Long-term process improvement examples are adaptations to data ownership and business processes and adaptations to the source systems capturing the data. See Figure 15.3. Build your business case using the modern PAF model:

- The data quality prevention and appraisal costs:
  - Implementing policies and procedures that need time and training
  - Performing audits
  - Statistical process control

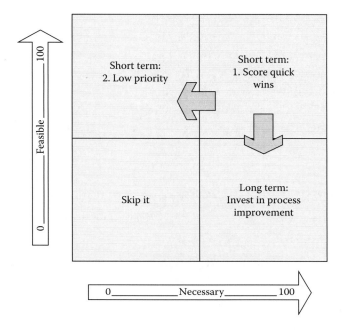

FIGURE 15.3
Data quality strategies should be included in the business analysis.

- The cost of substandard data quality:
  - Rework
  - Delays
  - Wrong decisions
  - Handling customer complaints
- Loss of customers is an opportunity cost to be derived from lifetime value analysis at best or an estimated guess at worst.

Even if some costs such as loss of customers and the cost of wrong decisions are hard to quantify you will be amazed how quickly you can break even between the prevention and appraisal costs and the gain in efficiency.

Data Quality Checklist

I know; I promised not to use too many checklists, but this is an unavoidable one if you are tackling the data quality issue. Rather than waiting for accidents to happen, this checklist will make all parties concerned aware of the data quality issue. "All parties" means: the business process owners (and beware if there are none in your client's organization), the database administrators (DBAs), data entry employees, and everyone playing a role in the BI project: extract, transform, load (ETL) designers, data warehouse DBAs, report designers, power users, report consumers, analysts, and a special profile I call the subject owners. They can be the business process owners or functional management, but make sure you identify them from the beginning of the project. The checklist looks at the past, present, and future of data quality drivers.

History Review of the Data Sources

Q.1: When was the last system conversion or migration to a new source system?

Q.2: When were there minor or major changes in the source system?

Q.3: Were new user profiles, purposes, or data entry methods added to the source system?

Q.4: Did the context in which the system was used change over time?

Comment:: The company may have been acquired or merged with another company, taking over their system or imposing the company's system on the other organization. It may have internationalized its business model, having to adapt to local data aspects, such as legislation, mail formats, and the like.

Q.5: Can you track the age of data elements?

Comment: Not all systems used timestamps or records such as insert_date or update_date to track changes of data elements. Some attributes lose all value over time, like national statistic qualifications or industry sector indicators.

Q.6: How are data elements updated or enriched?

Present Situation Review

Q.1: Can you give me an overview of the data input validation systems, processes, and procedures?

Q.2: What are the guiding principles in data quality assurance?

Q.3: What are the levels of slack allowed in customer data capturing?

Q.4: Do you use a root account model in your customer identification approach?

Q.5: What business rules apply to the data in this system?

Comment: Only consider the high-level business rules, for example:

- One customer can be served by many account managers.
- If a customer buys more than €300,000 per annum, a group account manager will supervise all sales activities hands-on.

Q.6: Is there a management policy in place for data quality and is every party concerned aware of this policy?

Q.7: What percentage of the source data is accurate? How do you check this key performance indicator (KPI)?

Q.8: What is the relationship with other systems on issues such as consistency, business rules, completeness, time-based integrity, and referential integrity?

Future Outlook

Q.1: Are any (new) KPIs on data quality defined by management?

Q.2: If so, are there any plans in place to attain these KPIs?

Q.3: What data quality roles and responsibilities are foreseen for the BI system?

Comment: Think of profiles such as legacy owners, data warehouse DBAs, business analysts, and the like.

Q.4: Do you have a return on investment (ROI) model or a budget for data quality in the data warehouse?

16

Business Analyst's Toolbox

OVERVIEW

This section integrates all previous topics into the major deliverables a business analyst has to produce: from the initiation phase until the transfer of the system to the organization. The answers to the questions and business analysis issues mentioned in these chapters will have to be ground, blended, and mixed with your vision of the strategic possibilities of information management and the information management aspects of the strategy process that unfolds itself before you through observation, interviews, reading reports, and checking source systems and their users to deliver the milestone document that will give direction to and provide the momentum for the project startup: the project charter.

The deliverables such as the business case and the requirements will be rewritten, developed, and fine-tuned throughout the entire project life cycle. But before we get there, some other deliverables will be produced. Especially in large organizations, this step-by-step approach will pay off to meet your biggest challenge: creating acceptance for change and removing fear of the unknown.

The toolbox's contents:

- Project direction document template
- Interview summary template
- Business analysis deliverables template
- Business case document template
- Project charter template
- Best practice sharing template
- Generic interview guide
- Generic business object definitions

PROJECT DIRECTION DOCUMENT TEMPLATE

Introduction

The main purpose of a Business Intelligence (BI) project direction document is to make an inventory "as is" and "to be" of the strategy process with regard to initiating a BI project. In other words, C-level management has expressed the idea that a BI solution might be the answer to current problems or future opportunities. Your job as an analyst is to assess the viability of this idea via a quick scan resulting in this project direction document. The interviews address high-level issues including:

- What is the level of confidence about the causal relationships between the major business processes of the organization such as marketing, sales, production, purchasing, and external actors such as trends, competitors, and your organization's referee on performance: the customer?
- Are the organization's goals shared by all levels?
- How is the reporting process today?
- What are the advantages and disadvantages of this process?
- What crucial information is missing?
- What decisions could improve on quality with this information?

We refer to all Business Intelligence issues in this book in case your interviewee wants to take more time to come up with more detail. But trust me, the kind of people you're interviewing will have a tight schedule to answer your questions and to read your project direction document. The document needn't reach literature status but it should contain brief and concise answer to the following topics:

- What is the background of this idea?
- How would we define the project?
- What could the project organization structure look like?
- How will we communicate the project in the organization?
- What is the initial business case for the project?
- What tolerances can we allow for time, budget, and quality?
- How will we control the project's progression?
- How will we manage the project's quality?
- What is the interdependency with other planned or ongoing projects?

- What are the major project risks?
- What do we conclude:
  - NO GO?
  - Examine it further?
- GO: probe deeper and draw up the project charter to take the decision to the next level?

Let us look a little bit more at the project management aspects as this may be beyond the business analyst's scope; she will provide input for the project manager and it wouldn't be the first BI business analyst operating as a de facto project manager because the content and the context of a BI project demand more than a pure-play project manager who has no or little BI knowledge.

DOCUMENT'S CONTENTS

The sections can be developed sequentially, which assumes reiteration of the interviews with the client's information sources.

Project Background

Use all available ammunition: quotes from C-level management, the organization's mission statement, quotes from managers, clients, and suppliers that provide contextual information for the BI project.

Project Context

In this section a detailed analysis of the strategy process is necessary as this will actually give direction throughout the project's life cycle and beyond. This section provides more detail than the previous one. Here you will assess the capability maturity model (CMM) level of BI, the major project risks, and the interdependency with other projects.

Business Case

We refer to the special section on this topic. Suffice it to say that at this stage the business case is a sketch, which will become a detailed drawing during the project as more information is made available and more facts and figures are discovered.

Project Definition

This section addresses the objectives in broad terms of the BI project, the project scope, and the deliverables. It also describes what the project is not and it clearly states the assumptions on which the project definition is based.

Project Organization Structure

Describe the main roles: who is on the steering committee or the project team and who are the single points of contact to obtain initial information for this document, and in the case of a GO for the development of a project charter, who will be contacted for further information.

Project Approach

This is a high-level account of resources, time, money, and quality needed to reach the initial objectives. It will also address the contents and the means of communicating the project in the organization as a part of change management any project requires. A planning of the major phases and the assumptions on which this planning is based completes the approach. Add optionally the methodologies used for the development.

INTERVIEW SUMMARY TEMPLATE

The primary objective of the interview summary is a quality check to assess if the business analyst has understood all the issues, definitions, relationships, wishes, and constraints the interviewee has communicated during the interview. It may also serve as a documentation item for newcomers in the organization who wonder why the Business Intelligence system is built the way it is. This template will help you to structure the information in such a way that the transition to the analysis is easily made.

Background Information

Use this section to describe why this project is initiated and why the interview took place with the interviewee. Because the interviewee is either a user, source owner, or some other form of stakeholder, you need to make this very clear from the outset of the project.

Roles and Responsibilities

Describe the role of the interviewee in the BI project and in the company. In case you are not certain of the interviewee's role, use the conditional tense. Table 16.1 provides you with a checklist of BI relevant roles and responsibilities.

Business Processes

In this section you describe the major business processes discussed during the interview.

Interaction with or Ownership of Business Processes

Some organizations use the concept of BPOs (business process owners) who manage a cross-functional process to deliver value for an internal or external customer. In that case, it is relatively easy to chart the process and the data that are produced and used along the way. If there are no BPOs

TABLE 16.1

Checklist of BI-Relevant Roles and Responsibilities.

Role in the Business Intelligence project	Principal responsibilities
Sponsor	Back the project that supports the sponsor's initiative
Steering committee	Translates the strategic initiative into project goals and govern the project.
Project Manager	Manages time, resources and money to deliver the product within budget, time and quality constraints. The project manager will produce the boundaries within which the analysis will take place.
Domain expert	Provides knowledge about the business processes involved in the analysis.
Source expert	Provides knowledge about the data sources
Application expert	Provides knowledge about how, when, why etc... the data are captured.
Risk manager	Provides the risk perspective on data, processes, applications,...

in the company, it will be your task to document the important processes (sales, procurement, inventory management, etc.) and the interaction of the interviewee with parts or the whole of the process.

Interview Summary

The easiest way to structure the interview summary is in a Q&A form to produce unambiguous and verifiable sentences for the interviewee. I would even suggest using quotes for aspects of the interview that matter greatly or that will have an impact throughout the data warehouse development phase, for example, "I want the reports before the opening of the stock market, every morning of the working week."

Open Issues—Questions

Anything that needs to be solved, decided, or avoided to push the BI project farther and where the interviewee can help.

Next Steps

Tell the interviewee what is going to happen after the interview, for example, "See the person you recommended me," or "Check the source data for the existence of x, y, or z."

BUSINESS CASE DOCUMENT TEMPLATE

Introduction

Making a business case for Business Intelligence has for a long time been a no-brainer. In most cases, all you needed to do was prove that painstaking and costly problems to produce reliable reports would be history with a proper BI system. Lately, this is just not enough anymore. Your added value as a business analyst lies not in calculating the benefits from remedying a problem, but from presenting opportunities, preferably strategic opportunities, for the client organization and calculating their strategic value.

Nevertheless, you will still meet clients who are only interested in direct savings or revenue improvement so I address these issues in this chapter. Throughout your interview sessions, your focus has to be on the business case. It helps if you dispose of an arsenal of generic improvement results from previous BI projects. If you do, skip this chapter but if you don't, make sure these are always in the back of your mind when talking to the business. Although I have named it "Template" it is almost impossible to produce a form like a document template that can be filled out and be done with it. The business case is client- and situation-specific as the example in Chapter 6 demonstrates.

Efficiency Economics

Ad Hoc Reports

Check if the organization spends a lot of time on ad hoc reports and calculate these savings in terms of person-hours times hourly rate.

Asset Management

Optimizing the availability of assets and administering the right dose of maintenance at an acceptable risk of unexpected defects will increase the return on assets. This is harder to calculate; approximation via scenarios with a defendable percentage reduction in maintenance costs sheds light on this opportunity.

Absenteeism Reduction

The combination of tasks, competences, customers, supervisors, and managers can provide input for improved Human Resources Management (HRM) policies which in their turn can reduce the absenteeism.

Reduction in Coordination Costs

Organizations that improve their BI system can reduce the number of coordination meetings between the various departments and reduce the number of steps they have to go through to come up with the right figure.

Improved Negotiation Position

Asymmetric information in exchange of goods and services has been the topic of many doctoral dissertations: a buyer who can predict the selling price of his suppliers, an HRM manager who has a clear view on churn risks per job description, and so on. Opportunities galore!

Revenue Improvement

Pricing

Pricing is the Midas formula that can turn any business venture into gold or . . . mud. The business case for better pricing is not easy to calculate unless you dispose of marketing research data about your customers' price perception. Yet, the client does not need a detailed business case to see dollars or euros to acknowledge the value of a smarter pricing system to see its value. The summit of pricing analysis is the Bayesian payoff matrix in Table 16.2. The intention of this revenue improvement tool is to reduce the minuses by better cost calculation, better estimate of customer value and better capacity planning.

Qualification Improvement

A BI system can provide quick matching and reference information to help salespeople qualify better, faster, and more accurately.

Customer Valuation Improvement

By providing more than the complete (long-term) financial facts on customers and combining these with customer interaction data, external marketing data, and risk analysis data, the organization can improve the quality of its decision making. But the road is long and difficult; let there be no false expectations created.

TABLE 16.2

Better Pricing Strategies as a Business Case

Your Strategy\Customer Expectations	Anticipated Lower Price	Anticipated Correct Price	Anticipated Higher Price
Price is too low	Irrelevant	–/–	–/–
Price is too high	Irrelevant	–/–	–/–
Correct price	Irrelevant	+/+	–/–

Improvement in Order Cancellations

There are many reasons for canceled orders. On the sales and marketing side an overzealous order taker may be neglecting the credit analysis of new customers, on the operations level there may not be sufficient insight in the fulfillment capacity, resulting in optimistic delivery date promises, and in the financial department overly sensitive credit scoring may reject creditworthy customers. These are just the most commonly known examples of information deficiencies BI may help to overcome.

Improved Forecasting

As Yogi Berra stated so eloquently, "Prediction is hard, especially about the future." Organizations have a lot to gain by even the slightest decrease in the mean average percentage error (MAPE). Your job as an analyst is to chart the MAPE of past predictions, compared to the actual outcome and develop scenarios to reduce this MAPE with a payoff. In a trade organization with an inventory of 10% of its yearly turnover, an improvement in the MAPE of 5% can lead to a reduction of the inventory of 2%, in other words, 20% lower inventory carrying costs. More on this topic in Chapter 9.

STRATEGIC OPPORTUNITIES

Information Value for Your Customers

If your client can improve marketing efficiency and efficacy by providing better and timely information to her customers, she will be interested. When UPS and DHL invested large sums in a parcel-tracking system via the Internet, powered by a data warehouse so their customer could follow the parcel's trajectory, they could not calculate the system's value in advance. But the system proved to be a differentiator and the basis for premium pricing.

Faster Response to Changing Conditions

"Time-to-market" is an example illustrating the importance of swiftly responding to changing consumer preferences; especially in the fast-moving consumer goods market, the smallest product adaptations or enhancements can make the difference between success and failure.

Quality of Decisions

This may seem an esoteric concept to the reader, yet what gives you the greatest comfort: knowing that you have covered as many aspects, perspectives, and scenarios possible before taking an important strategic decision that will affect your results profoundly for the years to come, or a group consensus around a couple of best estimates based on experience and gut feeling?

BUSINESS ANALYSIS DELIVERABLES TEMPLATE

Introduction and Overview

This template suggests the major deliverables to be produced at the end of the business analysis process. It is based on Lingua Franca's project management and business analysis methodology "FlexIS," which is the result of 20 years of practical experience of scores of people on scores of projects. We have learned from pioneers like Bill Inmon, Ralph Kimball, Séan Kelly, Dan Linstedt, and many others.

The template can be used as a specifications document to provide the necessary input for a technical scope and quote in terms of person-days, quality level(s), throughput time, and organization of the project. This document is the ultimate goal of your work as a business analyst: to reduce the risks of misunderstandings, redundant work, and even complete failure of the BI project. This document provides the input for the BI project charter. A template for the project charter is later in this chapter. We hope you will use it as a guide for your own project and not as a tight corset that prevents you from making your own mind up about the subjects, their level of detail, and the formulation of the project scope and the deliverables. The business case describes an office supplies company that sells directly to large-volume customers and has a chain of retail outlets. The example in italics is developed throughout the template to provide the reader with a coherent roadmap.

Overview of the Deliverables

1. High-level situation analysis
2. Purpose of the BI project
3. Stakeholder matrix
4. Business requirements
5. Project management constraints
6. Scope of the product
7. Data requirements
8. Presentation methods
9. Security requirements
10. Other requirements
11. Project plan and task list
12. Documentation
13. Glossary

High-Level Situation Analysis

This deliverable is the result of your discussions with general and functional management, business process owners, business controllers, customers, suppliers, and other stakeholders. It contains the following paragraphs:

1. General assumptions
2. Environmental situation and perception of external drivers
3. Perception of internal drivers
4. The 4 Cs
5. Strategic goals
6. Functional goals
7. Translating the goals into critical success factors (CSF), key performance indicators (KPI), and measures

These paragraphs will provide the context and the input for not only the BI project but also for IT governance decisions. Therefore, the conclusion should address the decision-making structure and decision-making process that aligns IT with the business.

General Assumptions

The first paragraph documents the fundamental paradigms, values, and beliefs of C-level management. It tries to capture the culture in which the

BI project will thrive, survive, or perish. So for all those of you who think this is a "soft" aspect, think twice, as I have seen many BI projects deliver a 100% technical success combined with a 100% organizational adoption failure.

Environmental Situation and Perception of External Drivers

Most companies perform strengths, weaknesses, opportunities, and threats (SWOT) analyses, so you will probably find some useful elements in these exercises. Yet, some challenging may be necessary as most SWOT analyses are performed by marketing departments and a BI project may look farther than the market aspects.

Perception of Internal Drivers

Cost drivers are either known and will enhance the depth and level of sophistication of the BI project or—and that is the majority—they are the object of a BI project. We refer to Chapter 7 on ABC and BI . But other internal drivers need to be charted for the BI project:

HRM: The bonus system(s) for management and employees can affect the way of doing business. Lack or abundance of certain resources may also influence it.

R&D: The level of R&D effort and the technology adoption degree of the organization certainly affects the business.

The 4 Cs

What does the company already know about these 4 Cs and what does it need to know to survive or improve its way of conducting the business?

Customer knowledge
Cost knowledge
Competitive knowledge
Competencies

Strategic Goals

Make sure you get the most out of this section. Many organizations communicate very generic objectives and goals to the outside world (and some of them even do it to their internal audience!). This may be nice for a press release but it is just not enough for a thorough business analysis document.

We all know the worn out expressions such as, "We aim to be close to the customer and because of this customer intimacy, grow faster than the market growth rate: by 7% instead of 3% market growth rate."

A strategic goal, to my knowledge, is a goal that can only be reached by sticking to long-term commitments that have the potential to create a unique differentiator from the competition. If you use this definition you will be surprised to see how few organizations can formulate strategic goals. The next step is to obtain the priorities of the strategic goals by formulating all mutually exclusive combinations in your questioning. For example, if you have to choose between increasing market share and reducing variable costs per unit sold, what would be your priority? This allows the interviewee to clarify the strategy further. Let us consider a few possible answers to this question:

1. I would choose for a market share increase because I am sure the variable unit costs will drop by 10% with every increase of 1% market share. Now is the time to ask on what data these assumptions are made because you need to have very good BI stuff and external data at hand to come up with this conclusion. Or, is it an assumption of a zealous marketing manager?

2. I would choose reduction of variable cost per unit because there is no need for further differentiation of the product by adding expensive features to the product. Or market share can increase with or without these add-ons.

3. I don't know, or I am not really sure. If your interviewee is honest, this answer will provide input for the BI analysis and the scope of the project.

Translating the Goals into CSF, KPI, and Measures

Management has to prioritize the strategic goals and identify each goal's success factor. This in turn can lead to an information requirement for the BI system. Critical success factors always include an active verb in their expressions. The CSFs describes the internal or external influence factors used in scenarios for business plans under high uncertainty conditions. If the interviewee has an opinion on how these CSF influence each other you will get valuable information on causal relationships that may affect your BI analysis and the approach to the data model and source analysis.

A strategic CSF could be: to develop a new business potential of €10 million, the information requirement would be the BI system should provide data on business potentials per product group. A KPI that quantifies this requirement could be: build a pipeline of 150 prospects with a value of minimum €65,000 per prospect.

There are, of course also CSF that are not as easy to translate into key performance indicators let alone influence them, such as the market growth for high bandwidth connections should cross the five million households mark before we can launch our gaming on demand initiative. If these figures are not provided by an external source your KPI will remain an academic issue.

Functional or Business Process Goals

These are derived from the overall strategic goals to render these general and long-term goals operational. Although most organizations use the concept of critical success factor to define the elements necessary for it to achieve its mission and key performance indicators to quantify strategic goals and measure the strategic performance of the organization and its parts, many organizations still group these CSFs and KPIs on an intermediate level and refine them further to build functional scorecards for HRM, marketing, and the like. For example, marketing needs to take stock of the customer potential for three new products. Or operations needs to reduce the cost of inventory by refining the forecasting methods.

A functional KPI example would be: operations has to deliver 95% of all parcels within the same day; the information requirement would be straightforward: measure the throughput time of each parcel between leaving the warehouse and the addressee's signature on the driver's PDA. Nevertheless, the lowest "grain" for a high-level analysis should be the corporate CSF and KPI. In a later phase, the functional or process scorecards may be included.

IT Governance Structure

In their book *IT Governance, How Top Performers Manage IT Decision Rights for Superior Results*, Peter Weill and Jeanne Ross (2004) examined the structure and the processes of aligning IT and business and making the key decisions in the right forum. The authors not only described IT governance; they also formulated best practices based on research of over 300 organizations.

The descriptive part is of great value to the business analyst who wants to put the BI project in a larger framework of IT governance. When the book changes from a descriptive into a prescriptive tone, I from a Business Intelligence business analyst point of view have to accept their arguments with some reserve and propose a modest descriptive attitude for the business analyst in a BI project. The authors themselves have put a lot of refinement and moderation in their conclusions but I am afraid this is going the same route as many studies have gone before: a study of 4,000 pages is boiled down into a 250-page book, which in its turn is reduced to four PowerPoint slides at conferences and in consulting workshops.

Although their study suggests best practices for all kinds of organizations, I see two obstacles that prevent me from incorporating their prescriptions into a Business Intelligence project startup: the significance of the results and the survey method itself.

The MIT-Sloan study was a worldwide and general IT study (Weill and Ross, 2004). So all kinds of IT investments were examined in this general study as were the scope of my book in the Western world and Business Intelligence, which can only be a fraction of the MIT-Sloan study. And then there is the method of using a survey and correlating its results with outcomes of complex business processes such as return on assets (ROA), return on investment (ROI), profit, or growth, which remains questionable. I have participated in a number of management surveys, both as an interviewer and interviewee which taught me the multiple sources of bias that can devaluate the research results dramatically.

Let me illustrate just one (psychological) source of bias: managers want to look rational. So, when I conducted research on the market readiness for biodegradable plastics in the early 1980s in Belgium, the results looked very encouraging. The majority of decision makers in local government, industry, agriculture, and opinion leaders in the media and academic world were very keen to adopt this new product range. Overnight success was at hand. Nevertheless it took more than a decade, government incentives, and compulsory legislation before biodegradable plastics became a success.

There was nothing wrong with the research method, the sampling method, nor the analysis. Years later, during a qualitative study in plastics, I found out that there was an irrational resistance against "plastics that wouldn't last." Our respondents were educated in the conviction that nondegradability was an essential aspect of plastics. So, if a simple and straightforward management survey like this one failed to produce reliable results how can a complex issue such as:

a) Decision making about
b) Investments in
c) Large organizations be singled out on their impact on
d) ROA–ROI–Profit–Growth?

Let us take a closer look at these four aspects.

a) Decision making

You probably have read some of Henry Mintzberg's articles or books (or my little Chapter 4 as a tribute to the master) where he takes out his sharp scalpel and cuts away the rational layer of managerial activities and presents his observations of what really happens. His insights on how organizational configurations are driven by social and even emotional drivers should open our eyes for sources of bias when surveying and comparing one organization type with another. It would seem impossible that the MIT–Sloan sample has produced a stratified sample of all organization configurations and their attitude toward information technology.

The decision-making process on technology issues is seldom purely rational. Within any organization type there are tech-savvy factions, coalitions of sceptics, innovation enthusiasts, and plain adversaries of new technology. The outcome of the decision-making process may be a rational summary and statement of direction but underneath the factions will remain in their irrational positions.

b) Investments

No cause of business impact is harder to quantify from a scientific point of view than an investment: you cannot create a control group that contains identical organizations that did not invest in the same manner as the test group. So, your guess is as good as mine.

c) Large Organizations

The larger the organization, the harder it is to factor out single sources of success. Large organizations combine financial strength, a vast reservoir of talent, assets that create an entry barrier to competition, market strengths such as market share and market penetration, brand value, efficiency bonuses based on learning curves, best practices, and economies of scale, and yes, they also have an IT infrastructure. So, how do you single out the IT governance as determining contributor to profit, growth, ROI, or ROA?

There are cases of IT as a contributor to these four outcomes galore but the decision-making process that led to these investments is almost impossible to factor out. The conclusion that joint decisions between IT and the business as Weill and Ross (2004, pp. 135–136) state is about as far as I am willing to go. But I guess this principle goes for any joint decision between business and technology people.

Imagine a car manufacturer where technology specialists build a production line without consulting the execs from HRM, finance, marketing, IT, and so on. This would probably be state-of-the-art producing lots of problems for the business.

d) ROA–ROI–Profit–Growth?

Ay, there's the rub. What are we comparing with what? Let me raise just three questions out of a dozen to illustrate my point.

- How do you compare return on assets which is the return on the entire left side of the balance sheet, or the result of structural measures, enabled by past, present, and future profits, with profit which is at the bottom of the income statement or the result of business processes enabled by the financial structure on both sides of the balance sheet? The decisions on the capital–labor intensity mix are a determining strategic choice for the organization to defend its presence in the market! Do you see the circular reasoning?
- When we measure return on investment , how do we factor out the net added value of the IT component in the investment portfolio?
- Growth–profit could be the subject of a tradeoff analysis of a "snapshot approach" but if you take the "movie approach," how do we estimate the measure in which growth will automatically lead to future profits or how profits fuel future growth?
- Last but not least: what the study could never produce is whether the organization has chosen the right financial goal out of these four options which could turn the results of the study upside down.

So, yes, communication, exchange of ideas and knowledge in a complex decision-making situation will always yield better decisions. That is the very reason I suppose you are reading this book: to make the business communicate better with IT and vice versa. By no means let my critiques in this research diminish the value of Weill's and Ross's book (2004). It has put the issue of IT governance on the agenda of every business that wants to utilize IT seriously as a competitive factor. It is with gratitude and full credit to their work that I use their model for assessing the direction and level of communication in the organization on IT issues. The following schemas are ideal deliverables for a business requirements document for a Business Intelligence project and are based on the theories in Weill's and Ross's book:

1. The five key IT governance decisions
2. IT governance archetypes
3. How enterprises govern
4. Common governance mechanisms

The Five Key BI Governance Decisions

1. BI principles decisions:
   a. In what measure do we value data quality in the transaction systems?
   b. If we have a tradeoff between security issues and potential gains from better distribution of information, which direction do we choose?
   c. Do we choose a proactive or a reactive attitude toward our BI users: do we deliver only the required information or do we make suggestions for enhancements?
2. BI architecture decisions
   a. Do we follow the general architecture policies or is there a compelling reason to choose an alternative route?
   b. If we need alternatives, where will they be of importance: in databases, extract, transform, load (ETL) tools, BI server(s), or client software?
3. BI infrastructure decisions
   a. What are the shared IT services the data warehouse will use?
   b. What part of the infrastructure will be organized per department or business unit?
   c. What are the access methods for the information consumers: local client PC, PDA, Web based, or VPN?

4. Business application needs
   a. Specify the business need.
   b. Specify the urgency.
   c. Present alternative solutions.
5. Prioritization of investments in BI
   a. How will we evaluate the priorities?
   b. Who will handle conflicting interests?
   c. Which user profiles will be served first?
   d. Which subject areas will be tackled first?

BI Governance Archetypes

It is my and many colleagues' experience that in most successful BI projects, anarchy is a nonexistent archetype, albeit that the BI project is often used as a means to stop the access dump and spreadsheet anarchy where every do it yourself (DIY) BI person claims his figures are the right ones. All other archetypes occur and as far as BI projects are concerned, are situational; see Table 16.3.

Based on about 50 "lessons learned" reports from BI projects, at least two major factors influence the archetype: The importance attributed to IT: when I was in the mail-order business in the early 1980s, IT was considered a strategic asset. Twenty years later, there are still industrial and service organizations where IT is at the bottom of the food chain. The other factor is the organizational configuration; in entrepreneurial organizations the duopolistic or business monarchy model dominates. In machine bureaucracies the feudal and business monarchy archetype is common. In the 1990s, IT monarchies were observed in organizations that thanked their existence to IT, mobile phone companies, or e-commerce organizations, although we see a shift to IT duopoly nowadays.

TABLE 16.3

BI Governance Archetypes

Style	Who Has Decision or Input Rights?
Business Monarchy	A group of business executives or individual executives (CxOs). Includes committees of senior business executives (may include CIO) Excludes IT executives acting independently.
IT Monarchy	Individuals or groups of IT executives
Feudal	Business unit leaders, key process owners, or their delegates
IT Duopoly	IT executives and one other group (e.g., CxO or business unit or process leaders)
Anarchy	Each individual leader

How Enterprises Govern BI

The matrix (Table 16.3; archetype × governance decision) for both input and decision making is then constructed to illustrate where the decisions are prepared and made.

Common Governance Mechanisms

Large organizations spend a lot of effort on coordinating mechanisms. Table 16.4 comes from the 2003 MIT–Sloan School Center for Information Systems Research and can be used by the BI analyst to position the project in the IT governance mechanisms used at the client's site. Be on the lookout for one or more of these coordinating mechanisms and make use of them throughout the entire project, from initiation to the lessons learned phase.

Purpose of the BI Project

The purpose of the BI project deliverable may need only a general description in terms, for example, the BI project needs to produce the necessary profitability analyses to determine the value of our top revenue contributors. But in larger organizations with multiple decision makers those general terms need a specification and translation per decision maker. In the examples we elaborate on the previous general description.

> Finance goals: To determine the top revenue customers by using a Pareto algorithm in the reporting tool that analyzes the entire active customer database linked to the invoice and direct costing data on a yearly basis.
> Marketing goals: To define the database of active customers as the analysis object by correctly integrating or consolidating the customers on account management level and on legal entity level as well as on network value by identifying the revenue generated through reference sales.
> Operation's goals: To identify the cost of quality per customer as a means to produce alternative customer valuation procedures as experience showed that customer input can seriously affect the company's profitability.

In some organizations even this is not enough. In that case we advise partitioning the goals further into BI process-based goals including the

TABLE 16.4

Governance Mechanisms

Mechanisms	Objectives	Desirable Behavior	Undesirable Behavior Observed
Executive and senior management committee	Holistic view of business, including IT	Seamless management incorporating IT	IT ignored
Architecture committee	Identify strategic technologies and standards—enforcement?	Business-driven IT decision making	IT police and delays
Process teams with IT membership	Take process view using IT (and other assets) effectively	End-to-end process management	Stagnation of functional skills and fragmented IT infrastructure
Capital investment approval and budgets	Consider IT as another business investment	Prudent IT investing: different approaches for different investment types	Paralysis by analysis. Small projects to avoid formal approval
Service-level agreements	Specify and measure IT service	Professional supply and demand	Manage to SLA, not business need
Chargeback	Recoup IT costs from business	Responsible use of IT	Arguments about charges and warped demand
Formal tracking of business value of IT	Measure IT investments and contribution to business value often using Balanced Scorecard	Makes transparent: goals, benefits and costs	Separates IT from other assets Focus on money, not value

risks accompanying every goal. Again in Table 16.5 we elaborate further on the finance goals to illustrate the level of detail.

Stakeholder Matrix

The stakeholder matrix is a simple but powerful presentation of who (as a person or a role) is involved in the project and why he or she is involved. We think of involvement on four levels or roles where one person can assume one or more:

- Client or sponsor: The person, department, or role who pays for the BI project. In a transactional project there can only be one sponsor but in a BI project, there may be many.
- Customer: The person, department, or role who benefits directly from the BI project.
- Stakeholder: The person, department, or role affected in a positive or negative way by the BI project.
- User: The person, department, or role who will use the BI products hands-on, that is, the reports, the front-end tool, or the analysis database.

We use the elements from the previous deliverable to elaborate on the goals, as in Table 16.6.

Business Requirements

The business requirements, which have been captured during the interviews, need to be presented in an understandable format to both the business and the IT community.

4.1. Use Cases

A good translation platform is the business use case, which basically describes the scenario of how users interact with the system. More on use case and scenario writing can be found in the works of Suzanne and James Robertson in *Mastering the Requirements Process* (2007) or many handbooks on Unified Modeling Language (UML). See Figure 16.1 for an example of an AS IS Business Use Case that describes the present and tedious manual process of customer profitability analysis. We propose to

TABLE 16.5

Example of BI Process-Based Goal Statement

Goal	Ability	Risk	Mitigation
Assemble all revenue and cost data on a per customer basis	Identify coherent revenue and direct cost data in the source systems that have the same granularity (e.g., sales order line/work order line/invoice line	There are no coherent cost data per customer in the source systems available	Take a representative sample and calculate the direct cost per customer manually to produce representative cost of goods sold percentages.
Extract a list of active customers	Identify active customers that fit a companywide definition	No companywide definition available	Initiate a process on management level to produce a single definition and foresee more than one customer perspective in the BI project that can be mapped afterward to the single customer definition.

TABLE 16.6

Example of a Stakeholder Matrix

Role (Name if Known)	Sponsor	Customer	Stakeholder	User
CEO (Jim Beam)	The CEO is sponsor because he is aware of the strategic value of the BI project as new competitors affect the company's margin			The CEO will use a Top 10 report of large volume customers who demand his personal attention
CFO (Jack Daniels)		The CFO will follow up the evolution of direct costs per top customer and will adjust with the COO		The CFO will use at least 4 volume and revenue reports: one per business unit
Account Managers		The account manager will need to adjust her sales strategy to improve the margins where critical		The account manager will need individual customer profitability reports
Database Administrators			The DBAs will have to monitor the ETL processes on a 24- hour basis which will force them to adapt their staff planning and work schedule	
Controllers			The controllers avoid tedious repetitive work which needs to be done for cost analysis	The controllers will be the gatekeeper to all cost reports, validating the results

FIGURE 16.1

Use case example: the customer order point (COP). The triangles in the supply chain represent the inventories and the rectangles represent high-level process steps. The model illustrates the two opposites in management: reduction of inventories and risk versus the highest possible service levels due to inventory build-up.

develop an AS IS and a TO BE version so the parties involved can get an image of the project and the transitions or changes it incurs.

4.2. Report Requirements Description

The next level of detail is also one all parties can understand: a description of the minimum reporting requirements, including the additional possibilities overlooked by the concerned parties. The latter proves your skills as a seasoned business analyst.

Each report requirement description should include the following descriptives:

- What are the measures and by which dimension should they be presented; for example, I want a volume report per product line per customer per year to date, year minus one, and year minus two.
- Refine the previous expression by adding the granularity and the drilldown possibilities; for example, by "customer" I mean every individual value-added tax identification (VAT) number, not the department who ordered the product; the time drilldown stops at a weekly level.

- Description of derived or "static" attributes that may not be present in the foreseen data warehouse solution; for example, totals per week per account manager or store type, parking lot surface, and so on.
- Users of the report.
- Presentation options (screen, pdf document, spreadsheet, executable, etc.).
- A layout example if necessary. This feature depends on the degrees of freedom the front-end tool offers its users.
- Business rules that may affect the comments, presentation, or other user aspects of the reports; for example, "A customer is a party that has bought at least one product within 12 months."

Project Management Constraints

Some practitioners consider this to be beyond the scope of a business analyst and leave this to the project manager but I disagree. A project manager will need some decision-making elements to come up with a realistic plan she can follow up. If the project manager has no knowledge of the analysis aspects you will lose precious time explaining all the business and technical aspects of a BI project. I prefer to make a draft proposal that can later be defined by a full-time PM practitioner in the case of large projects. But for projects smaller than 250 person-days I would prefer to keep the project management in the hands of the analyst. Any project has to deal with these five important constraints:

- Budget
- Project Information management
- Time (throughput and execution time, milestones, etc.)
- Organization
- Quality

Check the typical BI product constraints:

- Operating environment
- Database environment
- ETL tool
- Front-end tool
- Load windows
- Latency

- Refresh rate
- Simultaneity of report use

Check other external constraints:

- Legal
- Political
- Cultural

Now it is time to come up with the input for the development team: the scope and the data requirements will largely determine the cost and related elements of the development phase.

Scope of the Product

The scope defines the boundaries of the BI project. It describes the facts, the dimensions, the sources, and the iterations on a high level. One of the graphical aids Ralph Kimball developed is the data mart bus (see Figure 16.2), a matrix depicting the major business processes and the affected dimensions.

	Facts	Measures, Grain & Use	Customer	Region	Product	Retail_outlet	Employee	Budget_Revision	Unit_of_Measure	Date	Time_of_Day	Chart_of_Accounts	Update Frequency	Technical Dimension
Marketing	**Sales Order**	Detailed sales analysis at order line level. Measures include sales & volume, order- and sales tickeline counts	●	●	●	●	●	●	●	●	●	●	Daily	
	Budget Sales	Sales budget in unit price × volume = revenue and standard unit cost × volume = direct cost	●	●	●	●	●	●	●	●	●		Daily	
Finance & Operations	**Journal Entries**	Detailed GL transactions					●	●			●	●	Daily	
	General Ledger Balance	GL balance on a monthly basis									●	●	Monthly	
	Invoices	Detailed analysis at client- and supplier invoice line level, including credit notes, excluding internal transactions.	●	●	●	●			●	●	●	●	Weekly	
	Budget Finance	Financial Budget for **Sales, Purchases, Cost of Goods Sold and HRM Costs**	●	●	●	●	●	●	●	●	●	●	Monthly	
	Cost_of_Quality	Operational tracking of error costs per order and customer	●	●	●	●	●				●	●	Daily	

FIGURE 16.2
Bus matrix example.

A good scope description also considers the parts (sources, dimensions, facts, etc.) that are not in the scope to avoid all possible ambiguities. The scope is also a reflection on the business and report requirements indicating clearly which requirements will be dealt with and which will not be in the delivered product at the end of the project. In the case of strong demand for a certain feature that is not in the scope, prepare for a sound explanation the business sponsor can understand: a lack of money, time, resources, skills, assets, and the like, so the business sponsor can take action in case she wants her requirements in the scope; for example, this bus matrix for the company covers—on a conceptual level—all facts and dimensions the data warehouse should contain.

Data Requirements

Data requirements descriptions in a business analysis deliverable need only describe the target data. See Figure 16.3. By indicating the source of each attribute the technical analysts can pick it up from there and do the technical analysis and the data profiling. Depending on the complexity of the project, the number of sources, and the client's organizational

---

What ISO 11179-4:2004 Has to Say about Data Definition Requirements

1 Data Definition Shall:

a) Be stated in the singular
b) State what the concept is, not only what it is not
c) Be stated as a descriptive phrase or sentence(s)
d) Contain only commonly understood abbreviations
e) Be expressed without embedding definitions of other data or underlying concepts

2 Data Definition Should:

a) State the essential meaning of the concept
b) Be precise and unambiguous
c) Be concise
d) Be able to stand alone
e) Be expressed without embedding rationale, functional usage, or procedural information
f) Avoid circular reasoning
g) Use the same terminology and consistent logical structure for related definitions
h) Be appropriate for the type of metadata item being defined

---

FIGURE 16.3
Data definition requirements according to the International Standards Organization.

structure, this analysis can go two levels deep: the entity level and the attribute level.

Always check for the existence of a corporate data model. Organizations that have a corporate data model give proof of information management discipline that avoids redundant work and looks for clarity of definitions and consistency in data management. In most organizations this is an ongoing project, so don't expect a 100% ready source for your entity and attribute definitions and descriptions.

Describe the major entities needed for the data warehouse and list their subject area(s) to which the entity contributes information. Make sure you know if the entity is a corporate standard entity and list the data definition owner, the source application, the number of records, and whether history tracking is necessary and security issues may occur.

If needed, add the necessary attributes to the list, performing the same checks as for the entity to which they belong and add the application reference record, whether data profiling is required and, if available, a list of values. If the attribute and its related parents and children need a hierarchy, a grouping, or an aggregate navigation table in the data warehouse, do not forget to indicate it if your analysis uncovered the need for it.

Presentation Methods

The presentation methods description can take two directions: either the front-end tool is known in advance which strictly determines the presentation possibilities, or the tool selection takes place in a later phase of the project. In that case, a good business requirements document should provide sound input for the tool selection track.

For obvious reasons I do not give an illustration of the presentation method description based on the commonly known tools. If you go to the vendors' websites, you will find ample information. It is more useful to provide input for tool selection. Figure 16.4 provides you with a checklist.

Business Security Requirements

We restrict the notion of security to the business aspects such as technical security which should be covered by the technical people creating backup plans, storage redundancy, firewalls, and what have you to prevent the loss of integrity, availability, and physical removal or copying of records.

Feature	Explanation
General Usability and Visualization Features	
• Ease-of-use	A general evaluation based on the various degrees of computer literacy in the organization.
• Screen design	
• Task compatibility	Does the tool fit the task(s) the user has to perform with it?
• Conditional formatting	For example, if [invoiced.sales] < [budgeted.sales] by more than 5%, **Color** ([invoiced.sales]) = RED
• Style sheets supported (css)	Can you easily adapt the reports to your house style for consistent web-based reporting presentations?
• Drill-down supported on elements in graphs	
• Support for PDAs and BlackBerrys	
• Subtotal Points	Does the tool allow insertion of subtotals without having to develop extra SQL code?
• Number of graphs and visualizations	

(a)

FIGURE. 16.4
Presentation, usability, and functionality criteria for a BI front-end tool.

Security requirements can have an enormous impact on the project's complexity. Even more than the scope, security demands can affect the development's throughput time, the processing time for ETL, and the report servers. Although there may be reasons for strong security such as in the case of client self-service reporting environments or HR data such as salaries, make sure you are not creating a large opportunity cost on top of the technical costs. We refer to the essence of business intelligence as described by Gartner, "Information Democracy will emerge in forward-thinking enterprises, with Business Intelligence information and applications available broadly to employees, consultants, customers, suppliers, and the public. . . .

Functional Aspects and Presentation methods	
• Role-based dashboarding and reporting	Can I present the same report in different formats, based on report user roles?
• Common drilldown paths stored in repository	A feature that speeds up the drilldown processing
• Do drilldown paths depend on the role users have?	
• Standard reports can be adjusted	
• Can the adjustments be saved for the individual user	
• Export to Excel, formatting included	
• Export to PDF	
• Attach notes to figures	
• Distribute notes	
• Notes can be linked to specific dimension member	
• Full syntax of SQL SELECT supported	Can the designer use the common SQL dialects to build queries?
• SQL SELECT supported by menus	
• Can SQL SELECTs be done by an end-user?	
• Basket analysis supported	Basket analysis demands calculations after the query result set is presented on the client. Not all tools support this feature.
• Write-back facilities	You don't want to do this but…
• Keeps history when figures are changed	
• Support for slowly changing dimensions	
• Displays two options (historical and actual)	
• Support for Balanced Scorecards	Can you build strategy maps linked to the perspectives?
• Define impact of one KPI on another	Can you map dependencies between KPIs?
• BI self-service supported	
• Scheduled distribution of reports/dashboards	
• Publish and subscribe	
• Is the product real-time aware?	

(b)

FIGURE. 16.4 (CONTINUED)

In increasing order of complexity, these are the common security demands:

Report level security: a certain report user only has access to his pre-determined set of reports and cannot look into other reports, nor change the report definition that might give him access to other records.

OLAP, or view level security: the user group has read access to the entire OLAP cube or view tables in the database.

Database table level security: the user group has read access to specific tables in the database.

Database row or column level security: the user group has access to specific columns or rows in a specific table in the database.

Other Requirements

This chapter is meant for anything you might want to describe—cultural aspects, users and their level of computer literacy, sensitive aspects embedded in the organization's history—anything that could influence the outcome of the project is worth mentioning in this chapter.

Project Plan and Task List Proposal

A very high-level project plan and a list of the tasks for all parties involved may make things clearer for the technicians and will help them to grasp the expectations of the client organization. A small data warehouse project with a throughput time of one year and only four milestones tells a different story than a large data warehouse project with ten milestones to be met in eighteen months! High-level dependencies between project phases enhance the insight of the technical guys in the pitfalls of the project.

Documentation

Documentation, the orphan of any IT project, needs special attention in business intelligence because of its particular aspects:

A BI project's success is user driven: if she can't find the information to improve her use of the system, or interpretation of the data, she will abdicate and turn a technical success into a project failure.

A BI system integrates data from various sources and recycles these data into usable information. Nevertheless in case of doubt, good documentation will provide the context for better interpretations and quality checks.

BI systems evolve over time, as do the source data in transactional systems. Good documentation helps the technicians keep track of the system's evolution.

Therefore, the documentation track starts with the writing of the first business analysis documents.

Glossary

A glossary avoids verbosity, misunderstandings, and plain chaos. Over and over I have had to deal with misconceptions about terms used in analysis documents leading to efficiency losses and near-disaster. It may not be the sexiest aspect of a business analysis process but it is elementary and necessary and it will give you a sense of control and direction which is a prior condition for a successful analysis process.

PROJECT CHARTER DOCUMENT TEMPLATE

Overview

As soon as the initial business requirements have been agreed upon it is time to move the project to the next phase and have the customer sign off on a project charter. This charter will elaborate on the requirements with a focus on guiding principles throughout the project. Although it is not a formal contract document, I have seen many organizations use it as such. So be careful to address all the issues that will or can or should influence the outcome of the project.

This template is a suggestion of how a business analyst could present a project charter to be used as a general guidebook during the project. Its main purpose is to reassure the project sponsor and all other stakeholders that there will be a consistent navigator steering the project toward success and managing everyone's expectations in a correct way.

Every chapter may vary in length and level of detail in response to the organization's sensibilities. We consider you smart enough to fill in the suggested chapters intelligently. These are the principal chapters:

1. Project Scope
2. Project Organization
3. External Relationships and Dependencies
4. Project Approach
5. Project Resources
6. Risk Analysis
7. Business Case
8. Initial Project Plan

Project Scope

In the business requirements document, the product scope was expressed in a hybrid, business-technical way using the data mart bus matrix. Now it is time to make things clearer for the business sponsor by also distinctly defining the scope also in terms of complete business process descriptions, functional descriptions, and describing the various functional levels in the organization that will benefit from the project and its product(s).

A good explanation of the business themes per management level and per management function will make things clear for all parties involved. Avoid technical jargon but don't let this free you from producing a consistent, verifiable, and precisely formulated scope description. Finish this chapter by adding the latest version of the data mart bus matrix and a high-level description of the reports the project will deliver.

Project Organization

This is the part where the project organization is charted: to make sure all project management functions or roles are taken care of, the steering committee, the project team, and the reporting procedures are outlined. The steering committee consists of the senior user, the senior supplier, and the budget holder or sponsor, and, in the case of a larger organization, the program manager.

The project team consists of the customer, the project manager, and the business analyst to make sure equilibrium between formal project management aspects and intrinsic product quality is obtained. I have learned that if you give the upper hand to a project manager with little knowledge of the special aspects of a BI project, all deadlines and budgets will be met but the quality issues will emerge long after the project is delivered.

External Relationships and Dependencies

No project is an island in the corporate sea of initiatives, be they formal or informal. Identifying these initiatives and their potential, as well as their estimated or known impact on the BI project is crucial. Check for the classics, that is, ISO quality projects, business process re-engineering, platform migration projects, management reshuffling, mergers and acquisitions, new government regulations compliance initiatives, and so on.

Project Approach

The project approach, together with the project resources chapter, is the basis for an effective project plan. It contains the basic choices for the project direction such as: choice and prioritization of the iterations, an overview of the project phases, and, if possible, the principal work packages.

Project Resources

A description of the necessary internal and external resources, and an estimate of their time and cost provides further input for the budget and the project plan. Make sure you include the interviewees, the client's DBAs, and other client resources in the project charter. Nothing is more frustrating for a project than a lack of commitment from the client's resources once the project is launched.

Risk Analysis

Managing risks is essential in a business intelligence project. And trust me, there are many risks involved. To name but a few:

- The customer's engagement: Users, clients, other stakeholders, and especially the master data owners. Make sure you have risk management processes covered with the business sponsor.
- Scope control: I always warn my clients about scope control issues. It is not the major changes that appear on the radar and are dealt with

accordingly (either accept the change via a change request process or postpone or reject the change) that are the risk; it is the scattered, small, and local adjustments that may add up to major delays and cost overruns on the project.

- Insufficient expression of the customer's needs: "I can only say what I want when I see the results of the BI project," is a common statement in some form or other during the scoping phase. If you fail to reduce this important risk, you have a serious problem defending your added value in the business intelligence project.

- External factors will always pose a threat to your project: Changing legislation, availability of external data, pressure groups, or any external force can influence the outcome of the BI project.

- Execution: Any plan is only as good as its execution. Along the way all sorts of obstacles and stumbling blocks will be on your path. Make sure your project plan allows for slack to tackle these problems.

Business Case

We refer to the business case template and underline the fact that a business case assessment is a continuous process based on continuous improvement of information quality and reduction of uncertainty of the estimates and forecasts.

Initial Project Plan

In this chapter we make clear agreements on:

- Quality management
- Risk management
- Change management process
- Documentation and co-ordination of knowledge and knowhow

Overview of the Initial Project Plan

Always state your "school of thought" in project management, in most cases PMI BOK or PRINCE2. Any good project management method has at least the following characteristics:

- Process oriented, with a focus on the business case as the driving force
- Use of controllable and manageable project phases that

- Result in delivering concrete physical products and management products such as meeting summaries, risk logs, issue logs, and so on, at the end of every phase

The initial project plan contains:

- An overview of all the deliverables
- An overview of the activities
- A planning and estimate basis for time, cost, and quality level
- An overview of the project milestones

Planning Basis

After you have completed the project scope and the project approach sections with the client, you have described the input for this item. Now it is time to document these and other factors as a planning basis: assumptions about the available data sources, assumptions about the complexity of the ETL, and anything else that can influence the throughput time, cost, and quality of your project plan.

Global Planning

Table 16.7 illustrates the level of detail needed in a project charter:

Quality Management

Mention the subject, method, and objectives of the data quality management throughout the project for:

- The source data
- Customer expectations

TABLE 16.7

Global Planning Table

Data Mart	# PersonDays	T.T.	E.S.	E.F.	L.S.	L.F.
Finance						
Operations						
Sales and Marketing						
Quality						
Competence management						

Note: The components of this global planning table are the number of man days, the throughput time (T.T.), the earliest start (E.S.), earliest finish (E.F.) and the latest start (L.S.) and latest finish (L.F.). Note that in this stage you don't document any dependencies between the project phases or work packages.

- The extract, transform, load process (ETL)
- The presentation layer

Risk Management

Describe the various risk management procedures you foresee to prevent, avoid, reduce, accept, or transfer the project risks.

Change Management Process

The classical change management process should be sufficient for most BI projects: log the change requests, prioritize them with the customer, make an impact analysis per change (or combination of changes if they are interdependent), and ask for approval.

Documentation and Coordination of Knowhow

Make sure you have procedures for documentation and exchange of knowledge between the various actors in the project. All too many projects have failed, long after delivery of the BI environment, due to bad maintenance.

Preliminary Architecture

Although architecture presentations should need more qualification during the project itself, there is some added value in a preliminary architecture description to ensure that the customer is aware he is engaging in change of his IT environment: new servers, new platforms, new software are needed, and pictures speak louder than words. See Figure 16.5. The older systems need to be loaded once where the systems in use will need incremental loads on a daily basis. In this section some thoughts about the modeling approach may also be expressed.

Gantt Chart

If all the previous chapters are approved by the customer, it is time to come up with a draft project plan of the first iteration where details and dependencies may come into the picture. Now your project charter is ready for the contract phase where the customer will probably negotiate on price, throughput time, and quality. As drastic as the changes to this project charter may be after the negotiation phase, you dispose of a good baseline description and a benchmark to assess the impact of the negotiations on the project.

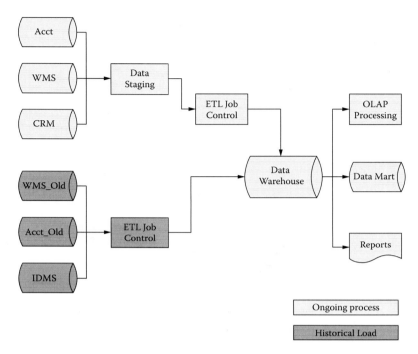

FIGURE 16.5
Example of a high-level BI project architecture.

BEST PRACTICE SHARING TEMPLATE

Overview

This template serves both as an interview guide to elicit knowledge from the best practice owner and as a structure of 11 topics to be inventoried and described to deliver an effective knowledge sharing document. The template is based on a template as published by Luc Bouquet (2010):

1. Title page
2. Executive summary
3. Best practice identification
4. Reason(s) why this is a best practice
5. Definitions
6. Resources for the best practice
7. How the best practice works
8. Specific instructions

9. Cost
10. Application area
11. Contact information

Title Page

A title is worth 75% of your message's communication power. Make sure your title mentions the activity closely tied to a measurable benefit; for example: increase query response times with a factor two or more. The title introduces a compelling story, told by a person in the organization. Make sure the story is in natural language and if the storyteller is not too timid you may enhance his communication power by depicting a photo of him. Catalog marketers know that adding a picture to a message increases the attention value of the message itself as people are attracted by faces of other people.

Executive Summary

The management summary should be as simple as possible without losing the context or the essence of the message. Two subtitles containing a maximum of 100 words each should do the trick: the problem and the solution. Why 100 words? Because that is on average what a person can read and understand in one minute. Surely any executive will be able to spare two minutes to be informed about a new way of working in her department?

Best Practice Identification

Make sure your audience can find the best practice via a number of search keywords such as:

- The RACI information (RACI = responsible, accountable, consulted and informed persons)
- The product(s) and process(es) affected by the practice
- The customers
- The ValidFrom and ValidTo dates
- Contextual keywords such as:
  - Function(s)
  - Department(s)
  - Technology
  - Discipline

Reason(s) Why This Is a Best Practice

Why do we do anything in an organization? Choose the ones that are appropriate:

- Increase customer satisfaction
- Increase revenue
- Decrease costs
- Reduce waste
- Improve the environment
- Decrease cycle time
- Reduce employee turnover

Definitions

Don't expect your readers to get the meaning of all the important concepts used in your best practice description. Avoid misunderstanding or down-right averting their attention from what you have to say. Define the concepts by telling what they are, what they aren't, and give examples. Your audience will reward you with extra attention and goodwill.

Resources for the Best Practice

Sum up the resources needed:

- People and their competences
- Software
- Equipment
- Consumables
- Documentation

How the Best Practice Works

Here is the meat of your document. Use all available means to convey the message unambiguously as you are implicitly or very explicitly writing instructions. Think of:

- Stepwise instructions
- Flowcharts
- Pictograms
- Photos

Specific Instructions

This section is only useful if you have to "branch out" your instructions to subaudiences who need specialized instructions. Subtitles such as "For security personnel only" direct the reader to the right section in the best practice.

Cost

You have already amply motivated the reader with the benefits; now it is time to come across with the cost of the best practice, leaving nothing untold:

- One-off costs such as investments
- Recurring costs
- Indirect effort such as study or training
- Direct effort

Application Area

This section is only necessary if the best practice identification section may not be able to provide unambiguous metadata about the best practice. If the risk exists that the wrong people may be attracted to this practice then you should clearly indicate which reader is best served with the practice and which one isn't. If the best practice is errorprone for novice users, here is the place to communicate the risks.

Contact Information

Name the persons and their relationship with this practice: the single point of contact, the owner, or the practice leader in the organization are three roles that may be of interest to the reader.

GENERIC INTERVIEW GUIDE

Introduction

I have expressed my disbelief in interview checklists for skilled Business Intelligence analysts. They impair natural conversation, rich in context, rapidly zooming in on the issues at hand instead of walking a treadmill and killing all spontaneity and creativity that so often leads to real innovative Business Intelligence solutions. Then why this interview guide?

Because you will meet executives who like to prepare for an interview and ask for a copy of this interview guide in advance. Because you want to make sure you have covered all aspects of the business. Fine, here it is. But do me one favor: don't put it in front of you. Learn it by heart or do whatever you want with it, just don't put it on the table. You are having an explorative discussion, not an oral exam.

How to Introduce the Interview Guide

I always use this introduction text as a basis:

> The specification of a data warehouse project is fundamentally different from the specification of a transaction system. In fact, the BI system must be capable of answering—or at least supporting the analytical process that leads to answering—business questions which do not even exist in the organization at its moment of inception. Therefore, consider this interview as a creative exploration of the enhanced possibilities of your job if this system were able to produce perfect and relevant information.
>
> This interview is not just about your present job; it is mainly about your future job, supported by better information.

Then I usually add an example of information I know the organization wants desperately in a simple and comprehensive form such as a graph and a data view of the graph, positioning it as one of the possible deliverables of the BI project.

Generic Interview List

Frame of Reference

- Charting the frame of reference of the organization is done by asking the following generic questions of all stakeholders. The following themes are the foundation of all interviews:
- Could you describe your business to me: the main drivers, your business objectives?
- What is the principal focus of your business: customer intimacy, operational excellence, or product leadership?
- What is the principal generic strategy of your organization: cost leadership, focus, differentiation, or a combination focus and one of the other two?

- What data and which elements and resources do you need to succeed?
- How are these data used?
- Which data do you share with colleagues, suppliers, customers?
- Down to what analysis level do you need the information (e.g., individual customer, department, etc.)?
- What is the lowest level of detail in your present report requirements?
- What are the principal hierarchies you need to structure or classify data, processes, facts, or principles? What are relevant timeframes for your department or business unit?
- Which available reports do you use now? With what frequency? Where do these reports come from? What is the information you want to extract from these reports? And what do you do once you have the necessary information?

You see, these are very simple, straightforward questions and themes. The principle is that you, not your interviewee, has to tackle the difficulties of requirements analysis.

Generic Questions

- What is your role in the organization?
- What are your responsibilities?
- What information, results, and other deliverables do you need to produce at what time?
- Which data (often/sometimes) are missing to make the best possible decision?
- What legal, commercial, logistic, and other management terms do you use regularly and how do you define these terms?
- Which processes:
  - Do you design? (D)
  - Do you lead? (L)
  - Do you execute? (E)
    - (For example, Financial reporting for the central bank = L
    - Reports for the stockholders = D, L
    - Analysis of the figures = D, L, E)
- What information do you use to determine the level of success of your department/job/team?
- How do you classify products, customers, coworkers?

- What reward systems does your department/business unit (BU) use?
- What criteria would you put forward to determine the success of this data warehouse/BI project?

Finally

Which of these dimensions are relevant to you?

1 - Product
2 - SKU
3 - Location
4 - Time of day
5 - Date
6 - Employee
7 - Customer
8 - Asset type
9 - Transport/shipment mode
10 - Freight forwarder
11 - Asset
12 - Competitor
13 - Sales channel
14 - Natural/general ledger account
15 - Document type
16 - Vendor
17 - Others that are typical for your organization type (i.e., coverage, broker, or insured party in insurance)

Have I forgotten to ask you anything that might be of importance to the project?

INTERVIEW GUIDE PER FUNCTIONAL AREA

Strategic Decision Making

What is your long-term perspective for your organization?
Which trends support your views?
Which is your basic strategic choice: improve efficiency or increase the commercial impact?

If you chose the latter, do you prefer an increase in customer intimacy or in product leadership?

Please rank the following high-level critical success factors:

- Meeting the financial objectives
- Internal customer satisfaction
- External customer satisfaction
- Optimum capacity use
- Risk control
- Continuous quality improvement
- Skilled and available people

What causal relationships do you see between these CSFs?
Which of the KPIs below are the ones you can determine/influence/use in your job?

- Customer satisfaction survey results
- Percentage use of available capacity
- Employee satisfaction survey results
- Competences that need to be developed
- Workplace absenteeism in percentage of available labor days
- Staff turnover
- MTBF (mean time between failure)
- Evolution of the order entry
- Percentage revenue from products less than three years on the market
- Conversion rate from quotes into orders
- Customer lifetime value
- Percentage conformity of delivered goods and services
- Number of solved and unsolved complaints per time period
- On-time pickup of external or internal carriers
- Cost per ton/km
- Deviations in specs per delivery
- Number of changed or canceled orders
- Percentage of processes within the quality norm
- Number of person-hours absorbed for rework
- Inventory turnover

- Return per square meter of office/outlet/warehouse/factory floor
- Maintenance costs per location
- Provisions for maintenance costs per location
- Risk inventory per location

Finance and Controlling

Do you use the Du Pont method* for your income statement and balance sheet analysis?

Do you use transfer pricing and if so, based on which principles?

- Cost plus?
- Sharing the margin? (Transfer price – Total Cost)/(Market price – Transfer price)
- Other

Do you use categories for cost accounting? For example,

- Direct variable costs (raw material, direct labor)
- Indirect variable cost (office supplies, indirect labor, e.g., maintenance, supervision, lubricants, etc.)
- Direct constant costs (depreciation or rent of machines, warehouses,,etc.)
- Indirect constant costs (office space, car rent, etc.)

What is the structure of your breakeven analysis?

Could you describe the audit process?

- Processes
- Procedures
- Audit trail

Is there an economic and technical description of the principal assets? Who decides on tradeoffs among financial performance, operational performance, and risk profile of these assets and on what decision basis?

---

* The Du Pont analysis method decomposes ROI and ROE into their determining factors, which provide valuable and fundamental analysis of the operations and the use of assets.

Marketing

What forecast method(s) do you use?

Which external and internal data and information do you use for the forecast?

Do you use SWOT analysis? If so, what are the quantifiable elements in this analysis and what are the sources of data and information?

How do you calculate market share(s)?

What information do you have about your competitors?

- Revenue and volume
- Income statements and balance sheets
- Market share(s)
- Cost accounting
- Other

What improvement initiatives are under scrutiny/planned/in progress/ being evaluated?

Do you use formal descriptions of brand personalities or branding strategies? If so, which attributes, advantages, and values are linked to your brand(s)?

What three- to five-year trends influence your decisions today?

What pricing strategy do you use:

- Target costing?
- Breakeven as a basis?
- Competitive pricing?
- Cost plus?
- Other

Sales

How do you report your sales pipeline and what are the measurable, relevant phases?

Describe your business development process and the data you collect during this process.

What is the average sales cycle's duration?

How many people are involved in the sales process on the customer's side and what are their profiles?

When are you vulnerable to your competitors?

What are your winning arguments to beat the competition?

Describe the expense account reporting and approval process.
What information that you deliver to the customer is valued highly?

- Are there missing pieces of information?
- Does the information arrive in a timely fashion?
- How much effort in time and money do you spend to get the information to your desk?
- Are there internal information suppliers involved in this process?
- Do they charge you or do you know their cost?

What sales improvement initiatives are under scrutiny/planned/in progress/being evaluated?

Logistics and Operations

Do you forecast demand from sales forecasts throughout the entire supply or service delivery chain?
What external and internal data and information do you use to plan your capacity?
What are their sources?
How do you evaluate external partners?
What efficiency improvement initiatives are under scrutiny/planned/in progress/being evaluated?
How do you evaluate the feasibility of these initiatives?
Do you use marginal cost accounting to evaluate efficiency improvements?

METADATA CHECKLIST

The importance of good metadata cannot be underestimated. That is why, from the beginning of this project initiative, we have to pay attention to this important aspect.

Metadata for Integration

The following data about the available data need to be documented:

- Source
- Target: output/other program(s)/other files/tables

- File name
- Field name
- Keys (foreign/primary)
- Used for
- Owner of the data element
- Owner of the application
- User applications
- Data type
- Length
- NULL rule
- Default rule
- Data entry domain values
- Indexes used
- Conversion rule
- Derivation rule
- Aggregation rule
- Logging statistics
- Version
- Release
- Valid_From_Date and Valid_to_Date

Metadata for Transformation

In a next stage of the analysis, when the extract, transform, load process is being defined, we need to add the following information:

- Processing rules for derivation and calculation of data
- Business definitions of tables where the data appear
- Business definitions of data type admissible values
- Hierarchy of the data

GENERIC BUSINESS OBJECT DEFINITIONS

Overview

In a data warehouse or data mart as well as in the analysis tool you can distinguish three types of dimensions:

Generic dimensions such as date, time, currency, location, and so on. The only business analysis issues with these dimensions is the question about the level of detail of a time dimension, or the completeness of the DATE dimension; that is, do we include all nonworking days per country and so on.

Contextual dimensions that add situational context to the data. Dimensions indicating the origin of data, batch source, or audit trail are good examples and of course these may vary depending on the subject area. Again, from a business analysis point of view these are no-brainers: you either need them or you don't.

Decision dimensions that contribute to both the analysis and the decisions to be made. Whereas the two previous types may explain business questions, they are hardly within the sphere of influence of management. The decision dimensions you will encounter in any data warehouse and BI project are: *customer, organization, employee, partner, territory,* and *product.*

In the following pages we attempt to formulate a generic and broad enough definition for these important dimensions. Use these definitions as a starting point for your exploration and tailor them to the customer's needs and wishes. They can also help you to check how the organization handles master data.

DEFINING THE PRINCIPAL ASSET OF AN ORGANIZATION: *CUSTOMER*

Introduction

Few information objects are more loosely defined than *customer.* At least that has been Lingua Franca's experience in the past 20 years of customer relationship management (CRM) and BI practice. So here are my two cents: a generic definition of *customer* you can use to challenge your client organization's definition. Creating a clear and elaborate definition of this principal asset will not only improve the BI user's communication effectiveness; it will improve sales and marketing operations greatly as people realize the specifics of each customer type. In a way this definition is an externalization of tacit knowledge of experienced sales and marketing people.

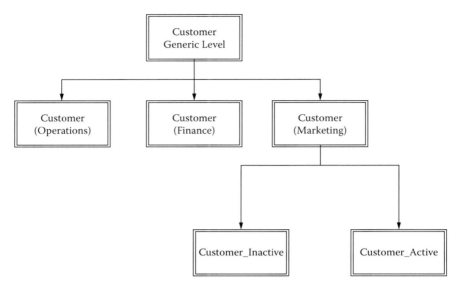

FIGURE 16.6
Customer taxonomy.

Taxonomy of *Customer*

Any organization embarking on a BI project for sales and marketing purposes will have to adopt the taxonomy shown in Figure 16.6 if it wants to avoid political infighting on definitions, analysis of the results, and management decisions. Note that the concept of inactive and active customers is related to marketing and not to finance and operations as their perspectives do not allow this division. Invoices and delivery notes may have a long lifespan for legal purposes, for instance: product traceability, warranty, or insurance.

Generic Definition of *Customer*

All [entities] are defined in an unambiguous way. Although most organizations have a tendency to declare, "We are different," I have only come across organizations that reduced the definition instead of enhancing or extending it. To make sure the definition is usable worldwide I have given some country-dependent examples of [Registration Database] below.

> [Customer <Generic level>]: A [Customer] is a [Party] that has one or more [Transactions] with a [Seller] either in process or settled as recorded in a written or oral Contract.

The [Seller] is in this case a [Legal Entity] which is part of the selling organization.

A [Party] is in this case a [Private Person], a [Public Entity], a [Collective Entity], or a [Legal Entity].

[Private Person]: is a living human being who can be defined by a social security number, an ID number, or a Name/Address combination. In the case where the [Private Person] has an official economic activity he can also be identified by a number in the [Registration Database] for [Legal Entities]. In that case the [Private Person] is considered as a [Legal Entity].

[Public Entity]: is a government organization that is (in some countries) identified via a number in the [Registration Database] for [Legal Entities] and or a Name, type of organization (e.g., Ministry, Public Health Organization, etc.), and Address combination.

[Collective Entity]: is an organization that is an assembly of other [Parties] that has no formal identification in the [Registration Database] for [Legal Entities] but acts in a directed way. Examples are: political parties, trade unions, churches, special interest groups, and purchase groups.

[Legal Entity]: is an organization that is identified via a number in the [Registration Database] for [Legal Entities] or a Name, type of corporation, and Address combination.

[Transaction]: an exchange of services or goods from the [Seller] with money, goods, or goodwill from the [Customer].

[Settlement]: the acceptance of goods or services by the [Customer] and the payment of money or goods or the emergence of goodwill to the [Seller].

[Registration Database]: contains minimum the name and address of the organization, the organization type, its board of directors, the capital, and a unique number.

For example, in the United States, most states require a tax identification number, in France it is le Registre National du Commerce (RNCS), in the Netherlands, Kamer van Koophandel (Chamber of Commerce), and in Belgium: Kruispuntbank Ondernemingen/ Banque-Carrefour des Entreprises.

Specific *Customer* Definitions

Although these definitions cannot be considered as canonical, I hope they will inspire you to make client-specific definitions. Some may say, "Why not add the notion of internal customer?" but I am afraid this will take us too far as this internal customer concept is even more specific to the organization.

> [Customer <Operations>]: a [Customer] who has a delivery in process or has been delivered a product or service.
>
> [Customer <Finance>]: a [Customer] who has received an invoice or a credit note.
>
> [Customer <Marketing>]: a [Customer] who has contacted the organization with the intention of doing business with the organization.
>
> [<Active> Customer <Marketing>]: a [Customer] who has contacted the organization with the intention of doing business with the organization in a period no longer than x months, "*x*" being an organization-specific period.
>
> [<Inactive> Customer <Marketing>]: a [Customer] who has contacted the organization with the intention of doing business with the organization for a period longer than x months, "*x*" being an organization-specific period.
>
> [Customer <household>]: a group of customers belonging to an ultimate parent [Customer] on the basis of legal and organizational criteria.

ORGANIZATION, A MEANINGFUL CONCEPT?

J. Watson Wilson is widely quoted as saying, "If you dig very deeply into any problem, you will get 'people'." Organizations are social systems so some analysts may conclude that the organization dimension is just an aggregate of people in a certain configuration, for example, the marketing people, the finance people, the people from the eastern regional office, and so on. I think this is just a part of a complex reality that constitutes an organization.

Organizational behavior theory sees the organization as the interaction between people and how they form formal and informal groups, structure that defines the formal relationships within the organization, technology that has a lot to do with the expected output of the organization, and the environment in which the organization operates. People,

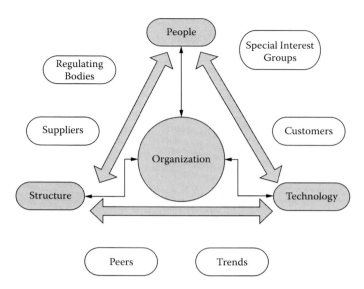

FIGURE 16.7
Schematic view of the organization concept.

structure, and technology are the constituents of organization but they also interact with each other outside the organization. The environment interacts with the organization and with its three constituents separately. See Figure 16.7.

So, let us accept the fact that DIM_ORGANIZATION, from a business intelligence point of view, is more than a rollup of DIM_EMPLOYEE. What exactly do we define and how do we define it to produce a meaningful concept for BI purposes? Let me work my way up from a minimalist approach up to a more sophisticated (but not always workable) concept.

The Many Definitions of *Organization*

The minimum definition of *organization* is people working together to transform input into output. This low-level process view is the narrowest definition I can find. Some examples are:

- The paint department is the organization that paints the finished goods.
- The customer service organization handles all enquiries, complaints, and other nontransactional communication from customers.

Let us take it a step further. *Organization* is an entity of people working together and sharing organizational goals that constitute the very reason why the organization was defined as such. The organization defines these goals and follows up on its performance which is reported to other organizational units. Some examples are:

- The marketing department is responsible for defining markets, market segments, and creating and following up on the marketing plan to make sure the company has the most effective and efficient exchange of goods and services with its customer base.
- The business unit School Books is responsible for the educational market and manages the entire supply chain, sales, and marketing to serve this market segment.

Moving on: "organization" is a group of people or other organizations that operate according to shared principles or values or ideas. Some examples are:

- The trade union defends the rights of the workers vis à vis the company management.
- The project group "equal opportunities" monitors the company's equal opportunities policy in recruiting and selecting employees and promoting or demoting employees.

EMPLOYEE OR PARTNER?

Ouch, this is a tricky one. In many countries "employee" is a legally defined concept, namely a person hired by an employer who has the right to supervise and give orders to the employee. Yet, many organizations prefer to use subcontractors and self-employed resources to do the job to reduce social liabilities for redundancies. Legally speaking, these are not employees but they certainly are human resources. Therefore, I prefer the latter term as a generalization of employee.

A human resource, then is an individual who provides physical or cerebral labor for another person or an organization in exchange for money

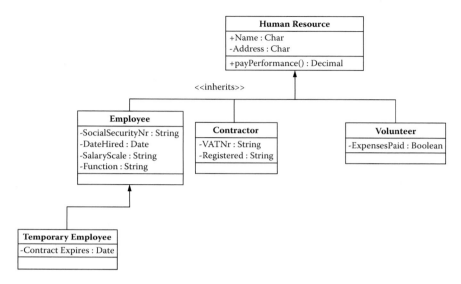

FIGURE 16.8

An example of a UML diagram, illustrating the options for human resources.

or a nonpecuniary reward as is the case in many nongovernmental organizations or in political parties and other volunteer organizations. There has to be some form of integration in the organization otherwise the term "human resource" would be inappropriate and "subcontractor" or "supplier" would be a better term. See Figure 16.8.

So, how do you count human resources? "Head count" as defined by the U.S. Small Business Administration (website) narrows it down to "employees":

> The number of employees of a concern is its average number of persons employed for each pay period over the concern's latest 12 months. Any person on the payroll must be included as one employee regardless of hours worked or temporary status. That is, it is a "head count." The number of employees of a concern in business under 12 months is based on the average for each pay period it has been in business.

Try to reconcile this with the Dutch definition of head count in a multinational company which includes all human resources in the organization including interns, job students, self-employed, contractors, and so on.

PRODUCT

From a process management point of view, a product is the output, the result of a process that has transformed input under a set of conditions, for example, a chemical process or a physical process. From a project management point of view, a product is the result of an agreement between the client and the contractor to produce a result at the end of the project. A project also produces management products including progress reports, risk and issue logs, and the like.

In its broadest marketing sense, a product is any object (a commodity, an artifact) offered in the market to satisfy a need. A product can be tangible or intangible (also called a service). Most tangible products for the consumer market are identified by a unique identifier on it: an EAN* Code (or UPC† as it is called in the United States). Other products have their own code system, for books: ISBN, pharmaceutical products: Pharmacode,‡ and so on.

Products can be analyzed on various levels and in different appearances. Let's examine these different product levels and appearances further to make sure we have an unambiguous understanding of the analysis object "product" during our business analysis process.

- Product item: This is the lowest grain, describing a a specific version of a product that can be designated as a distinct offering among an organization's products.
- Product line: A cluster of closely related product items that are considered a unit because of marketing, technical, or end-use considerations.
- Product group: Also called a product family, is a combination of goods or services that use the same production processes, share characteristics, and in most cases serve the same customer segment.
- Product category: This is a term that defines the positioning of the product in the retail outlets. For example, a chocolate muesli bar can be positioned in the breakfast, sports nutrition, or snack cat-

---

* EAN: European Article Numbering
† Unique Product Code
‡ For example, the *Club Interpharmaceutique* in France which defines and categorizes all medicine with six figures and a seventh modulo 11 figure.

egory. Each of these categories has Its own specific way of reaching a customer segment.

- Product portfolio: also called product assortment, Is a higher hierarchy of product groups.
- Product bundle: This is the combination of two or more products that enhance each other's selling power by optimizing the customer's value for money perception. Well-known examples are personal computers and bundled software or a car and an insurance policy.
- Product set: There is some ambiguity about this concept. I have … set = two or more packages of the same product and a combination of related products in a special package; for example, 10 packets of different flavors of crisps in a bag may be defined as a set but this may also be the case for three bottles of wine with two wine glasses and a corkscrew in a wooden case being considered as a set. What distinguishes the latter from a bundle is the indivisibility of the offer whereas a bundle can always be "unbundled."
- Product packaged units: The number of product units per package which is the product sales unit. such as a 30-piece chewing gum box.
- Product daily recommended dose: A common denominator used in the pharmaceutical and the food supplement market to abstract from the product form (i.e., 500-mg capsules compared to nose drops, etc.).

All these instances of the product mix can be the object of our analysis.

TERRITORY

In the early 1980s, the first salesforce automation tools saw the light. And soon data modelers found out that there was a lot to gain in normalizing the database to its full extent. One of the findings was that "Address" should not be used as an attribute in *company* and *contact* tables but should be considered as a separate entity. As a consequence, all 2.0 versions approached it this way, unaware of the potential beyond the horizon. In those days GIS systems were not mainstream but already the analytical possibilities of this modeling approach were used in large sociological studies such as ACORN (A Classification of Residential Neighbourhoods) in the United Kingdom and mail-order companies used the potential for canvasing, targeting their clients' neighbors.

Territory, as an object is not a social construct like *customer* or *employee*. It is defined in an absolute, mathematical way, namely a chain of topographical coordinates describing a point, a line, or an area on the surface of this planet. But territory is also assigned to people and organizational units using a geographical aspect. The *territory* object can be modeled on two levels: the pure GIS level, combining spatial information, cartography, and database technology and the second, derived level which models geographical aspects using the topographic coordinates (longitude, latitude, and elevation) as a reference point, line, or area for roads, zip codes, borders, and so on. Territory master data tables for general business use need no extra GIS functionality or data as most BI tools can get the job done with these coordinates.

Geographical Aspects of *Territory*

Geographical sales territories are a good candidate. Do not confuse this type of sales territory with other types depending on other (master) data such as customer type, product, sales channel, and the like. Other commercial geographical area denominations including Nielsen areas, residence type, zip codes, and delivery routes belong to this category.

Appendices

OVERVIEW

The Appendices are intended to make sure the reader has the basic knowledge about Business Intelligence and to clarify the author's perspective on the concepts used. Appendix B "Business Intelligence from 1960 to Today" on the history of BI, not with the intention to be complete but to make the link between the developments in strategic management focus and the developments in BI. Appendix C defines the major data warehouse architectures in "The 101 on Data Warehousing."

How Do You Become a BA4BI?

You can do it the hard way, like so many before you: by costly trial and error. Some organizations apparently wouldn't want it any other way as they do not invest in specialized training programs. But as BI has grabbed the boardroom's attention, this segment is shrinking rapidly. A small telephone survey among 100 major Benelux companies revealed that 70% are looking for training programs specifically targeted at analysis for Business Intelligence. In this section I describe the skill sets that can be developed during a training program.

A business analyst for Business Intelligence (BA4BI) masters five important skill sets:

- Data knowledge
- Application knowledge
- Process knowledge
- BI skills
- Interpersonal skills

Data Knowledge

The analyst has to connect data quality issues with master data management based on data profiling and data lineage analysis. This data knowledge can only exist partly out of context, on a pure technical level. This is the level where the data domains are fixed, the null handling is defined, and low-level business rules, the cardinality, and referential integrity are described. You simply cannot analyze data fully without knowing its context. What processes, supported by which applications create, use, or alter the data? What are the various perspectives on the data? Therefore you need to acquire knowledge about these processes and applications.

Application Knowledge

The source applications that capture the recordings of facts such as sales orders, invoices, payments, hiring and firing, and so on are—except for legacy systems—*n*-tier applications where database, business rules, and the presentation layer are clearly separated. Although the market for these systems is consolidating around 10 major players, there is still a lot of customization of these systems and on a departmental level smaller systems may still be in use as these departments need less functionality.

It may be a good idea to provide students with some information on the major players in enterprise resource planning (ERP): the general architecture, aspects of the data model concerning master data, and the commonly used dimensions such as customer, region, human resource, product, sales channel, and so on. Also, an overview of best practices in order management, customer relationship management, inventory management, and the like can contribute to a better understanding of how online transaction processing (OLTP) applications work. But it is clear that no generic curriculum can fully provide you with sufficient knowledge about the source applications. This can only be acquired on the job.

Process Knowledge

This is where most analysts for BI fall short as they only focus on the business processes that affect the data requirements, ignoring the important context of other processes such as the strategy process, IT governance processes, and functional processes which even in the best end-to-end process management organizations won't go away too soon.

Business processes produce more data than the information system captures. Understanding the fine nuances between what happens and what is registered contributes to high-quality requirements gathering. This is the spot where an experienced business analyst can show the client additional opportunities, he was not aware of for Business Intelligence.

Understanding the strategy process starts with understanding the strategic drivers and how they interact with each other and with the organizational and functional units and the business processes. Processes including costing and pricing, marketing, sales, research and development, and supply chain management are subject to these higher level processes and cannot be understood in their entirety without understanding their link with the big picture. Specific processes such as credit analysis and fraud detection may be considered somewhat detached from these higher level processes but they operate in an environment defined by marketing, finance, and operations. So contextual knowledge of these higher level processes is always favorable for better business analysis deliverables. Remember, you are not a passive receptacle for business requirements; it is your duty to point out opportunities and threats to your client.

BI Skills

Can there be something like specific BI skills? Yes and no. Analytical skills, planning skills, change management, and developing a business case are not confined to the BI universe but they certainly are a specialization, useful for producing a project charter for BI projects that stick. BI governance and vision management skills are in the same league but they support the longer term BI processes and embed these in the organization.

Interpersonal Skills

This goes without saying: a business analyst who is not skilled in interview techniques, requirements gathering, workshops, brainstorming, prototyping, and mediation between opposing factions may have the highest technical qualifications possible; she will fail in her job without these "soft skills."

APPENDIX A: WHAT TO ASK ON YOUR JOB INTERVIEW

Introduction

This section is based on the assumption that nobody graduates as a seasoned business analyst for Business Intelligence. You are probably already a business analyst, experienced in agile software development or you are a BI developer who wants to turn her career around or an information analyst who wants to take his analytical skills upstream, where the information is produced. Whatever your starting point, the following questions for your job interview will attract your attention to the key aspects that shape the environment in which you will be working.

Questions

1. What is the organization's configuration?
   Tip: Use Mintzberg's typology (Entrepreneurial, Machine Professional, Diversified, Innovative, Missionary, Political)
2. How is governance implemented; that is, who decides on IT principles, architecture, business application needs, and investments in general? Who provides the input and who decides?
   Tip: IT monarchies, IT–business duopolies or business monarchies are the winners. Beware of distributed decision making either in the business units or process groups. These are killing fields for BI projects and therefore your future as a BA4BI!
3. What level of formalization is customary in the organization?
   Tip: Look at the level of formal recordings, documentation and agreements on requirements gathering, analysis, development, unit and system tests, user acceptance tests and production.
4. What is the amount of BI functionality the average BI developer produces in the organization?
   Tip: The answer to this question ("don't know" or "x # of functionality" will help you to determine the BI project maturity of the IT organization. Don't be surprised if the first answer comes up.
5. What are the lessons learned from previous BI projects?
   Tip: Probe for technical, organizational and even social and psychological lessons. BI is about decision making processes and therefore a mixed project (social and technical).
6. How is customer satisfaction measured?
   Tip: The ideal measurement is a customer survey combined with the measure in which the business case is realized.

APPENDIX B: BUSINESS INTELLIGENCE FROM 1960 TO TODAY

Introduction

A historic perspective can contribute a lot to a better understanding of the customer's BI culture. Therefore I have assembled a few historic facts and figures relevant to the business analyst's profession. For a full account of the history of BI, I refer the reader to D.J. Power (2007). Although the author uses an obsolete term as "Decision Support Systems," the paper is a very complete and comprehensive overview. I recommend it to every analyst who wants to master all aspects of the trade.

The Early Years

From the beginning of time in the computer age, men have asked themselves whether a computer would be able to think like a human being. Authors such as Karel Čapek predicted robots in the 1920s and scientists including Alan Turing were dealing with this question in the 1950s. Related (marketing) terms such as "thinking machines" and "artificial intelligence" went farther on that track leading to expert systems in the medical realm like MYCIN. But at the same time a more prosaic approach evolved from World War II's new discipline: Operations Research. Scientists at the RAND Corporation such as George Dantzig started to use computers for optimization and planning purposes. The 1950s and 1960s were the planning era, when strategic management was reduced to careful planning and executing the plan. Henry Mintzberg (1994) lucidly describes the end of the planning era during the Vietnam War when it soon became clear that strategic management should take more into account than quantitative figures like body counts.

IBM launched the concept of management information systems (MIS) which in most cases were purely financial and operational descriptive statistics in static reports. In the early 1970s, management discovered the possibilities of the decision support systems (DSS). The model-driven DSS concept especially gained momentum as almost every serious vendor from IBM to Comshare supported the idea of information systems supporting not only structured but also semistructured and unstructured decisions. Nevertheless, DSS remained a top-down approach and the hierarchical databases under the hood were inflexible, expensive, and not very intuitive.

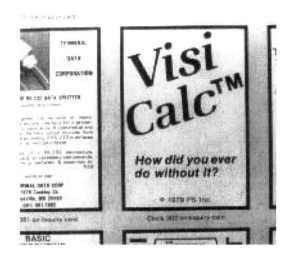

FIGURE A.1
The first branded spreadsheet product for the PC: VisiCalc.

As Professor Power states in his paper, McCosh and Scott-Morton's book (2007) on DSS was very influential in Europe and European business schools began to introduce management information systems courses in their curriculum. I remember my first MIS/DSS course in 1981 which was confined to an introduction to programming in BASIC and working with a spreadsheet called VisiCalc (Figure A.1) stitched together with a chapter on the importance of good management information.

Emergence of the Data Warehouse

The inflexible and poorly maintained EIS and DSS systems soon proved the need for flexible, data driven support for decision making. Enter the data warehouse, a relational database made of fact tables containing the measured facts like sales amount, invoiced amount, number of widgets produced and so on and dimension tables containing the perspectives on these measures like region, product, customer. Enter also the operational data store (ODS) to improve on microscopic analytics like fraud detection and the processing of massive amounts of data.

From the early 1980s until today gurus such as Bill Inmon, "the father" of the data warehouse and Ralph Kimball "the doctor of DSS" elaborate further on the data-driven concept. Especially Ralph Kimball evolved the concept from a purely technical solution for a business question into a business-driven, bottom-up process. His publications (1996, 1998, 2000, 2002) always have a chapter on the business case. In Europe, Séan Kelly (1996) evangelized the need for the data warehouse using mass customization as the principal business driver. Later Peppers and Rogers (1997) upped the ante with 1:1 marketing requiring even greater amounts of data for their marketing business case.

The Business-Driven Business Intelligence Era

The business-driven BI environment is a natural evolution of the data-driven approach with an eye on the business case. Already in the late nineties there was talk of data warehouse verticals with pre-modeled generic solutions for telco, banking, fraud detection, retail, and what have you. Although they did not always realize their promise, they did focus on rapid deployment, business drivers, and ease of use which later reflected in three new developments: the service oriented architecture (SOA) the data vault from Dan Linstedt, and the data warehouse appliances, in other words software as a service (SaaS) for BI. Where the data vault modeling approach reduces rework time for rapidly changing data capture priorities, the data warehouse appliance reduces the setup time and setup cost of a data warehouse. The SOA data bus allows near real-time data warehousing and reduces the need for an ODS for low complexity analytics.

APPENDIX C: THE 101 ON DATA WAREHOUSING

This Appendix helps you to get a quick grasp of the main concepts and best practices in data warehousing. For an in-depth study of the foundation layer of Business Intelligence, we refer to three schools of thought: Bill Inmon (1992, 1997, 2008) with his top-down corporate information factory and DWH 2.0 approach, Ralph Kimball (1996, 1998, 2000, 2002) with a bottom-up data bus architecture, and Dan Linstedt (2008) promoter of the data vault method. But to help you make your choice with which author to start, here's the 101.

Business Need

You have (and if not yet, you will as soon as you start as an analyst for BI) heard it over and over again: "I want a timely and accurate report, based on one version of the truth on clients, products and revenue." Or, "I want to target my customer more accurately and get a better insight in my cost and revenue drivers." Maybe you heard this one: "I can't detect trends and emerging evolutions unless I set up a study and by the time the results are there, they are already obsolete." All these are variations on one theme: the reporting as it is conceived on top of transaction systems offers me a fractional, incomplete, and inaccurate view of the complex reality that constitutes my organization's environment. Sometimes the business need is a compelling demand from governmental bodies like Basel II reporting or Sarbanes–Oxley regulations or an external event triggers the need for a data warehouse: mergers and acquisitions and a listing on the stock market impose high demands on the information needs.

So there you are: in the middle between an anxious and impatient business sponsor and the IT department with all its legacies, relics from the past, and exciting new projects at hand, leaving you with myriad applications, databases, data dictionaries, and what have you to create the tower of Information Babylon.

Technology Barriers

But we have clean new applications from the last generation, using the same development frameworks, programming languages, and a single database technology so where's the problem? I'll tell you where the problems are.

Denormalization versus 3NF: The database is designed for fast encoding and retrieving single transaction lines and is completely normalized to support this. Only by integrating data around subject areas can we present a holistic view of business issues. The subject area can be functional (i.e., marketing, finance, sales) or it can be process-based (i.e., from order to invoice, from invoice to receivables, from raw material to finished goods).

Definitions: The definitions of the objects are tuned for operations, not for decision making and vary as a function of time, department, or process. A customer from an accounting perspective is quite a different species from a customer defined by marketing people.

Open to multiple sources: Business Intelligence can and should go farther than the organization's source systems alone. BI systems that connect with the outside world provide far richer context and a better decision basis but then you will almost certainly be confronted with different technologies and database systems than the one your organization so neatly implemented companywide.

Let's go a little bit more into the details.

Denormalization versus the Third Normal Form

You don't have to be an SQL guru to understand that the more joins between tables you have to make to come up with a query result, the more processing power and time you need to scan all these tables whereas a denormalized approach may create a larger data volume and store redundant records but respond to queries in fractions of a second instead of minutes or hours.

A picture says more than 1,000 words. Have a look at the denormalized model in Figure A.2 where the central fact table is nothing more than the preconceived join of all dimensions with one or more recorded measures such as claims transactions amount, per party, per policy, per organization, and so on, yielding a quick and accurate response. *Every dimension in the figure has a one-to-many relationship with the fact "Amount" representing the paid out claims. More on this in the section "The Solutions."*

I am not even going to try to show you the data models from the source systems (although it would illustrate that the process to get to this simple STAR schema is not a walk in the park). In some legacy systems the date field had to be reconstructed from four records: one for day, month, year, and century. At least they didn't have any problems with Y2K conversions

Definitions

A large logistic organization used what I can only describe as a "departmentally dependent product definition." I am sure some of you will recognize this case. The core activity of the organization was getting goods from A to B, storing them temporarily and getting them from B to A. To market this service they had developed eight different sales channels who all differentiated this basic product to match the expectations of their market segment. By doing so, they created over 4,000 variations on this simple activity creating a nightmare for operational and financial analysis.

The data warehouse exercise led to a layered product definition with the core attributes and definition as a foundation for all sales channels who then could add layers for operations and costing, marketing, and sales. Offering reports with this layered product dimension, every decision

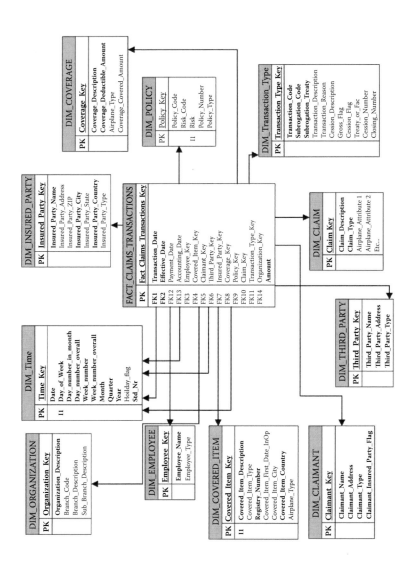

FIGURE A.2

A STAR schema for an insurance company, the result of intensive manipulation of data coming from more than 150 source tables.

maker in the organization knew the common grounds on which he would have to meet his KPIs for the group level, leaving him enough freedom to define his departmental KPIs.

Open to Multiple Sources

I do not mention the name of a large ERP vendor who positioned a custom-built data warehouse as a natural extension to his OLTP solution giving clients the impression that all you needed was the entire suite and you're all set. I beg to differ. The data warehouse should be conceived as an exchange platform for information regardless of the sources tapped. The investment in a corporate data warehouse is so large that you cannot afford rework deep down the line. So you need a flexible open architecture that can accept new data flows coming from new applications, acquired companies with their specific IT systems, vendors of commercial information, government bodies such as the Department of Trade or intercompany organizations such as LIFFE and NYBOT.

Solutions

Components

Regardless of the analysis and development methodology used, the same generic components can be distinguished in a data warehouse.

Source Systems

This is where you will perform the reality check with the messiest part of the data warehouse components: the source systems. Figure A.3 shows a real-world example of an organization where "the only constant is change" as Heraclites and others have said.

The webshop is not integrated in the CRM application and is not linked to the master data nor to the "All_Contacts" database in the CRM app. The order fulfillment is partly a legacy app loved by the logistic workers who are very resistant to change so we can't tell when the new ERP application will make this dinosaur extinct. Pricing rating and charging are, for security and audit reasons, run by the financial department which is not always focused on maintaining customer relations and there is no link between the product data and the general ledger to name but a few shortcomings. As most apps use a subset (the dotted lines) of master data (or other sources) and add their perspective to the subset we are faced with departmental clients who only

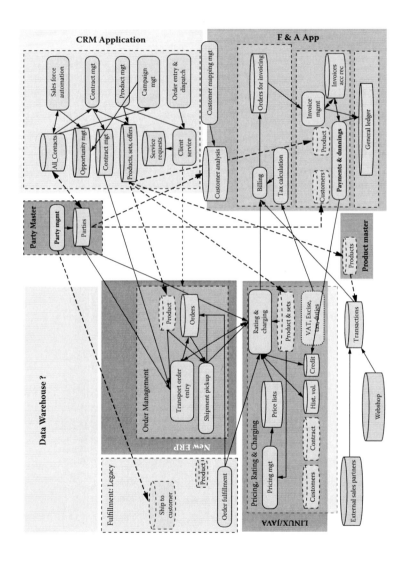

FIGURE A.3

A real world example of an application landscape of source systems. The dotted lines indicate that subsets of the data are used and full lines indicate 100% reuse of the data.

trust their own source data even if they would eventually prove to be less reliable than other source data. Welcome to the real world!

Data Staging Area

When you take in all the data from these sources, you may need to accomplish a few things:

- Get the transfer done rapidly (so simple extract queries, no joins, just imports or copies, please)
- Dispose of a separate processing and storage platform to perform complex operations for data cleansing and massaging the data to a convenient and uniform shape.

Target Database

In 90% of the sites I visited, classic row-based relational database systems (RDBMS) were used to store the BI data for querying. The other 10% were columnar databases like Sybase IQ and Red Brick which became Informix and later DB2. Columnar databases are far more efficient in loading, querying, and use of storage space. But because most organizations already have a RDBMS license they consider an extra technology platform at extra cost too much of a burden for the initial project. As the data warehouse grows and the problems with querying and disk space become evident, the organization is already too far committed to the platform to change course. As the RDBMS vendors are constantly working to mitigate the flaws in their technology for BI, their clients stay on board. There is some buzz about correlation database management systems (CDBMS) but as with object-oriented database management systems (OODMBS) I have never seen one at work in a data warehouse.

Extract, Transform, Load Process

For an in-depth introduction to the subject read *The Data Warehouse ETL Toolkit* (2004) by Ralph Kimball and Joe Caserta. It provides you with the complete picture whereas this section is just a quick sketch. The ETL process is a designed and patterned plan specific to a project and to an agreed data warehouse architecture to extract the raw data from source systems, transform these data to make them useful and usable for analysis and reporting and loading these data into a target database designed and optimized for querying. There are many questions and issues to address before the actual process is launched. Here are a few examples to illustrate ETL is not a walk in the park:

- Null handling strategies: do we insert a dummy value, do we refrain from loading, do we insert a default value, and so on?
- Free text conversion: agree on rules that handle all free text possibilities into coded values.
- Defining lookup values.
- Addressing the surrogate key values and keeping the natural keys or not.
- Addressing late-arriving facts.
- Data cleansing: before, during, or after extract?
- Partitioning strategies: by date, region, and the like?
- Indexing strategies in the target database: the tradeoff between performance versus flexibility and disk space.
- Slowly changing dimensions: update to overwrite the old value? Insert new fact and IsCurrentFlag? or with a ValidFromDate and ValidToDate?

APPENDIX D: SURVEY FOR A BI PROJECT FOR THE PURCHASING DEPARTMENT

Introduction

The objective of this survey is to get a rapid view of the BI situation with the large user community of buyers and buying managers from the Purchasing Department. The survey focuses on three business questions:

Do you know the departmental objectives?
Do you know your personal objectives?
Do you have an opinion on how BI can contribute (better) to meeting these objectives?

The survey is pretested before it is sent to the user community. Complete confidentiality and anonymity is guaranteed as no one needs to fill in names or staff IDs. At the end of the survey, the respondents are asked to indicate their age category and functional level but they are not obliged to do so nor will the survey be considered invalid should such information be lacking.

A Few Caveats

Think in advance of some ways to boost the response rates: introduce the survey to the team leaders, promise to pick up the results with a ballot box (to guarantee anonymity), or any other creative idea you may come up with. Promise a feedback session to interested people. They may be your staunched allies or your fiercest enemies; get to know them and give them the chance to come out with their contribution.

Example

Please indicate whether you agree with the following statements on a scale of 7 points ranging from 7: entirely to 1: not at all. Some questions will ask you to fill in your comments or suggestions. Please write them down in clear and readable handwriting.

Thank you in advance for your cooperation.

	1	2	3	4	5	6	7
1. The mission of our department is to provide value to the organization through:							
a) informed purchasing decisions							
b) increase the company's gross margin							
c) intensify the relationships with our business partners							
2. The mission of our department is also to follow up and communicate on subjects like:							
a) market trends							
b) supplier performance							
c) supply chain performance							
d) total life-cycle cost of raw materials, components, and finished goods							

3. The three major critical success factors for our department are:
   a) _____
   b) _____
   c) _____

4. My three major key performance indicators are:
   a) _____
   b) _____
   c) _____

	1	2	3	4	5	6	7
5. I expect more efficiency from my reporting environment.							
6. I have all the reports I need.							

7. If you need more reports, which would you consider:
   a) absolutely necessary: _____
   b) optional: _____
   c) nice to have: _____

8. Do you have any comments or suggestions?

9. What age category are you in?

Age category	Tick
18–25	
26–35	
36–45	
46–55	
56–65	
66 +	

10. What is your functional level?

Level	Tick
Clerk	
Team leader	
Middle management	
Analyst	
Junior buyer	
Buyer	
Senior buyer	

Please make sure to return this survey before (date).

Bibliography

BOOKS

Alesina, Alberto and Spolaore, Enrico. *The Size of Nations*, Cambridge, MA: MIT Press, 2003.

Arnold, John, Cooper, Cary L., and Robertson, John T.: *Work Psychology, Understanding Human Behaviour in the Workspace*, 3rd edition, Harlow (UK): Pearson Education, 1998.

Barquin, Ramon and Edelstein, Herb (Eds.): *Planning and Designing the Data Warehouse*, Upper Saddle River, NJ: Prentice-Hall, 1997.

Baumol, William. *The Free Market Innovation Machine.*, Princeton, NJ: Princeton University Press, 2004.

Chailland, Gérard: *Anthologie mondiale de la stratégie*, Paris: Robert Laffont, 1990.

Crosby, Philip. *Cutting the Cost of Quality: The Defect Prevention Workbook for Managers.* Original edition Boston 1967 Industrial Education Institute, republished at SQuality College Bookstore, 1990.

Davis, Keith and Newstrom, John W.: *Human Behaviour at Work*, 8th edition, New York: McGraw-Hill, 1989.

English, Larry, *Improving Data Warehouse and Business Information Quality*, New York: John Wiley & Sons, 1999.

Feigenbaum, Armand, V. *Quality Control: Principles, Practice and Administration; An Industrial Management Tool for Improving Product Quality and Design and for Reducing Operating Costs and Losses.* New York: McGraw Hill, 1951.

Gansor, Tom, Totok, Andreas, and Stock, Steffen: *Von der Strategie zum Business Intelligence Compentency Center (BICC), Konzeption – Betrieb – Praxis*, München: SIGS Datacom GmBH – Carl Hanser Verlag, 2010.

Handy, Charles. *Gods of Management*. New York: Oxford University Press, 1978.

Heskett, James L., Sasser, W. Earl Jr., and Schlesinger, Leonard A.: *The Service Profit Chain*, New York: Free Press, 1997.

Hofstede, Geert: *Allemaal Andersdenkenden.* Amsterdam-Antwerp, 1991, Contact Edition (originally published in English: *Culture & Organisation, Software of the Mind*).

Hofstede, Geert; Hofstede Gert-Jan; Pedersen, Paul P. *Werken met Cultuurverschillen.* Amsterdam-Antwerp: Contact Editions, 2004, (originally published in English by Intercultural Press: *Exploring Culture First*).

Hollingshead, A.B., and McGrath, J.E. Computer-assisted groups: A critical review of the empirical research. In Guzzo, R.A., Salas, E., & Associates (Eds.). *Team Effectiveness and Decision Making In Organizations* (pp. 46–78). San Francisco: Pfeiffer, 1995.

Imhoff, Claudia; Inmon, William; and Ryan Sousa. *Corporate Information Factory.* Hoboken, NJ: John Wiley & Sons, 2001.

Inmon, W.H.: *Building the Data Warehouse*, New York: John Wiley & Sons, 1992.

Inmon, W.H., Strauss, D., and Neushloss, G.: *DW2.0 The Architecture for the Next Generation of Data Warehousing*, San Francisco: Morgan Kaufmann, 2008.

Inmon, W.H., Welch, J.D., and Glassey, Katherine L.: *Managing the Data Warehouse*, New York: John Wiley & Sons, 1997.

Inmon, W.H., Zachman, John A., and Geiger, Jonathan G.: *Data Stores, Data Warehousing and the Zachman Framework*, New York: McGraw-Hill, 1997.

Juran, Joseph M. *Juran's Quality Handbook*, (6th Ed.) New York: McGraw Hill, 2010.

Kaplan, Robert S. and Atkinson, Anthony A.: *Advanced Management Accounting*, Englewood Cliffs, NJ: Prentice-Hall, 1989.

Kanter, Rosabeth Moss. *The Change Masters*. New York: Simon & Schuster, 1983.

Kelly, Séan: *Data Warehousing, the Route to Mass Customisation*, Chichester, UK: Wiley & Sons, 1996.

Kennedy, Paul: *The Rise and Fall of the Great Powers: Economic Change and Military Conflict from 1500 to 2000*, New York: Random House, 1987.

Kimball, Ralph: *The Data Warehouse Toolkit*, New York: John Wiley & Sons, 1996.

Kimball, Ralph and Ross, Margy (Eds.): *The Data Warehouse Toolkit: The Complete Guide to Dimensional Modeling*, 2nd edition, New York: John Wiley & Sons, 2002.

Kimball, Ralph, and Merz, Richard: *The Data Webhouse Toolkit*, New York: John Wiley & Sons, 2000.

Kimball, Ralph, Reeves, Laura, Ross, Margy, and Thornthwaithe, Warren: *The Data Warehouse Lifecycle Toolkit*, New York: John Wiley & Sons, 1998.

Kimball, Ralph, and Caserta, Joe. *The Data Warehouse ETL Toolkit*. Indianapolis: Wiley, 2004.

Leliveld, Rob and Vink, Maurits Jan: *Succesvol invoeren van zelfsturende teams*, Baarn, The Netherlands: H. Nelissen, 2000.

Linstedt, Daniel, Graziano, Kent, Hultgren Hans: "The Business of Data Vault Modeling", 2008, via www.lulu.com

McGovern, Ambler, Stevens, Linn, Sharan and Elias: *A Practical Guide to Enterprise Architecture*, Upper Saddle River, NJ: Prentice-Hall Technical Reference, 2004.

Ména, Jesus. *Data Mining Your Website*, Woburn: Butterworth Heinemann, 1999.

Mintzberg, Henry: *Mintzberg on Management*, New York: Free Press, 1989.

Mintzberg, Henry. *The Structuring of Organizations*. Englewood Cliffs, NJ: Prentice-Hall, 1979.

Mintzberg, Henry; Lampel, Joe; Quinn, James B.; and Ghoshal, Sumantra. *The Strategy Process*. New Jersey: Prentice Hall, 1991.

Mintzberg, Henry: *The Rise and Fall of Strategic Planning*. New York: The Free Press, 1994

O'Rourke, Patrick James: *Eat the Rich*, New York: Atlantic Monthly Press, 1998, p.1.

Peppers, Don, and Rogers, Martha. *Enterprise One to One*. New York: Currency, 1997.

Peters, Tom. *The Circle of Innovation*. New York: Knopf/Borzoi, 1997.

Poe, Vidette, Klauer, Patricia, and Brobst, Stephen: *Building a Data Warehouse for Decision Support*, Upper Saddle River, NJ: Prentice-Hall, 1997.

Porter, Michael E.: *Competitive Strategy*, New York: Free Press, 1980.

Power, Daniel J. "A Brief History of Decision Support Systems" 2007, http://dssresources.com/history/dsshistory.html

Redman, Thomas. *Data Quality, the Field Guide*. Woburn: Butterworth Heinemann, 2001.

Robertson, Suzanne and Robertson, James: *Mastering the Requirements Process*, Boston: Addison-Wesley, 2007.

Rummler, Geary A. and Brache, Alan P.: *Improving Performance*, San Francisco: Jossey-Bass, 1985.

Senge, Peter. *The Fifth Discipline: The Art and Practice of the Learning Organization*. New York: Doubleday, 1990.

Smith, Eliot R. and Mackie, Diane M.: *Social Psychology*, 3rd edition. Philadelphia: Psychology Press, 2007.

Thomsen, Erik: *OLAP Solutions*, New York: John Wiley & Sons, 1997.

Tiwana, Amrit: *The Knowledge Management Toolkit*, Upper Saddle River, NJ: Prentice-Hall, 2000.

Van Grembergen, Wim: *Strategies for Information Technology Governance*, Hershey and London: Idea Group Inc., 2004.

Weill, Peter and Ross, Jeanne: *IT Governance, How Top Performers Manage IT Decision Rights for Superior Results*, 2004.

Weill, Peter, and Ross, Jeanne W. *IT Governance: How Top Performers Manage IT Decision Rights for Superior Results*. Boston: Harvard Business School Press, 2004.

Wintzen, Eckart. *Eckart's Notes, (1st. Ed.)*. Rotterdam: Lemniscaat Publishing, 2007.

Zachman, John A.; Inmon, William H.; and Geiger, Jonathan G. *Data Stores, Data Warehousing, and the Zachman Framework Managing Enterprise Knowledge*. New York: McGraw-Hill, 1997.

ARTICLES

Aldag, Ramon J. and Fuller, Sally Riggs: Beyond fiasco: A reappraisal of the groupthink phenomenon and a new model of group decision processes, *Psychological Bulletin* 113: 533–552.

Bouquet, Luc: *eNewsletter, CIDM* August 4th, 2010, http://www.infomanagementcenter.com/enewsletter/2010/201008/index.htm.

Davenport, Thomas: Competing on analytics, *Harvard Business Review* (January), 2006.

Friedman, Benjamin: Capitalism, economic growth and democracy, *Daedalus* 136(Summer), 2007.

Henderson and Venkatraman: Strategic alignment: Leveraging information technology for transforming organisations, *IBM Systems Journal,* Vol 32, No. 1, 1993.

Kahneman, D. and Frederick, S.: Representativeness revisited: Attribute substitution in intuitive judgment. In T. Gilovich, D. Griffin, and D. Kahneman (Eds.), *Heuristics and Biases,* New York: Cambridge University Press, 2002, pp. 49–81.

Kahneman, D., and Tversky A. Judgment under Uncertainty: Heuristics and Biases. *Science*, New 185, (4157), pp. 1124–1131, Sept. 27, 1974.

Kahneman, D., and Tversky A. Prospect Theory: An Analysis of Decision under Risk, *Econometrica* (pre-1986); pp. 263–291, March 1979.

Kahneman, D. and Tversky, A. The Framing of Decisions and the Psychology of Choice, *Science*, New Series, 211, (4481), pp. 453–458. Jan. 30, 1981.

Kahneman, D. "Maps of Bounded Rationality, a Perspective on Intuitive Judgment and Choice." Nobel Prize Lecture. December 8, 2002.

Lewin, Kurt. Frontiers in Group Dynamics, *Human Relations*, Volume: 1, Issue: 1, Sage Publications, Pages: 5-41, 1947.

Maslow, Abraham H. A Theory of Human Motivation, *Psychological Review*, 50, 370–396, 1943.

Mintzberg, Henry. The Manager's Job: Folklore and Fact, *Harvard Business Review*, March/ April, pp. 163–176, 1990.

Moser, Karin S: Wissenskooperation: Die Grundlage der Wissensmanagement-Praxis, *Wissensmanagement – Praxis, Einführung, Handlingsfelder und Fallbeispiele. vdf Hochschulverlag AG an der ETH* Zürich, 2002, pp. 97– 113.

Power, D.J.: A brief history of decision support systems. *DSSResources.COM*, World Wide Web, http://DSSResources.COM/history/dsshistory.html, version 4.0, March 10, 2007.

Romer, Paul: Endogenous technological change, *Journal of Political Economy*, 98(5), Part 2: The Problem of Development: A Conference on the Institute for the Study of Free Enterprise Systems (October), 1990, pp. S71–102.

Schiffauerova, A. and Thomson, V. A review of research on cost of quality models and best practices, *International Journal of Quality and Reliability Management*, Vol. 23, No. 4, 2006.

Waterman, Robert, Jr., Peters, Thomas, and Philips, Julien: Structure is not organisation, *Business Horizons* (June), 1980.

CONFERENCE PAPERS

Barabba, Vincent P.: The market-based adaptive enterprise: Listening, learning, and leading through systems thinking: An appreciation of Russell L. Ackoff. In *Proceedings of the Russel L. Ackoff and the Advent of Systems Thinking Conference*, Villanova University, Villanova, PA, March 4–6, 1999.

Kahneman, Daniel: Maps of bounded rationality: A perspective on intuitive judgement and choice. Prize Lecture, Princeton University, Department of Psychology, Princeton, NJ, December 8, 2002.

Verlaeten, Marie-Paule: Policy frameworks for the knowledge based economy: ICTs, innovation and human resources. In *An OECD Global Forum Brazil*, September 2002, e-mail: marie-paule.verlaeten@mineco.fgov.be.

WEBSITES

Accentures Press release (December 11, 2008) http://newsroom.accenture.com/article_display.cfm?article_id=4777 U.S. Small Business Administration. http://www.sba.gov/content/guide-size-standards

Index